Rethinking Teacher Supervision and Evaluation

Third Edition

T0355125

Praise for *Rethinking Teacher Supervision and Evaluation*

A concise collection of practical ideas on how principals can improve teaching and learning, Kim Marshall is a former administrator who knows from experience how to ensure that teachers receive the support and guidance they need to be effective in meeting the needs of students. An invaluable resource for instructional leaders.

—**Pedro A. Noguera, Ph.D.,** *Dean of Rossier School of Education and Distinguished Professor of Education*

In *Rethinking Teacher Supervision and Evaluation*, Kim Marshall challenges the conventional perspective on teacher evaluation, urging us to perceive it not merely as a set of obligatory transactions but as a system capable of transformative leadership moves. This paradigm shift, according to Marshall, holds the potential to cultivate true collaboration, strategic actions grounded in research, and ultimately, improved learning for teachers, effective leadership decisions, and tangible progress in student achievement.

Kim Marshall introduces a novel approach, emphasizing mini-observations and reflective post-visit conversations as key components. These elements, he argues, enable school leaders to construct a comprehensive understanding of teachers' strengths and areas for improvement. Notably, this method relies on multiple data points rather than a single observation, providing a more nuanced and accurate evaluation.

What sets this text apart is its practicality. Kim Marshall offers actionable suggestions that render it an invaluable resource for both emerging and experienced school leaders. The proposed strategies empower leaders to navigate the complexities of teacher evaluation with finesse, making informed decisions based on a holistic understanding of each teacher's performance.

Moreover, the text advocates for transformative changes in the existing evaluation system, positioning it not as a mandatory exercise but as a catalyst for positive outcomes. Kim Marshall's innovative ideas, outlined in this book, present a compelling argument for reshaping our approach to teacher evaluation. It is, undeniably, the resource needed to usher in a new era of evaluation that prioritizes the growth and success of students, teachers, and school leaders alike.

—**Dr. Gloria McDaniel-Hall,** *Associate Professor, National Louis University, Chicago, IL*

Ample research now tells us that principals can be crucial to student learning, especially so for disadvantaged students. This book helps us understand *how* principals can matter, embedding a discussion of high-impact strategies for improving instruction into an insightful overview of the most relevant research, information that should be part of every principal's training.

—**Charles M. Payne,** *Henry Rutgers Professor of Africana Studies and Director of Joseph C. Cornwall Center for Metropolitan Studies at Rutgers, The State University of New Jersey-Newark*

This book serves as a manual for everyday supervisors looking to help teachers improve their practices. The mini-observation strategies will help us build the muscles to coach teachers toward closing the knowing–doing gaps of planning and implementing effective lessons.

—**Dr. Hoa Tu,** *Superintendent, New York City Public Schools*

Kim Marshall's *Rethinking Teacher Supervision and Evaluation* is the most practical, compelling source you'll find on this topic. If we heed his irrefutable case for frequent classroom visits and specific, targeted feedback, then instructional quality—and student outcomes—will absolutely improve.

—**Mike Schmoker, Ed.D.,** *Author, Speaker, and Consultant*

One of the great joys of teaching and leadership is the opportunity to watch a master at work. Great teachers, as Marshall demonstrates, enthrall us not because are magicians, but because they work hard, take feedback, and improve every day. The challenge is this: How do we take our current teaching staff to that level? How do be build the next generation of expert teachers? In this Third Edition of *Rethinking Teacher Supervision and Evaluation*, Marshall provides the roadmap to do just that. His mini-observation system has a uniform goal of instructional excellence, but does not take a one-size-fits-all approach to classroom observation. Best of all, Marshall provides teachers and administrators not only with a goal of effective practice, but also with specific guidance on many traditional practices to be avoided. If we aspire to see more great teaching, then we need to see more effective observation, feedback, and support for teachers at every level. Whether you are observing veteran staff members or the growing number of new teachers who have had little or no pedagogical training, this book will help. To be clear, this is not just a book for administrators – it is a lifeline for teachers who are weary of ambiguous and inconsistent evaluation systems. They deserve a roadmap for how to improve, and this book is the GPS to great teaching.

—**Douglas Reeves,** *Author, Fearless Schools*

Kim Marshall, an award-winning principal, author, consultant, and mentor to school leaders, leverages his extensive career experience into this compendium of practical wisdom on the important topic of teacher observation and evaluation. Marshall begins by debunking many current supervision and evaluation practices, then builds a case for more demonstrably efficient and effective ways of offering feedback that actually improves teaching and learning. This updated version of his classic book includes new insights, including the potential of Artificial Intelligence to support the teacher observation/feedback process. I consider this 3rd edition of *Rethinking Teacher Evaluation and Supervision* an indispensable guide to any current or aspiring school leader or instructional coach.

—**Jay McTighe,** *Education author and consultant,*
and Coauthor of the Understanding by Design® series

"Kim Marshall's new book is a master class in teacher supervision and evaluation. All current and prospective supervisors stand to benefit from its deep insights, clear explanations, and spot-on guidance."

—**Susan Moore Johnson, EdD, Jerome T. Murphy,** *Research Professor,*
Harvard Graduate School of Education, Massachusetts

Rethinking Teacher Supervision and Evaluation

How to Shift the Conversation to Coaching, Continuous Improvement, and Student Learning

Kim Marshall

Third Edition

JB JOSSEY-BASS™
A Wiley Brand

Published by John Wiley & Sons, Inc., Hoboken, New Jersey.
Published simultaneously in Canada.

Chapter 3 – "Let's Cancel the Dog-and-Pony Show" in Phi Delta Kappan, November 2012

Chapter 3 – "How Principals Can Reshape the Teaching Bell Curve" in The Journal of Staff Development, August 2015

Chapter 4 – "Rethinking the Way We Supervise, Coach, and Evaluate Teachers" in Education Gadfly, February 20, 2019

Chapter 7 – "Getting Teacher-Evaluation Rubrics Right" in Rubric Nation: Critical Inquiries in Education, Tenan-Zemach & Flynn (editors), Information Age Publishing, 2015

Chapter 8 – "Test Prep: The Junk Food of Education" in Education Week, October 1, 2003

Chapter 8 – "Using Student Learning in Teachers' Assessments" (with Douglas Reeves) in Edutopia, April 30, 2018

Chapter 8 – "In Praise of Assessment (Done Right)" in Phi Delta Kappan, March 2018

Chapter 8 – "Merit Pay or Teacher Accountability" in Education Week, September 1, 2010

Chapter 9 – "Interim Assessments: A User's Guide" in Phi Delta Kappan, September 2008

Chapter 10 – "Rethinking Differentiation: Using Teachers' Time More Effectively" in Phi Delta Kappan, September 2016

Chapter 12 – "Should Supervisors Intervene During Classroom Observations?" in Phi Delta Kappan, October 2015

Chapter 13 – "The Big Rocks: Priority Management for Principals" in Principal Leadership, March 2008

Chapter 14 – "Quality Assurance: How Can Superintendents Guarantee Effective Teaching in Every Classroom" in The Councilgram, March 2013

Chapter 15 – "The Big Picture: How Many People Influence a Student's Life?" in Phi Delta Kappan, October 2017

Chapter 15 – "Mini-Observations: A Keystone Habit" (with Dave Marshall) in School Administrator, December 2017

For general information on our other products and services or for technical support, please contact our Customer Care Department within the United States at (800) 762-2974, outside the United States at (317) 572-3993 or fax (317) 572-4002.

Wiley also publishes its books in a variety of electronic formats. Some content that appears in print may not be available in electronic formats. For more information about Wiley products, visit our web site at www.wiley.com.

Library of Congress Cataloging-in-Publication Data is Available

ISBN 9781394265251 (Paperback)
ISBN 9781394265268 (epub)
ISBN 9781394265275 (epdf)

Cover Design: Wiley
Cover Image: © kali9/Getty Images; © SolStock/Getty Images

For Lillie and Dave, skillful and intrepid teachers

Contents

The Author

Kim Marshall was a teacher, central office administrator, and principal in the Boston public schools for thirty-two years. He now advises and coaches principals, teaches courses and leads workshops on instructional leadership, and publishes a weekly newsletter, the Marshall Memo, summarizing ideas and research from sixty publications (www.marshallmemo.com). Marshall has written several books and numerous articles on teaching and school leadership. He is married and has two adult children; both are teachers: one in Boston, the other in Philadelphia.

Acknowledgments

First and foremost, I am grateful to my wife, Rhoda Schneider, for her support, wise counsel, and keen eye, and to Lillie Marshall, Dave Marshall, Katherine Marshall, and Laura Marshall.

Christie Hakim at Jossey-Bass believed in this book from the beginning and persuaded me to write it, and she and her colleagues contributed mightily to first edition, including Leslie Tilley (special thanks for helping reformat the rubrics), Julia Parmer, Hilary Powers, Kate Gagnon, and Pam Berkman. The second edition benefited from close attention from Kate Gagnon and Tracy Gallagher. The third edition was the brainchild of Ashante Thomas, and I am grateful for her encouragement, guidance, and attention to detail.

A loyal group of friends and thought partners have shaped this book over the years: Roshone Ault, Justin Baeder, Paul Bambrick-Santoyo, Roland Barth, Dick Best, Kitty Boles, Joanne Bragalone, Barney Brawer, Andrew Bundy, Lorraine Cecere, Emily Cox, Rudd Crawford, Larry Cuban, Joan Dabrowski, Charlotte Danielson, Jenn David-Lang, Gerry Degnan, Ted Dooley, Ellie Drago-Severson, Moshe Drelich, Karen Drezner, Rick DuFour, Kathleen Elvin, Alexandra Fagan, Sarah Fiarman, Kathleen Flannery, Ray Fugate, Michael Fung, Vikki Ginsberg, Amelia Gorman, Mary Grassa O'Neill, Maureen Harris, Mary Ellen Haynes, Bill Henderson, Jay Heubert, George Hill, Jeff Howard, Toni Jackson, Shahara Jackson, Mark Jacobson, Barry Jentz, Fred Jones, Lois Jones, John King, Khalek Kirkland, Sandi Kleinman, Diane Lande, Gerry Leader, Doug Lemov, Mike Lupinacci, Nick Marinacci, Keith McElroy, Jay McTighe, Carol Merritt, Nancy Milligan, Sandy Mitchell-Woods, Pedro Noguera, Mairead Nolan, Penny Noyce, Bill O'Neill, Maria Palandra, Andy Platt, Brandon Ray, Doug Reeves, Mark Roosevelt, Josh Roth, Mary Russo, Jon Saphier, Mike Schmoker, Pamela Seigle, Mark Shellinger, Ken Shulack, Vicki Spandel, Sue Szachowicz, Wyllys Terry, Nick Tishuk, Pete Turnamian, Betsey Useem, Mike Useem, David Vazquez, Jamey Verilli, David Ward, Bob Weintraub, Rick Weissbourd, Grant Wiggins, Dylan Wiliam, and Sara Zrike.

Finally, I am grateful to the teachers at the Mather School, who tutored me as these ideas germinated, and to the budding principals, seasoned coaches, and honchos in New Leaders for New Schools, who have contributed in ways they cannot imagine: Cami Anderson, Monique Burns, Jann Coles, Ben Fenton, Stephanie Fitzgerald, Kris Klasby, Mark Murphy; Jon Schnur, and Vera Torrence; my New Leaders coaching colleagues; and all New Leaders principals.

Finally, my special thanks to Athie Tschibelu, who went above and beyond the call of duty to help launch one of the first components of this book.

Introduction

Principal evaluation of teachers is a low-leverage strategy for improving schools, particularly in terms of the time it requires of principals.

—Richard DuFour and Robert Marzano

This quote strikes many educators and parents as shocking and counterintuitive. Isn't giving teachers evaluative feedback an essential part of a principal's toolbox for improving teaching and learning?

But when I ask groups of educators what helped them improve in their early years in the classroom, their responses (via anonymous polling) tell a different story. Here's what participants in a recent webinar had to say:

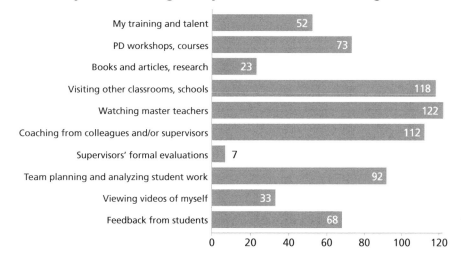

As a new teacher, the top four for improving your teaching and your students' learning?

Category	Value
My training and talent	52
PD workshops, courses	73
Books and articles, research	23
Visiting other classrooms, schools	118
Watching master teachers	122
Coaching from colleagues and/or supervisors	112
Supervisors' formal evaluations	7
Team planning and analyzing student work	92
Viewing videos of myself	33
Feedback from students	68

I see similar results every time I ask this question, with "supervisors' formal evaluations" often getting zero votes. Far more likely to improve teaching and learning, say educators in a wide variety of settings, is informal input from colleagues, mentors, coaches, supervisors, students, various forms of professional development, and a modest acknowledgment of their own training and talent.

Facing Facts

This begs the question of whether teacher evaluation can be a player in improving teaching and learning in K–12 schools. As I've coached principals, given presentations, and read research for the *Marshall Memo* in the new millennium, several hard truths have emerged:

Hard Truth 1. Students learn a lot more from some of their teachers than from others. The egalitarian teacher norm described by Susan Moore Johnson (2012)—we're all equal in a very tough job—is belied by major differences in achievement from classroom to classroom. The results of a Tennessee study summarized here show a fifty-two–point spread in achievement between students who spent three years with the least-effective and most-effective teachers.

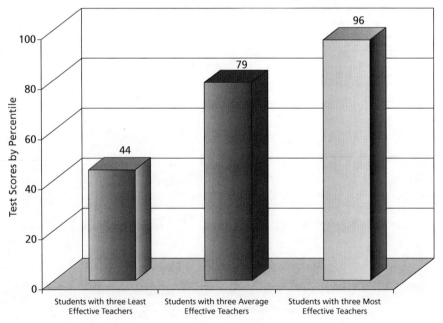

FIFTH-GRADE MATH SCORES ON TENNESSEE STATEWIDE TEST
BASED ON TEACHER SEQUENCE IN GRADES 3, 4, 5
(Second-Grade Scores Equalized)

Source: Sanders and Rivers (1996).

What made the difference? It was the cumulative impact of specific teaching practices used hour by hour, day by day, week by week, month by month. Books like *The Skillful Teacher* by Jon Saphier et al. (2008) and *Teach Like a Champion 3.0* by Doug Lemov (2021) have unpacked the techniques that explain why students learn so much more in some classrooms than in others.

Hard Truth 2. Every school has a range of teaching quality from highly effective to not so effective. Variation can be represented by a simple bell curve, which has a slightly different shape from school to school but conveys the same basic idea: there's always a range of teaching effectiveness.

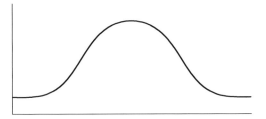

British researcher Dylan Wiliam said it well (2018, p. 183): "Today in America the biggest problem with education is not that it is bad. It is that it is variable. In hundreds of thousands of classrooms in America, students are getting an education that is as good as any in the world. But in hundreds of thousands of others, they are not."

Hard Truth 3. Vulnerable students have a greater need for good teaching than their more-fortunate classmates. Yes, a rising tide of effective instruction lifts all boats, but the maritime metaphor doesn't convey an important characteristic of schools: skillful teaching makes a bigger difference for students who walk in with any kind of disadvantage, including poverty, neighborhood violence, quarreling parents, learning disabilities, health issues, and ineffective teaching the year before. The study summarized here compared the impact of effective and ineffective teachers on students with different levels of preparation as they moved through fifth, sixth, and seventh grades:

In hundreds of thousands of classrooms in America, students are getting an education that is as good as any in the world. But in hundreds of thousands of others, they are not.

The Effect of Teachers Accumulates

Fourth-graders of all abilities who have three effective
teachers in a row will pass seventh-grade math test.

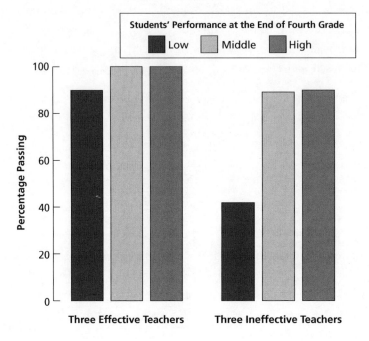

Source: Bracey (2004).

On the left are three cohorts of students who were lucky enough to have effective teaching three years in a row. They achieved at similarly high levels, even though some (the left-hand bar) started with much lower achievement than others.

The three student cohorts on the right are a matched sample who had three years of ineffective teaching. Those who started out with high and middle achievement (the two bars on the right) were still doing quite well at the end of seventh grade despite lower-quality teaching, but those who started out with low skills fell way behind.

With mediocre and ineffective teaching, we see a widening proficiency gap—the so-called Matthew effect, with the rich getting richer and the poor getting poorer.

This study and others like it show that vulnerable students dispro-portionately benefit from good teaching—the so-called equity hypothesis (Fullan, 2003). With mediocre and ineffective teaching, we see a widen-ing proficiency gap—the so-called Matthew effect, with the rich getting richer and the poor getting poorer. Conversely, with effective and highly effective teaching we see more-equitable student outcomes and narrowing proficiency gaps.

Hard Truth 4. Traditional teacher evaluations rarely have an impact in teaching and learning. This figure lays out the components of the "clinical supervision" model that's been standard practice in K–12 schools for almost a century:

Pre-obs.	Observation	Analysis, write-up, and proofreading	Post-observation
30 mins.	45 mins.	120 mins.	45 mins.

We'll go into more detail on the design flaws in this model in Chapter Three, but one problem jumps out: if a single evaluation takes four hours, a supervisor with twenty to twenty-five teachers (a typical caseload) is spending a lot of time each year on an activity that does very little to improve teaching and learning.

In some schools, these four hard truths converge in a perfect storm, with grievous effects on students' education:

- Many students have academic and other disadvantages.
- Too much teaching is mediocre and ineffective.
- Teachers are not effectively supervised and evaluated.

Tragically, this scenario is most common in economically embattled communities where the need for good teaching is greatest. The pandemic heightened these equity issues, and even though the emergency has passed, its lingering effects on student behavior and learning loss continue to erode teachers' and administrators' morale. It's more urgent than ever that schools use the most effective methods!

The Search for a Better Process

None of this is news to seasoned educators and policymakers, and experts have been hard at work looking for ways to improve teacher evaluation and student outcomes. Here are ten theories of action that have been used in some schools around the US, each followed by my concerns about its viability:

Double down on the traditional teacher evaluation model, investing heavily in training supervisors to ensure inter-rater reliability. Spending more time preparing administrators on a deeply flawed model will not improve outcomes. There might be more uniformity in write-ups, but they will remain an ineffective method for improving teaching and learning, taking up large amounts of supervisors' time that could be better spent, and adding to their cynicism about the process.

Use detailed rubrics to 4-3-2-1 score individual lessons. Rubrics are helpful descriptions of the many facets of teaching, but they're not suitable to evaluating a single lesson, during which a teacher can demonstrate only a small part of the overall palette of effective instruction. Rubrics are best used to evaluate each teacher's work at the end of the school year – more on this in Chapter Seven.

Bring in outside evaluators to backstop principals' evaluations. The idea is to have supervisors with more objectivity to supplement on-site supervisors, but educators from outside don't know the culture, curriculum, and personalities of a school when they parachute in and can't possibly visit classrooms often enough to give fair and accurate evaluations. Better to put the resources into supporting school-based supervisors with manageable caseloads and a better evaluation model.

Use anonymous student surveys as a significant part of teacher evaluations. Although students speak the truth about their teachers and their input can provide valuable pointers (and sometimes stinging rebukes), making surveys high-stakes (in Pittsburgh schools they were 15 percent of teachers' evaluations) can corrupt the process and prevent teachers from listening to their students' helpful suggestions.

Inspect lesson plans and classroom artifacts to ensure quality teaching. Yes, teachers need to be prepared for each lesson, but lesson execution is what matters. The time supervisors spend reading and commenting on lesson plans is better spent visiting classrooms (they can spot-check the lesson plan) and talking to teachers about how each observed lesson went. Asking teachers to submit "evidence" of their planning and assessments is also a poor use of their time—and a poor use of administrators' time going through reams of paperwork or digital files.

Use "real-time coaching" with supervisors intervening during problematic lessons. This idea will be discussed in more depth in Chapter Twelve; suffice it to say that this runs the risk of undermining teachers' authority with students and making teachers dread every visit by their supervisor. Except for dire emergencies, why not wait till after the lesson to talk to the teacher?

Evaluate teachers via lesson videos they submit. Videos can be powerful tools for reflection and professional development, but making them the medium for evaluation can become a digital dog-and-pony show. Most teachers will (naturally) hand in videos of excellent lessons and administrators won't have a sense of how things are going for students on a daily basis.

Use back-of-classroom cameras so supervisors can evaluate lessons remotely. Watching teachers via camera smacks of Big Brother and deprives the observer of the ineffable elements of a classroom that can only be picked up by being there in person, walking around, looking at classroom assignments, and chatting with a few students about what they are learning.

Use test-as-data transcripts and artificial intelligence (AI) to evaluate lessons. AI is amazing and can provide data on some aspects of a lesson—for example, who's doing most of the talking, even the emotional valence of classroom exchanges—but again, the physical presence of the supervisor in classrooms opens up so much more.

Use value-added measures (VAMs) and student learning objectives (SLOs) to evaluate teachers on their students' learning gains. There's no question that talking about student learning should be central to the supervisory and coaching process, but experts have shown that VAM and SLO methodology has serious flaws, making them a suboptimal way of having that conversation. We'll go into this in more detail in Chapter Eight.

Each of these ideas is problematic, either in concept or in execution, which reflects the frustrating juncture at which US educators find themselves today. So many well-intentioned reform ideas have failed to deliver on their promise; Charles Payne documented this in painful detail in his book, *So Much Reform, So Little Change*, Harvard University Press (2022).

So many well-intentioned reform ideas have failed to deliver on their promise.

So where does that leave us?

The focus has returned from grandiose nationwide plans and technological fixes back to the front lines: schools and districts, principals and superintendents and heads of school. Do they have no choice but continuing with the traditional teacher evaluation process?

I believe we can do better.

Let's start by imagining what teacher evaluation would look like in an ideal world. Every teacher wants their students to finish the year with the knowledge, skills, and habits of mind to be successful at the next level. To evaluate teachers on this aspirational goal, principals and other supervisors would need to answer three questions:

The intended curriculum. Are students being taught the right content for this grade or course, at the appropriate level of rigor?

The taught curriculum. Is the teacher using the most effective instructional strategies to teach that content?

The learned curriculum. Have all students made good progress toward mastery?

This is a tall order, but for the sake of argument, let's see how well the traditional evaluation process answers each question:

- Supervisors catch glimpses of the intended curriculum by looking at a few lesson plans before observations.

- They sample the taught curriculum in one or two evaluation visits.
- To assess whether the curriculum has been learned, supervisors look at students' work during classroom visits and perhaps analyze their grades and standardized test scores (although collective bargaining agreements often limit using student achievement as a factor in teacher evaluation).

In short, traditional evaluations are a woefully inadequate strategy for providing information in these three areas.

This book proposes a different approach to assessing each teacher's effectiveness, summarized here:

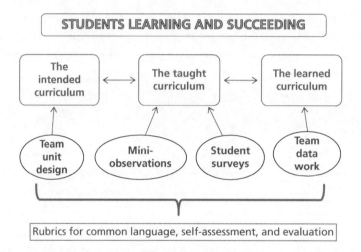

The goal is all students learning and succeeding. To get a handle on the intended curriculum, supervisors work with teacher teams on their curriculum unit plans. To assess the taught curriculum, supervisors make frequent, short, systematic, unannounced classrooms visits (mini-observations) and get additional insights in face-to-face conversations with teachers after each visit. Anonymous student surveys provide additional low-stakes insights on day-to-day teaching.

> *The goal is all students learning and succeeding.*

To see how well students are learning, supervisors look over students' shoulders during mini-observations, check in with teachers and look at student work during debriefs, and closely monitor teacher teams as they look at student assessments and work. All this information is pulled together, with input from each teacher's self-assessment, in detailed rubric scoring at the end of each school year.

This approach involves fundamental changes in the way supervisors handle the professional dynamic with teachers:

- From infrequent, announced, full-lesson observations to short, frequent, unannounced visits
- From extensive note-taking during full lessons to jotting insights on a possible "leverage point" in each mini-observation
- From lengthy formal write-ups to brief face-to-face conversations including appreciation and coaching, followed by a brief written summary
- From guarded, inauthentic communication with teachers to candid give-and-take based on authentic observations
- From teachers saying, "Let me do it my way," to teacher teams continuously asking, "Is it working?"
- From one-right-way evaluation criteria to constantly looking at new ideas and practices
- From infrequently evaluating *teaching* to continuously analyzing and discussing *learning*
- From top-down accountability to teachers and teacher teams taking on real responsibility for improving teaching and learning
- From cumbersome, time-consuming year-end evaluations to streamlined rubric scores
- From evaluating individual lesson plans to supervising the effectiveness of curriculum units
- From inadvertently sowing envy and division among teachers to empowering and energizing teacher teams and building trust
- From focusing mainly on ineffective teachers to improving teaching in every classroom
- From supervisors being mired in paperwork to continuously orchestrating schoolwide improvement

The Bigger Picture of School Leadership

Of course, there is more to getting good teaching and learning than supervision, coaching, and evaluation. This diagram, mirroring some of the insights in the poll at the beginning of this chapter, gives us the bigger picture in what's involved in improving teaching and learning in every classroom.

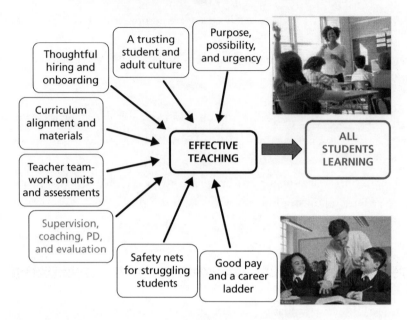

Yuri Arcurs/Alamy Stock Photo, Image Source/Alamy Stock Photo

Teacher evaluation has been a weak contributor in most schools. The mission of this book is to elevate teacher supervision, coaching, and evaluation to equal partner status, pulling their weight in the overall effort to ensure effective teaching and equitable, high student achievement.

Let's zoom out and get an even broader perspective, looking at one student's journey through a K–12 school district. This diagram shows the approximate proportion of each year that the student spends with each teacher.

K	Ms. King - Reading, Writing, Math, Science, and Social Studies + Homeroom	ART	MUSIC	PHYS.ED	LIBRARY	COMPUTER
1	Ms. Reid - Reading, Writing, Math, Science, and Social Studies + Homeroom	ART	MUSIC	PHYS.ED	LIBRARY	COMPUTER
2	Ms. Wilding - Reading, Writing, Math, Science, and Social Studies + Homeroom	ART	MUSIC	PHYS.ED	LIBRARY	COMPUTER
3	Miss Roche - Reading, Writing, Math, Science, and Social Studies + Homeroom	ART	MUSIC	PHYS.ED	LIBRARY	COMPUTER
4	Ms. Simms - Reading, Writing, Math, Science, and Social Studies + Homeroom	ART	MUSIC	PHYS.ED	LIBRARY	COMPUTER
5	Mr. Hastings - Reading, Writing, Math, Science, and Social Studies + Homeroom	ART	MUSIC	PHYS.ED	LIBRARY	COMPUTER

6	Math + HR	Social Studies	Science	English	Foreign Lang.	PHYS. ED.	MUSIC	ART	DRAMA	COMPUTER
7	English + HR	Foreign Lang.	Math	Social Studies	Science	DRAMA	COMPUTER	PHYS. ED.	MUSIC	ART
8	Social Studies + HR	Science	English	Foreign Lang.	Math	MUSIC	COMPUTER	ART	PHYS. ED.	DRAMA

9	Biology + Advisory	Algebra	World Hist	Spanish	English	Elective	PHYS. ED.	HEALTH
10	Geometry + Adv.	World Hist	English	Elective	Spanish	PHYS. ED.	HEALTH	Earth Science
11	English + Adv.	Chemistry	Algebra II	Spanish	U.S. History	PHYS. ED.	HEALTH	Elective
12	Civics + Advisory	Latin	English	PHYS. ED.	HEALTH	Elective	Pre-Calculus	Physics

For example, Ms. King, the kindergarten teacher, has students most of each day, but once a week students go to specials—Art, Music, Physical Education, Computer, and Library. The middle school this student attends is departmentalized, so students move from teacher to teacher, with one of them serving as homeroom (HR) teacher. The high school is also departmentalized, with one teacher responsible for advisory duties.

Moving through the grades from kindergarten to high-school graduation, this student has sixty-six subject-area teachers—and that doesn't count pullout special education teachers, counselors, tutors, substitutes, and all the other educators and support staff students come in contact with—probably more than one hundred by the time they graduate.

When I show this figure to groups of educators, I ask how many of their teachers they can remember. Usually only a few teachers stand out—a high-school social studies teacher who inspired a lifelong fascination with history, a second-grade teacher who made a biting comment that the student had terrible handwriting and would never amount to anything.

Teachers change lives, often for the better, sometimes for the worse. Every teacher wants to be the one who's remembered thirty years later for their positive contribution. Many won't have that dramatic an impact, but they're all part of the overall K–12 effort to graduate students who are well-educated, decent human beings.

Teachers change lives, often for the better, sometimes for the worse.

The reason I'm including this graphic is to make vivid the importance of *all* those teachers being effective. It's their cumulative impact, not just a few superstars, that counts. The job of the principal and other supervisors is making sure all students are getting good teaching every day and being vigilant for teaching practices that are not effective or even harmful.

This points to a system of supervision, coaching, and evaluation that has administrators in classrooms frequently, with a good eye for instruction, the human skills to bring out the best in teachers, and the courage to address mediocre and ineffective practices when they occur. The mission of this book is to give you a convincing description of such a system.

Here is a chapter-by-chapter summary.

Chapter One tells the story of my fifteen-year Boston principalship, during which my colleagues and I struggled against significant obstacles and realized that it's difficult to get major gains in student achievement without external standards linked to good assessments—and a better teacher evaluation process.

Chapter Two gives the blow-by-blow of my initial failure as a principal to get supervision and evaluation working well, and my discovery, with encouragement from teachers, of mini-observations—an effective way of getting into classrooms and giving teachers feedback.

Chapter Three analyzes the design flaws in the conventional supervision and evaluation process that explain why it almost never improves teaching and learning.

Chapter Four describes how mini-observations systematically sample daily class-room reality.

Chapter Five suggests ways that supervisors can be thoughtful and perceptive observers.

Chapter Six describes how supervisors can use what they learn in mini-observations to continuously affirm and coach teaching.

Chapter Seven describes how mini-observations, debriefs, visits to teacher teams, other points of contact, and teacher self-assessments culminate in end-of-the-year rubric evaluations. This chapter includes my revised teacher evaluation rubric.

Chapter Eight focuses on how student learning can be central to the supervision, coach-ing, and evaluation process, and several ways to deepen supervisors' focus on results.

Chapter Nine further broadens supervision, describing how supervisors can direct and support teacher teams (professional learning communities) as they look at interim assessment results, figure out learning problems, help struggling students, involve students in improving their own performance, and continuously improve instruction.

Chapter Ten looks at the fraught issue of differentiation and suggests a different set of look-fors in teacher preparation, lesson execution, and follow-up with struggling students.

Chapter Eleven broadens the usual definition of supervision to include supervisors working with teacher teams as they clarify learning goals and "backwards design" curriculum units—all of which helps teachers draw on each other's insights and wisdom and makes the supervisor a more perceptive and helpful thought partner during and after classroom observations.

Chapter Twelve asks whether supervisors should get involved in lessons while conducting mini-observations (spoiler alert—there are problems with this practice).

Chapter Thirteen analyzes supervisors' time management challenge—how they can fit all this into already-overflowing school days.

Chapter Fourteen suggests ways superintendents can support and direct the work of supervisors as they implement this model; this chapter includes my revised principal evaluation rubric.

Chapter Fifteen provides a very short summary of the book, frequently asked questions, and a wrap-up of the basic argument.

Sixteen Enhancements in the Third Edition

This edition is coming out eleven years after the second edition was published and benefits from everything I've learned in the intervening years from coaching principals, speaking and writing about this and other school leadership issues, and extensive reading for my weekly *Marshall Memo*. I've been surprised at how much my thinking has evolved. Here are some new elements:

- This introduction reflects a rethinking of the key issues, including the "four hard truths" about supervision and evaluation and the challenge that supervision and evaluation face if they want to be a player in improving teaching and learning.
- There's more emphasis on the issue of equity and the key role that effective, culturally competent teaching plays in closing proficiency gaps.
- My analysis of mini-observations has been rethought in a ten-point framework, which provides the organizational structure for Chapters Four through Eight.
- The coaching component of mini-observations is much more prominent throughout the book, playing a major role in continuously improving teaching and learning.
- I've clarified that mini-observations are the best observation strategy for principals and other supervisors, while full-lesson visits are appropriate for instructional coaches, peer evaluators, and lesson videos.
- The sequence of chapters has been changed, placing rubric evaluation immediately after the implementation of mini-observations to emphasize the close link.
- There are three brand-new chapters: making learning central to the supervision and coaching process, a way to rethink differentiation, and whether supervisors should chime in during informal classroom observations.
- There's been extensive rewriting and updating and chapters are shorter, which, along with new typography and my attempt to use shorter paragraphs and more bulleted lists, should make the book easier to read.
- There are several questions to consider at the end of each chapter.
- I've revised my teacher and principal rubrics, taking out the 4-3-2-1 scores at the top of each page, trimming one row on each page, and making numerous wording changes from suggestions made by frontline educators.
- Because the rubrics are more compact, the book is smaller and more portable.
- I've substituted *supervisor* for *principal* in most sections, emphasizing that the book is also geared to assistant principals, department heads, deans, and central office staff members—anyone who supervises and evaluates teachers.

- There are new poll graphs on questions I frequently ask educator audiences.
- I've included several new graphics that I hope will shed light on complex issues.
- I've made a number of references to the role ChatGPT and other large language models can play in curriculum unit design and lesson preparation.
- I've included answers to frequently asked questions in the last chapter to serve as a guide in persuading skeptics of the power of the mini–observations approach.

1

A Rookie Principal Learns
the Hard Way

We can, whenever and wherever we choose, successfully teach all children whose schooling is of interest to us. We already know more than we need in order to do this. Whether we do it must finally depend on how we feel about the fact that we haven't so far.

—Ronald Edmonds

I became principal of Boston's Mather Elementary School late in the summer of 1987, absolutely determined to boost student achievement and convinced that supervision and evaluation of teachers was central to my role as an instructional leader. Had I reflected more carefully on my prior experience as a teacher, graduate student, and central office administrator, I would have better anticipated some of the bumps that lay ahead.

Supervision as Seen by a Rookie Teacher

Fresh out of college in 1969, I began teaching at the Martin Luther King Jr. Middle School, an embattled part of the Boston Public Schools. Supremely ill-equipped to handle a self-contained class of twenty-five energetic sixth graders, I had a rough first year. A supervisor from Boston's central office visited several times and was highly critical, so my first exposure to teacher evaluation was one in which my job was on the line.

I was one of a number of rookie teachers at the King, and we all regarded this evaluator with fear and loathing. We groused about how the only things he seemed to care about were quiet students, a clean chalkboard ledge, and window shades pulled down at exactly the same

17

height. Disdain for this vision of good teaching was fiercest among those of us who were having the most trouble with classroom discipline. Imagine our glee when students turned the supervisor's Volkswagen Beetle upside down in the parking lot one spring afternoon.

But the man was right to criticize my teaching, and the point was driven home when I invited an education professor I'd met to observe my teaching. He sat patiently through a couple of lessons and said afterward that he hadn't seen "one iota of learning" take place. This was not exactly what I wanted to hear, but the comment, focused on student outcomes, was right on target—and it's been stuck in my brain ever since.

One of the school's assistant principals was assigned to the sixth-grade corridor, and he knew I was struggling. But with so many other crises in the building, what he gave me was a series of pep talks, not detailed feedback or substantive help.

Somehow I got through the year without being fired—perhaps an acute teacher shortage in Boston helped—and spent the beginning of the summer writing an article vividly describing my experiences (Marshall, 1970, "Law and Order in Grade 6E," published a little later in the *Harvard Bulletin*). After it came out, I received perhaps the most devastating evaluation an idealistic young teacher could receive:

> Your article clearly shows that whites do NOT belong in Black schools. With all your woes and problems, you forget that the 25 Black students you "taught" have had another year robbed from them (and people wonder why when they become adults they can't "make it" in society). It is unfortunate that you had to "gain your experience" by stealing 25 children's lives for a year. However, Honky—your day will come!
>
> —From one Black who reads the *Harvard Bulletin*

In my second year, inspired by a visit to a suburban summer school, I implemented "learning stations"—a decentralized style of teaching, with students working on materials I wrote on purple ditto masters the night before. Right away things were calmer and more productive. The principal was quite supportive of my unconventional teaching style, even bringing visitors up to my classroom from time to time. But I rarely got any direct evaluative feedback and was basically trusted and left alone.

In the 1970s, there was no Massachusetts curriculum to speak of, and measurable student outcomes weren't part of the conversation.

Did my students learn a lot? I believed they did, judging from weekly tests I created, but I was never accountable to any external standards. In the 1970s, there was no Massachusetts curriculum to speak of, and measurable student outcomes weren't part of the conversation. For the school's administrators, the important thing was that there were almost no discipline crises or parent complaints emanating from my classroom.

During these years, I operated very much as a loner, closing my classroom door and doing my own thing. At one point I actually cut the wires of the intercom speaker to silence the annoying schoolwide PA announcements. Here was teacher isolation at its most extreme; if World War III had broken out, my students and I might have missed it. I loved this professional autonomy, and my students had some great learning experiences, but how prepared were they when they moved on to seventh grade? That wasn't discussed.

A Quasi-Administrative Role

After eight years teaching sixth graders, I stepped out of my classroom to act as the King School's "education coordinator"—a grant-funded support role that allowed me to work on schoolwide curriculum improvement—and I began to look at grade-to-grade learning expectations. As I moved around the building, I noticed that the curriculum was highly fragmented, with teachers covering a wide variety of material without a coherent sequence from Grade 6 to 7 to 8.

I could also see that the quality of teaching varied widely, with no agreed-upon definition of best practice. But I couldn't get involved in evaluating my colleagues because I was still in the teacher bargaining unit, and even making coaching suggestions was tricky. After two years as education coordinator, I returned to the classroom, believing that I could have more impact teaching one group of students.

But I'd been bitten by the administrative bug, and this was reinforced as I pondered a series of *New York Times* articles about an intriguing wave of research on schools that somehow managed to get much better student achievement in high-poverty communities. One prominent exponent was Harvard Graduate School of Education professor Ronald Edmonds, who boiled down the formula for effective urban schools to five variables:

- Strong instructional leadership
- High expectations
- A focus on basics
- Effective use of assessment data
- A safe and humane climate

A 1979 British study, *Fifteen Thousand Hours* (Rutter et al., Smith, 1979), had a similar message, describing the "ethos" and expectations that made some schools much more effective than others. This vein of research emphasized the importance of the principal going beyond routine administrative work and being an instructional leader. I began to think seriously about becoming a principal.

To make that move I needed an administrative certification, so in 1980, I paid an emotional farewell to the King, where I had spent eleven formative years, and enrolled in Harvard's Graduate School of Education. I had the good fortune to study with Edmonds himself, and his searing comment on failing urban schools, quoted at the beginning of this chapter, became my credo.

I believed I was ready to be a transformational school leader, but during my year in graduate school, the voters of Massachusetts passed a tax-limiting referendum, sending Boston into a budget tailspin and forcing the district to close twenty-seven schools. There was no way I was going to be a principal, and I prepared to return to the classroom.

Then, through a chance connection, I was recruited to serve on the transition team of Boston's incoming superintendent, Robert "Bud" Spillane, a forceful advocate of high student achievement and school accountability. He and I hit it off immediately, and I ended up spending the next six years in the central office, first as a speechwriter, policy adviser, and director of curriculum, then, under Spillane's successor, Laval Wilson, as director of an ambitious strategic planning process. The *Nation at Risk* report of the National Commission on Excellence in Education dominated the national discourse during this period, and I found myself in the thick of Boston's response to the "rising tide of mediocrity" acerbically described in the report.

I was more convinced than ever that the real action was at the school level, and I begged the superintendent to make me a principal.

My central-office colleagues and I did some useful work—we produced a set of K–12 grade-by-grade learning expectations and curriculum tests—but throughout my six years as a district bureaucrat, I felt that our efforts to improve schools were like pushing a string. There weren't enough like-minded principals at the other end pulling our initiatives into classrooms, and we didn't make much of a dent in Boston's distressingly low student achievement. I was more convinced than ever that the real action was at the school level, and I begged the superintendent to make me a principal.

My Own Ship

In 1987, I finally got my chance. The superintendent put me in charge of the Mather, a six-hundred-student K–5 school with rock-bottom achievement and a veteran staff. As I took the reins, I believed I was ready to turn the school around because I had seen the urban educational challenge from three perspectives: an innovative teacher, a student of the research on effective urban schools, and a big-picture central office leader. Now I could really make a difference for kids.

How did it go? During my fifteen years as Mather principal, the school made significant gains. Our student attendance rose from 89 percent to 95 percent and staff attendance from 92 percent to 98 percent. Reading and math scores went from rock-bottom in citywide standings to about two-thirds of the way up the pack. In 1999, the Mather was recognized in a televised news conference for making the biggest gains in the MCAS (Massachusetts Comprehensive Assessment System, the rigorous statewide tests introduced the year before) among large elementary schools statewide. And in the spring of 2001, an in-depth inspection gave us a solid B+. I was proud of these gains and of dramatic improvements in staff skills and training, student climate, philanthropic support, and the physical plant.

But these accomplishments came in agonizingly slow increments and were accompanied by many false starts, detours, and regressions. Graphs of our students' test scores did not show the clean, linear progress I had expected. Far too many of our students scored in the lowest level of the 4-3-2-1 MCAS scale, too few were *proficient* and *advanced* (the top two levels), and our student suspension rate was way too high. Serious work remained to be done. In 2002, I was exhausted

> *Graphs of our students' test scores did not show the clean, linear progress I had expected.*

and concluded that I had done as much as I could and it was time to move on. Packing up my office, I hoped that my vigorous young successor would take the school to the next level.

Why weren't Mather students doing better? It certainly seemed that we were pushing a lot of research-based buttons, and if the Mather's student achievement had been higher, outside observers would have pointed to a number of "obvious" explanations: the hiring of a number of first-rate teachers, frequent classroom visits, extra funding, major improvements to the building and grounds, the daily *Mather Memo* communicating operational matters and research insights to all staff, and my seventy-eight-hour work weeks. Why weren't our test scores higher?

Looking back, I can identify a number of factors that made it difficult for me to get traction as an instructional leader: teacher isolation, uneven grade-level teamwork, curriculum fragmentation, poor alignment of teaching and assessment, the difficulty of assessing student writing, and accountability for student learning. Let's examine these challenges—hardly unique to the Mather—and then look at an external event that provided a partial breakthrough.

Teacher Isolation

In my first months as principal, I was struck by how cut off Mather teachers were from each other and from a common schoolwide purpose. I understood teachers' urge to close their classroom doors and do their own thing—that's the kind of teacher I had been! But the effective schools research and my experience in the central office convinced me that if Mather teachers worked in isolation, there might be pockets of excellence, but grade-to-grade progress would continue to be disappointing.

So I struggled to get the faculty to work as a team. In the *Mather Memo* and staff meetings, I focused on curriculum and best practices. I encouraged staff members to share their successes, publicly praised good teaching, and successfully advocated for a number of prestigious Boston Public Schools "Golden Apple" awards for the best Mather teachers. I recruited a corporate partner whose generosity made it possible, among other things, to fund occasional staff luncheons and an annual Christmas party. And I orchestrated a major celebration of the school's 350th anniversary in fall 1989 (the Mather is the oldest public elementary school in the nation), fostering real pride within the school and community.

But morale never got out of the subbasement for very long. Staff meetings were often dominated by arguments about discipline problems. As a young principal who was seen as being too "nice" with students, I was often on the defensive. We spent very little time talking about teaching and learning, and most teachers continued to work as private artisans, sometimes with great expertise, sometimes with painful mediocrity—and overall student achievement didn't improve.

Uneven Teacher Teamwork

Lacking the chops to unite the whole staff around a common purpose, I decided that grade-level teams were a more manageable arena in which to build collegiality. I figured out how to schedule common planning periods for each team (by sending the five classes at each grade level to specialist classes at the same periods), and same-grade teachers began to meet at least once a week and occasionally convene for after-school or weekend retreats (for which teachers and paraprofessionals were paid).

Lacking the chops to unite the whole staff around a common purpose, I decided that grade-level teams were a more manageable arena in which to build collegiality.

After much debate, we introduced looping, with all the fourth-grade teachers moving up to fifth grade with the same students and fifth-grade teachers moving back to fourth to start another two-year loop with new groups of students. Teachers found that spending a second year with the same class strengthened relationships with students and parents—and within the grade-level team—and a few years later the kindergarten and first-grade teams decided to begin looping, followed a few years after that by the second- and third-grade teams. That meant students moved through the school in three loops: K–1, 2–3, and 4–5, which had a very positive impact.

But despite the amount of time that teams spent together, there was a strong tendency for the agendas to be dominated by ain't-it-awful stories about troubled students, dealing with discipline and management issues, and planning field trips (we used external funding to pay for a full-time field trip bus, dubbed the Mathermobile). I tried to bring in training and instructional coaches to work with the teams, but I had limited success shifting the agendas of these meetings.

Years later, the idea of grade-level teams working as professional learning communities came into vogue, but this template and the research behind it weren't available to us. Grade-level teams looking at student work and common assessments and sharing techniques happened very rarely. In retrospect, I wish I had attended team meetings and guided them in this direction, but at the time I told myself that teachers needed to be empowered to run their own meetings.

Curriculum Clarity

During my years in Boston's central office, I led a team that spelled out grade-by-grade city-wide curriculum objectives. As a principal, I was chagrinned to see these expectations ignored in many classrooms. Mather teachers (like many of their counterparts around the country) often did their own thing, causing lots of problems as students moved from grade to grade. While teachers at one grade emphasized multiculturalism, teachers at the next had students memorize state capitals. While one team focused on grammar and spelling, another cared more about style and voice. While one encouraged students to use calculators, the next wanted students to be proficient at long multiplication and division.

These ragged hand-offs from one grade to the next had a real impact on staff morale. But teachers rarely spoke to colleagues in the grade just below about passing along students with important skills and knowledge. Why didn't they? That would have risked airing serious pedagogical disagreements and jeopardizing one type of staff morale—congeniality. But *not* having those honest discussions doomed the Mather to a deeper morale problem stemming from suppressed anger at what many teachers saw as students' uneven preparation for their grade. Morale was further degraded by disappointing standardized test scores, which became increasingly important and public as the years passed.

The lack of clear grade-by-grade curriculum expectations was also a serious impediment to my supervision of teachers. When a principal visits a classroom, one of the most important questions is whether the teacher is on target with the curriculum—but that's hard to define when no one is sure exactly what the curriculum is! If principals don't have a clear sense of what (for example) third graders are supposed to learn about fractions and what proficient fifth-grade writing looks like, it's awfully hard to give effective supervisory feedback. And it's impossible for a principal to address this kind of curriculum anarchy one teacher at a time. Supervision can't be efficient and effective until curriculum expectations are clear and widely accepted within the school.

Supervision can't be efficient and effective until curriculum expectations are clear and widely accepted within the school.

I saw this do-your-own-thing curriculum ethos as a major leadership challenge and tried repeatedly to get teachers to buy into a coherent K–5 sequence with specific objectives for the end of each grade. At an all-day staff retreat in a chilly meeting room at the John F. Kennedy Library overlooking Boston Harbor, I asked teachers at each grade to meet with those at the grade just below and then with those just above and agree on a manageable set of curriculum hand-offs. People listened politely to each other, but back in their classrooms, they made very few changes.

Undaunted, I brought in newly written Massachusetts curriculum frameworks and national curriculum documents, but these didn't match the norm-referenced tests our students were taking at the time and could be ignored with impunity. When the Boston central office produced a cumbersome new curriculum in 1996, I "translated" it into teacher-friendly packets for each grade level—but once again, these had little impact on what teachers taught. Visiting classrooms, I could comment on the *process* of teaching but had great difficulty commenting on *content*, which meant I wasn't addressing the heart of the matter—student learning.

The lack of coherent learning standards resulted in far too many of our students moving from grade to grade without the skills and knowledge they needed to be successful. At graduation each June, I shook fifth graders' hands knowing they were better prepared than most Boston elementary students—but still had major academic deficits. It was not a pretty picture, and I was intensely frustrated that I could not find a way to change it.

Teaching and Assessment Alignment

As I struggled to clarify the K–5 curriculum, it occurred to me that perhaps I could use the standardized tests that most Boston students took to get teachers on the same page (*what gets tested gets taught*, I'd been told more than once). The citywide assessment in reading and math at that time was the Metropolitan Achievement Test, given at every grade level except kindergarten, with school-by-school results helpfully published in Boston newspapers. I spent hours doing a careful analysis of the Metropolitan and, without quoting specific test items, presented teachers at each grade level with detailed packets telling what the test covered in reading and math.

Did teachers use my pages and pages of learning goals? They did not. The problem was that the tests teachers gave every Friday (covering a variety of curriculum topics with differing expectations and criteria for excellence) had a life of their own, and I wasn't providing a strong enough incentive for teachers to give them up. Besides, wasn't it wrong to "teach to the test"?

As hard as it was for me to admit, teachers were not being irrational. The Metropolitan, a norm-referenced test, was designed to spread students out on a bell-shaped curve and was not aligned to a specific set of curriculum goals (Boston's or any other school district's) or "sensitive" to good teaching (Popham, 2004a). In other words, it was possible for teachers to work hard and teach well and not have their efforts show up in improved Metropolitan scores. Teachers sensed this, and the result was cynicism about standardized testing—and the kind of curriculum anarchy I found at the Mather.

Although my foray into test-based curriculum alignment was unsuccessful, I had stumbled on an important insight. The key to getting our students well prepared by the time they graduated from fifth grade was finding high-quality K–5 learning expectations and tests that measured them. The problem was that we had neither. Without clear expectations and credible tests, I couldn't coax teachers out of their classroom isolation. For ten years I searched for the right curriculum-referenced tests and tried to clarify and align the curriculum—but until the late 1990s, I wasn't successful. This in turn stymied meaningful grade-level collaboration and meant that when I made supervisory visits to classrooms, I was largely flying blind.

> *Without clear expectations and credible tests, I couldn't coax teachers out of their classroom isolation.*

Assessing Student Writing

Another aspect of the Mather's balkanized curriculum was the lack of agreement among teachers on the criteria for assessing student writing. As was true in many schools, the same essay could receive several different grades depending on which teacher read it. The absence of clear, public scoring guides meant that students got very uneven feedback and most teachers lacked the data they needed to improve their classroom methods.

In 1996, the Mather staff made a bold attempt to solve this problem. Inspired by a summer workshop I attended with the late Grant Wiggins, an assessment expert based in New Jersey, we created grade-by-grade scoring rubrics that described the specific characteristics of student writing on a 4-3-2-1 scale in these domains of writing:

- Mechanics and usage
- Content and organization
- Style and voice

With exemplars of proficient student writing at each grade level, our standards were now clear (and demanding). We could be pretty sure that the same piece of student writing would get the same scores no matter who graded it. We began to give students quarterly "cold-prompt" writing assessments (they wrote on a topic with no help from their teacher or peers) in September, November, March, and June. Teachers scored the papers together and then discussed the results.

This process had great potential. We were scoring student writing objectively, we shared the criteria with students and parents in advance (no surprises, no excuses), we were assessing students' progress several times a year, and teacher teams at each grade analyzed students' work, gave them feedback, and discussed best practices for teaching writing.

But for several reasons, this initiative sputtered. Scoring and analyzing tests took too long (often several weeks went by from the time students wrote their compositions to the time we scored and discussed them), our graphic display of the data from each assessment didn't show clearly where students were improving and where they needed help, team meetings fell victim to the "culture of nice" (most teachers weren't frank and honest and didn't push each other to more effective methods), and we didn't involve students in the process of looking at each piece of writing and setting goals for improvement. Without these key elements, our writing initiative didn't bring about major improvements in classroom practice or significantly boost students' performance.

Student Learning

As the years went by, I became increasingly convinced that the most important reason student achievement wasn't meeting expectations was that we spent so little time actually looking at how much students were learning. The teachers' contract allowed me to supervise classroom pedagogy and inspect teachers' lesson plans, but woe betide a Boston principal who tried to evaluate teachers based on student outcomes. At one level, this resistance was well founded: unsophisticated administrators might be tempted to use norm-referenced standardized tests to unfairly criticize teachers for failing to reach grade-level standards with students who were not well taught in previous years.

The headlong rush through each year's curriculum was rarely interrupted by a thoughtful look every few weeks at how students were doing and what needed to be fixed to improve results.

But not looking at results cuts teachers and administrators off from some of the most useful information for improving teaching and learning. Most Mather teachers, like their counterparts in other schools, fell into the pattern of teach, test, and move on. The headlong rush through each year's curriculum was rarely interrupted by a thoughtful look every few weeks at how students were doing and what needed to be fixed to improve results.

At one point I asked teachers to give me copies of the unit tests they were giving—not the results, mind you, just the tests. Almost everyone ignored my request, which baffled and upset me. But when I checked in with a few teachers individually, I realized it wasn't an act of defiance as much as puzzlement at why the principal would be making such a request. Most teachers saw their tests as private artifacts that were none of my business.

Perhaps they were also self-conscious about the quality of their tests. *(Was he going to look for typos?)* Unwilling to push the point and distracted by other issues, I didn't follow up. In retrospect, collecting tests and talking about them with teacher teams might have led to some really productive conversations. If I had taken it a step further and orchestrated conversations about how students *performed* on the tests, then we really would have been cooking. But I almost never got teachers to relax about the accountability bugaboo and talk about best practices in light of the work students actually produced.

The *Aha!* Moment: Massachusetts Standards and Tests

Looking over the challenges I wrestled with in my first decade at the Mather, it's easy to see why we weren't more successful at reaching higher levels of student achievement. I was haunted by the knowledge that with each passing year, the proficiency gap between our students and those in more-effective schools was widening.

But how could we combat the hydra-headed challenges and get higher expectations, create a more positive culture, and convince teachers to work in teams on clearly defined learning outcomes? How could we avoid the Matthew effect, the Biblical prophecy that hangs over educators: "To those who have, more will be given, and they will have abundance; but from those who have nothing, even what they have will be taken away" (Matthew 13:12).

Like other struggling schools, we needed outside help—and it finally arrived when Massachusetts introduced rigorous external standards and high-stakes testing (the Massachusetts Comprehensive Assessment System, or MCAS) in 1998. What really got people's attention was that in a few years, students who didn't pass the tenth-grade MCAS in reading and math wouldn't get a high school diploma. When that message sank in, things changed quite quickly.

Right after our fourth graders took the first round of MCAS tests in spring 1998, we had a staff meeting and a highly respected Grade 4 teacher burst into tears. "No more Lone Ranger!" she exclaimed and pleaded with Mather kindergarten, first-grade, second-grade, and third-grade teams to prepare students better so that she would never again have to watch her students being crushed by a test for which they were so unprepared. You could hear a pin drop. This teacher's emotional plea shone a bright light on the problems that had been festering for years.

At first, there was resistance to the idea of preparing students for an external test. This wasn't surprising, given the years of working in isolation with idiosyncratic, personal curriculum expectations and contending with standardized tests that didn't measure much of what was being taught.

In a subsequent faculty meeting I asked Mather teachers to sit down and take a sampling of MCAS test items. After we got past some initial pushback ("Mr. Marshall, we're not children. This is a waste of time!"), teachers were impressed with the test questions. Here's what came out of this meeting:

- Although MCAS tests are hard, they measure the skills and knowledge students need to be successful in the twenty-first century.

- Success on elementary-grade MCAS tests is an essential steppingstone to getting a high school diploma.

- It is now possible to align our curriculum to external tests because MCAS items and Massachusetts standards are available online.

- Most of our current students are not prepared to do well on the MCAS.

- Nonetheless, our kids *can* reach the proficient level if the whole school teaches a well-aligned K–5 curriculum effectively over a period of years.

This was just where we needed to be in order to take the next steps.

We were fortunate that, starting in 1998, Massachusetts has had high-quality curriculum standards and assessments, and a remarkable level of transparency, making it possible to align our curriculum with the tests our students would take. Subsequently, the Common Core State Standards in English language arts and Mathematics and the Next Generation Science Standards led to further refinements in Massachusetts standards and clear, worthwhile learning targets.

Slim Curriculum Booklets and Achievement Targets

One limitation with the original 1998 Massachusetts curriculum frameworks and tests was that they covered only Grades 4, 8, and 10. As Boston's central office officials mulled over how to fill in the gaps, our Mather team decided we could do the job more quickly on our own. The state had published "bridge" documents to accompany the Grade 4 MCAS tests, and we set up committees that worked with consultants over the summer to tease back the Grade 4 standards to Grades 3, 2, 1, and kindergarten and up to Grade 5.

By that fall, we had slim curriculum booklets for each grade (about twelve pages each) containing clear learning expectations accompanied by rubrics and exemplars of good student work. Parent leaders helped us scrub the jargon from our drafts, and our corporate partner printed copies of the booklets for all teachers and parents. The curriculum summaries quickly became drivers for learning in every classroom—and were widely circulated in other Boston schools in what the superintendent at the time referred to as a "curriculum black market."

Embracing and extending the new Massachusetts standards was enormously helpful in each of the areas we'd struggled with for so long. Grade-by-grade MCAS-aligned targets put an end to curriculum anarchy and shifted the discussion in teacher teams from *what* to teach to *how* to teach it—that is, finding the best methods and materials to maximize student learning. Although teachers gave up some academic freedom in the process, their isolation from one another was greatly reduced because teams had a common mission and a clear focus.

External standards also helped our staff members confront the issue of expectations; having agreed that the new Massachusetts standards were appropriate and attainable (provided there was effective, aligned teaching from grade to grade), we could unite around a relentless push for *proficiency*—a term that acquired special potency when it was attached to the demanding third level on the 4-3-2-1 MCAS achievement scale.

External standards also gave us a more-focused mission statement and school improvement plan. Our purpose, we now saw, was to prepare students with the specific knowledge and skills to be successful at the next grade level so that fifth-grade graduates would be prepared to perform at a proficient-or-above level in any middle school. Such a simple and measurable purpose was unimaginable before the arrival of MCAS.

About the same time we took these steps, an outside consultant helped us agree on a schoolwide achievement target for reading, writing, math, and social competency four years down the road. Grade-level teams then spelled out their own SMARTS goals (specific, measurable, attainable, results-oriented, time-bound, and stretch) for that year to act as steppingstones toward the long-range target (see Chapter Eight for more details and samples). Each year, we updated the SMARTS goals as higher achievement and expectations moved up through the grades.

> *Our purpose, we now saw, was to prepare students with the specific knowledge and skills to be successful at the next grade level so that fifth-grade graduates would be prepared to perform at a proficient-or-above level in any middle school.*

Necessary but Not Sufficient

Ronald Edmonds often said that the existence of even one successful high-poverty school proved that there was no excuse for any school to be ineffective. With this message, Edmonds laid a guilt trip on educators who weren't getting results, and his stinging challenge might have jolted some educators into thinking more seriously about improving their schools.

But was Edmonds right that we knew in the late 1970s exactly how to turn around failing schools? Did the correlates from a few beat-the-odds schools provide enough guidance? Was he fair to thoughtful, hard-working school leaders who were struggling with barriers like those at the Mather? Was he perhaps a little glib about what it would take to close the gap?

There's no question that Edmonds and his generation of researchers gave us an inspiring vision by showcasing the schools that succeeded against the odds and highlighting the factors that seemed to make them work. It's a tribute to Edmonds and others that their "effective schools" lists have held up so well over the years.

But the early literature did not provide a sufficiently detailed road map to help a failing school out of the wilderness, and something else was missing: credible external standards and assessments. Without those ingredients, success depended too much on extraordinary talent, personal charisma, a heroic work ethic, a strong staff already in place—and luck. This allowed cynics to dismiss isolated urban success stories as idiosyncratic and claim that the urban school challenge was fundamentally unsolvable.

But Edmonds made an extraordinarily important contribution by getting three key messages into the heads of people who care about schools:

- Demographics are not destiny; children with disadvantages can achieve at high levels.
- Specific school characteristics are linked to beating the social class odds.
- We need to stop making excuses, get to work, and learn as we proceed.

Coupled with standards and good assessments, these insights have started us on the way to closing the proficiency gap. Recent research by Karin Chenoweth—including *Getting It Done* (2011) and *Districts That Succeed* (with Christina Theokas, 2021)—has updated the early research with exemplars of highly effective practice, and Education Trust's *Dispelling the Myth* website https://edtrust.org/dispelling_the_myth/ provides updated examples of beat-the-odds schools. Visiting such schools is one of the most transformational experiences educators can have.

Turning around failing schools and closing the proficiency gap continues to be difficult, especially in the wake of the pandemic. Principals and teachers can have the right beliefs and embrace standards, yet still run schools with mediocre student outcomes. In my years at the Mather and in my work coaching principals and reading extensively since I left the school in 2002, I have become convinced that belief and standards are not enough.

To be successful, schools need to radically improve the way they handle four key areas: curriculum planning, during-the-year assessments, teacher teamwork, and teacher evaluation—all of which can interact synergistically if they are handled well. The following chapters make the case for a new approach that promises to drive significant improvements in teaching and learning and actually close those persistent gaps.

Questions to Consider

- *Have you had experiences similar to Kim's as a new administrator?*
- *What has been the impact of high-stakes testing in your school?*
- *Are you persuaded by Ronald Edmonds's theory of action on school improvement?*

2 | Finding Our Way to a Better System

Frequent high-quality conversations with a skillful observer who has evidence about what went on and how it is impacting students can be immensely valuable to teachers. We should focus on that.

—Jon Saphier

Within a couple of weeks of starting as principal at the Mather in fall 1987, I plunged into what I considered the most important part of my job: sitting in on one or two classes a day, typing a page or two of comments that evening, and popping them into teachers' mailboxes, usually the next day. I was careful to keep my comments almost entirely positive, and many teachers appreciated the richly detailed feedback. Some wondered how I could capture so many direct quotes. (*Was he wearing a wire?)* But a few teachers were horrified by what they saw as evaluations in sheep's clothing.

Supervision Hits a Brick Wall

It wasn't long before the school's union representative filed a grievance, alleging that my write-ups were evaluative and therefore violated the contract. We had a preliminary hearing and I turned down the grievance, arguing that what I was doing was *supervision*—ongoing feedback to affirm good teaching and spur improvement—as distinct from end-of-year evaluations. How could teachers object to that?

But the union rep didn't buy my argument and took the grievance to the next level. I was horrified when my boss, the area superintendent, upheld the grievance. The contract language,

31

he said, specified that every time I did a lesson write-up, it had to be accompanied by the entire seven-page Boston Public Schools evaluation checklist and go into the teacher's personnel file.

Losing a grievance is not an ideal experience for a new principal, and it took the wind out of my sails. My concept of informal, appreciative write-ups and helpful feedback had been forcefully and publicly repudiated, and I didn't know what to do. In the months that followed, I visited classrooms less and less frequently. By my second year, I had retreated to the minimum requirement—one evaluation a year, which later became one every other year for teachers who earned an overall Excellent rating.

Deprived of during-the-year supervisory write-ups, I was determined to make the end-of-year evaluations as meaningful and helpful as possible. I asked teachers to let me know when they were doing a lesson they felt especially good about so I could see them at their best. But my invitation was greeted with chilly silence, and I had to take the initiative to schedule the required observations.

I procrastinated, and usually found myself doing a flurry of observations in the last week before the mid-May deadline, staying up late trying to do a good job on the write-ups, and cutting corners on follow-up conferences (I usually put evaluations in an envelope in teachers' mailboxes with a note asking them to sign and return them). Teachers rarely had anything to say; I got the required signature and little more.

I became increasingly doubtful about the whole process. Evaluation should be the tip of the iceberg, I believed, with supervision making up the much larger portion, where detailed information is gathered and there is a less formal atmosphere in which feedback can be given and problems can be corrected without final sanctions. Wasn't it absurd, I thought, for a teacher's official "grade" to be determined by one lesson?

It also wasn't surprising that many teachers prepared a glamorized lesson for the arranged evaluation visit and played it safe by not showcasing more-adventurous, risk-taking classroom activities. That's why, again and again, I came away from my formal evaluation visits with the uneasy feeling that I hadn't seen what was really going on in classrooms on a day-to-day basis—which was either better or worse than what I saw as the evaluator.

And when teachers got compliments or criticisms from me, it wasn't surprising that they didn't trust them or take them to heart. *What does he really think of my teaching?* I could almost hear them asking.

A good question, because a great deal was left unsaid. I had major concerns about the very conventional, teacher-centered instruction I glimpsed when I visited classrooms to deliver messages or deal with discipline problems, but didn't have enough information to put together a believable critique for individual teachers.

The contractual provisions, combined with a long history of distrust of administrators, conspired to keep teachers and me from talking with real honesty and authenticity about the heart of the matter—their teaching and students' learning. There was just the sigh of relief at the summative grade *(Whew, I got an overall Excellent!)*, and the papers were filed away without learning or improvement.

All this frustrated me no end. I believed that my failure to give teachers meaningful supervision and evaluation meant that I was not a real instructional leader and had little hope of turning around student achievement. I aspired to be the kind of principal who was always in classrooms and had useful insights that would help teachers make even more of a difference to kids. Good supervision and evaluation, I thought, were central to being a good principal, and I was blocked from doing that part of my job.

> *Good supervision and evaluation, I thought, were central to being a good principal, and I was blocked from doing that part of my job.*

Managing by Rushing Around

So I tried a different approach. I made a checklist of all thirty-nine classrooms and resolved to drop in on every teacher every day, either for an errand, to give a student or teacher a birthday greeting (this had become one of my trademarks), or just being visible. I felt that this way I would at least get a quick impression of what teachers were doing and how engaged and responsive students were. And because I wasn't writing anything down, I'd be flying under the contractual radar.

But it quickly became apparent that these drive-by visits were utterly superficial. All eyes were on me when I walked in (some teachers insisted on having their students stand up and chorus, "Good morning, Mr. Marshall!"), and regular instruction came to a halt. I wasn't hearing student-teacher interactions in classrooms and was in and out so quickly that I couldn't focus on the curriculum that was being taught or peek at students' work. For all my visibility, I didn't know much more about what was going on in classrooms than before. I certainly didn't know enough to say or write anything intelligent to teachers at the end of the day or add items with any validity or specificity to my evaluations at the end of the year. Was I "managing by walking around"? Not really.

There was another problem. My flying visits raised the anxiety level among teachers by making them wonder what conclusions I was drawing as I walked through their classroom every day without comment. *What was Kim Marshall thinking, and what was he going to do with the information he gathered?* I actually saw and remembered very little beyond the most general impression (teacher up and teaching, students quite attentive, lots of student work on the walls), but teachers thought I was filing away everything in my field of vision and feared the worst about real or imagined inadequacies in their classrooms.

The fact that I wasn't *communicating* anything to them created a tense communication gap that was not about to be closed: it was simply impossible for me to catch up with thirty-nine teachers before the end of the day; and even if I could talk to them all, what I had to say about their classrooms would have been utterly without substance.

I was back to seeing virtually no classroom instruction and cobbling together perfunctory, ill-informed evaluations at the end of each year.

So my quixotic attempt to see every teacher every day fizzled. With so little emotional and substantive payoff, I lost motivation and I soon fell into a pattern of six or seven desultory visits a day, driven by specific deliveries I needed to make. I was back to seeing virtually no classroom instruction and cobbling together perfunctory, ill-informed evaluations at the end of each year.

That's when I became an addict to HSPS—hyperactive superficial principal syndrome—very busy with lots of unimportant stuff. An administrative intern who shadowed me at one point documented an amazing two hundred interactions in a typical day—and that didn't count saying "Hi there!" to students I encountered around the school. Constantly in demand, juggling people and activities, racing around the building doing this and that, I became an intensity junkie as I dealt with a parade of challenges:

- A weeping girl with a splinter under her fingernail
- A fight in the cafeteria
- A teacher dealing with a dying relative
- A pigeon flapping around an upstairs corridor
- A parent cussing out the office staff about her child being bullied on the bus
- A jammed photocopier (I became an expert at pulling out little bits of paper so teachers could run off their worksheets)
- A discipline crisis in a rookie teacher's classroom
- The laminating machine grabbing the end of my favorite tie
- A paraprofessional having a seizure and requiring emergency medical care
- A call from the central office in support of the angry parent
- A teacher sending a misbehaving boy to the office for the umpteenth time
- Helping a delivery from a trucker who didn't do stairs
- And more, every single day

All this made me feel sort of important and kept me super-busy. But I knew that I wasn't dealing with the heart of the matter—the quality of teaching and learning.

Chatting with other principals and dipping into the professional literature, I realized I wasn't alone. It appeared that few principals were successful at getting into classrooms on a regular basis, and powerful, almost inexorable forces conspired to keep most of us from playing a meaningful instructional role. Here is how we analyzed HSPS:

- The principal trapped in a cycle of dealing with one crisis after another
- Each day so chopped up by interruptions that it's very hard to focus on deeper stuff (and this was before email)
- When the principal escapes from the office, wandering around without a systematic agenda and missing a lot
- Evaluation visits only when they are absolutely required and unrepresentative of teachers' everyday practice
- Teachers rarely getting feedback, and teachers and principals having few authentic conversations about teaching and learning
- Teachers accustomed to working in isolation, with mediocre teaching practices continuing in all too many classrooms

In my more morose moments, I concluded that this pattern had major consequences for the equitable education of all students. Those who entered school with disadvantages fell further and further behind. The gap between the haves and the have-nots got wider each year. A *real* instructional leader would be able to strategically push back against these forces, go beyond superficial management (while still meeting students' and colleagues' needs), and run a school that served all students. I clearly wasn't doing this—which made me a walking, talking gap-widener.

How was it possible to be an instructional leader, given the contractual wall preventing more-authentic classroom observations? I began to think that the reality of the modern principalship precluded meaningful supervision and evaluation. I wondered whether, as some have suggested, it was hopelessly idealistic for the principal to be more than a disciplinarian and crisis manager.

> *I wondered whether, as some have suggested, it was hopelessly idealistic for the principal to be more than a disciplinarian and crisis manager.*

An Idea Is Born

These questions gnawed away at me for another year. Then at a staff meeting in June 1993, our physical education teacher blurted out that Mather teachers didn't feel appreciated. I wasn't telling people often enough that they were doing a great job, he said. Lots of heads nodded.

He went on to say that with the college soccer team he coached after hours, he constantly told the players that they were terrific, even when they weren't, and Mather teachers needed to have their work praised in the same way.

As he spoke, my silent reaction was that this kind of cotton candy praise was meaningless and teachers would end up just as unsatisfied. But this exchange set a new train of thought in motion. The official evaluation process would probably remain captive to announced observations, checklists, comments, and ratings. But what if I gave more-frequent, less-formal feedback to teachers in a way that was substantive and helpful—a way that would make supervision more meaningful and might even improve teaching and learning?

The idea was based on three beliefs. First, all teachers, even those who are very effective, need reassurance, but praise from the principal must be based on specific examples of actual events in their classrooms, not just a glib, uninformed "Great job!" Second, teachers know they're not perfect, so if all they get is praise, they know that the principal is not leveling with them. Third, to do the best job for their students, teachers need specific, constructive feedback, delivered with tact and skill. To put these into action, my supervision would have to look something like this:

- **Frequent.** This would somewhat reduce worries about being caught at a bad moment, because one not-so-good observation would be balanced by plenty of others.
- **Short.** Frequent visits would necessarily take less time than standard evaluations.
- **Substantive.** But the visits would be long enough that I could focus on what was happening.
- **Unannounced.** Otherwise, I wouldn't be seeing everyday reality as students were experiencing it.
- **Face-to-face debriefs.** These needed to happen promptly or teachers would be left guessing about what I thought.
- **Low-key.** This would increase the chance of non-defensive reflection and a two-way conversation.
- **Nothing in writing.** I didn't want to lose another grievance.

I dubbed this scheme *mini-observations*, and as I started my seventh year as principal, I briefed teachers on it in the *Mather Memo* and prepared to swing into action.

I had forty-two professionals to supervise (thirty-nine teachers, the nurse, our special education team leader, and our student services coordinator) and figured that if I saw an average of four people a day, I could make a complete cycle of the staff every two weeks with time to spare. If I kept up that pace for the whole year, I would have visited each staff member a total of nineteen times. That was the goal. Here's what actually happened.

In September, even though I was absolutely determined to break out of HSPS and launch my mini-observations, I had great difficulty getting started. Every day there was a new list of reasons for not getting into classrooms. Our music teacher unexpectedly took early retirement and I had to find someone new—immediately! There were some glitches in the schedule that urgently needed to be fixed. Two new teachers were demanding their share of classroom supplies as well as carpets for their reading corners. We had to get our School-Site Council up and running to comply with the Massachusetts Education Reform Act. I needed to work closely with our new assistant principal to get her acclimated to the school. One pressing issue after another kept me from starting my mini-observations.

But as the days passed with no visits, I realized that the biggest barrier was in my own head. I was actually *nervous* about taking more than a superficial look at what teachers were doing. It was as if a force field surrounded each room, and even if I was already in someone's classroom on an errand, the invisible shield kept me from slowing down, turning it into a mini-observation, and taking a closer look at what was going on instructionally.

I knew what I wanted to do, I knew how to do it, and I knew how important it was. I just couldn't get started!

Part of the problem was my addiction to HSPS. I had grown to love the fast-paced, superficial way I'd been operating for years, never stopping in any one place or any one conversation for very long, constantly zooming around the school *doing stuff.* Another problem was the ambivalence of many teachers at having me in their rooms. Many craved affirmation and feedback, but they also wanted to be left alone, fearing that I might take them out of context, hurt their feelings, or come up with some fundamental criticism that would pose a threat to the way they had been teaching.

> *I knew what I wanted to do, I knew how to do it, and I knew how important it was. I just couldn't get started!*

I had fears and insecurities of my own. I would be walking in with no evaluation checklist or procedural script to hide behind. Would I be able to see what was really going on in each class? What if I missed something important and looked foolish? What if I didn't have anything intelligent to say? I had been writing lengthy end-of-year evaluations for years, but these were almost always delivered in an envelope and were rarely accompanied by face-to-face conversations. Doing a mini-observation and having a conversation afterward seemed quite a bit more challenging.

Mini-Observations Take Off

Enough! On the evening of September 29, I jotted a note in my diary and *shamed* myself into getting started. To make it easier, I told myself I would begin with the teachers who seemed least likely to be threatened by my visits. On the first cycle, I would concentrate on finding something positive to say—catch teachers doing good things. The next morning, I pushed through the force field and visited four classrooms for five minutes each.

It felt great! I was able to really *see* things when I slowed down and became an observer. And when I caught up with each teacher later on, I was able to share what struck me in a way that they appreciated.

- I complimented one of our Reading Recovery teachers on her patience working with a first grader who had virtually no reading skills, noting her gentle tenacity, hanging in there with him minute by minute.

- I reinforced a second-grade teacher for her restraint in pulling back from directing the whole class and allowing the kids to start working on their own (her tendency to over-direct instruction was something I had touched on in her evaluation the year before).

- I raved to our newly hired music teacher about the way he led a class singing "Fly Like an Eagle."

- I praised a third-grade Vietnamese bilingual teacher for having her students do mental math while they read Ping.

It felt good to give specific commendations; for once, I knew what I was talking about when I complimented something because I'd seen it with my own eyes, and each teacher walked away with something specific from the boss—which they might have shared with a significant other when they got home. The principal taking the time to observe instruction and give personal feedback—that was something!

The most striking thing was how much I was able to see in just five minutes.

The most striking thing was how much I was able to see in just five minutes. This flew in the face of decades of conventional wisdom—the deeply ingrained belief that every minute you're in a classroom you learn more, so you need to stay the whole lesson to make evaluative comments. But I found that five minutes was enough to have a substantive conversation. Counterintuitive but true!

Encouraged by this first day, I forged ahead, trying to do four quick observations a day. Some days I couldn't squeeze them in, but I completed my first full cycle of the staff in four weeks. Slow, but not bad for a beginner. I began my second round, and completed it in only three weeks. I had now racked up more than eighty observations with feedback. My confidence grew, and by December I had completed a cycle in two weeks. I was on a roll!

What proved most challenging was catching teachers later in the day and having an informal yet meaningful conversation about what I'd seen. In a few cases, I was able to give the teacher some feedback while I was in the classroom (if students were busy working in groups).

But most of the time, my feedback occurred when I caught up with the teacher during a break later that day or early the next.

If my comment was positive, I sometimes shared it with the teacher while other colleagues were within earshot; if I had something critical to share, I needed to talk to the teacher alone, which sometimes took some doing. My instinct was to have stand-up feedback conversations in a classroom, corridor, or parking lot; I didn't want to raise the anxiety level by summoning the teacher to my office.

On a few occasions, I picked a bad moment—a teacher was rushing to the bathroom between classes or preoccupied with something else. Sometimes several days passed before I found the right time and place to share critical feedback with a teacher. One teacher told me of her tension and annoyance when I kept her waiting over a long weekend. She wanted to know what I thought! But like most other teachers, she kept her cool and waited for me to track her down.

At first, people were dubious about mini-observations. I had introduced the idea at the beginning of the year, but teachers weren't sure what to expect. Several were visibly relieved when I gave them positive feedback after their first visit. One primary teacher practically hugged me when I said how impressed I was with her children's Thanksgiving turkey masks. But others were thrown off stride when I came into their rooms, and I had to signal them to continue what they were doing. I hoped that as my visits became more routine, these teachers would relax and be able to ignore my presence. And that's what happened in almost all cases.

From the beginning, five minutes felt like the right amount of time. That's how long it took me to get the feel of what was going on and think about my "teaching point." I found that if I moved around the room, looked at students' work, and listened carefully, I was always able to find something that could serve as a beachhead in my conversation with the teacher later on. On each visit, I asked myself, *What strikes me in here? What's interesting, different, or problematic? What is worth sharing with the teacher? What will give this teacher a new insight?* It could be anything in the room—the teacher's interactions with students, the lesson, the materials, or students' questions and insights.

> *I found that if I moved around the room, looked at students' work, and listened carefully, I was always able to find something that could serve as a beachhead in my conversation with the teacher later on.*

Developing a Style

I quickly learned to enter the room looking casual, upbeat, and non-officious (I never wore my jacket), giving a quick nod if the teacher caught my eye to signal that I didn't need to speak to the whole class. I never wrote down anything while I was there, even if I needed to remember something unrelated to the lesson (say, to pick up milk on the way home). I allowed the style of the lesson to shape the way I handled myself in the class. If it was teacher-directed, I would perch on a windowsill or a desk at the back of the room and watch the kids while listening intently to the teacher.

If students were actively working on something, I would circulate and look at what they were writing, sometimes chatting with students about what they were thinking as they did their work. Sometimes I worked for a few minutes with one student, getting a sense of what made the task easy or difficult. And sometimes I was able to chat with teachers about what they were trying to do—although usually I tried to maintain the fiction that I was invisible in the room so that the lesson could go on as normally as possible even though the principal was in there wandering around thinking goodness knows what.

As I got into a groove, I found that four or five teachers a day was a manageable number to cover. The brevity of mini-observations made it much easier to fit them into even the most hectic day. Many times, I was called to the office while I was in the middle of an observation, but I was almost always able to find something worth commenting on before I left.

On one occasion, a visitor showed up ten minutes early for an appointment. I gave him the school fact sheet, excused myself, and ran upstairs to fit in a mini-observation before we met. Nooks and crannies like this became much more productive. On a Friday just before a vacation, I visited a third-grade teacher during the last period of the day. The class was going full steam, and I joked with her later that she had passed the ultimate test—great instruction minutes before a vacation! If the class had been in an understandable state of flux, I wouldn't have counted that as a mini-observation. It was good to have that flexibility.

On the rare days when I managed to visit six or seven teachers (usually to try to finish a cycle by the end of a week—an artificial deadline that I nonetheless felt driven by), I found that the feedback started to suffer. It was impossible to catch up with that number of people and give meaningful individual comments within twenty-four hours—and my memory was stretched recalling the details to share with teachers the next day. So five mini-observations a day became my maximum.

After I completed my second cycle of observations—I'd done almost ninety visits with feedback so far—I began to feel more comfortable offering criticisms. In the third round, I told one teacher that a particular student seemed lost during an activity and wasn't getting help. I told another teacher that she needed to use a firmer tone when she gave directions and pause a beat to make sure all students were paying attention. And I commented on another lesson where there were three different activities going on—a tape recorder playing, a worksheet, and an explanation by the teacher on another topic—and some students appeared to be confused.

I wasn't always at my best. Visiting a first-grade classroom one afternoon, my eyelids began to droop. Chronically sleep-deprived, I was infamous among my fellow Boston principals for dozing off in boring administrative meetings. I didn't think this would happen during such short, active supervision visits, but in this class it did.

When I talked with the teacher later in the day, she hissed, "Mr. Marshall, you fell asleep in my math class!" I was truly embarrassed and apologized profusely, but as we talked, she acknowledged that it hadn't been her best lesson; she felt pressured by the upcoming standardized test and was teaching a low-interaction, drill-and-practice lesson. The truth was that she was a little bored with the lesson, too.

I made the decision early on to count brief observations only if active teaching was going on. If I came into a classroom and the kids were in transition, eating a midmorning snack, or taking a test, I usually left and came back later. I also decided not to focus on the nonclassroom areas of teaching—parent interactions, working with colleagues, professional development, and routine duties. If necessary, I would comment separately on those areas, or take them up in the formal evaluation every year or two in the required Boston checklist.

Keeping Track of Visits

Early on, I realized that I needed a way to record which teachers I had visited and what I saw. This was partly because I didn't trust my memory and wanted to be sure I didn't miss anyone, and partly to keep track of which subject was being taught each time around so I would be sure to see the full range—with homeroom teachers, reading, math, social studies, and science.

I created a one-page list of all forty-two staff members with a line after every name, made fifteen copies (the number of cycles I hoped to complete), and stapled them together at the top. Each evening, I jotted down a brief description for each teacher visited, for example, "Wed., Jan. 26—Kids writing autobiography sheets in cooperative pairs. Quite engaged." After we'd had the follow-up conversation, I added a checkmark to the left of the teacher's name. As it turned out, I was pleasantly surprised with my ability to remember what struck me in each classroom, even if a day or two passed, and I seldom needed to refer to my notes when I gave teachers feedback. But the checklist was essential for keeping track of where I'd been.

In the first couple of rounds, I visited teachers in random order, dropping into classrooms when I happened to be in a particular part of the building or if an errand took me into the room and it seemed like a good moment. After the first two cycles, I began to try to map out certain classrooms to visit in certain periods (working from a master schedule of the school that told me when math, science, reading, and other subjects were being taught).

But I found that teachers often changed their schedules and that my own plans were thrown off by random events. I did try to rotate the subjects I observed with each teacher, so if I arrived for an observation and found the same subject being taught as in my last observation, I left and came back later to see a different subject. I tried observing teams of teachers on the same day (for example, all the fourth-grade teachers one period, all the specialty teachers one day), but it almost never worked out because I was called back to the office.

Toward the end of December, as I neared the end of my fifth cycle, I noticed something interesting: I wasn't planning the sequence of visits, but the same four or five teachers were always the last to be seen. These were classrooms, I realized, where I felt unwelcome and awkward. When I walked into one of these classrooms, the teacher would say through gritted teeth, "Say good morning to Mr. Marshall, boys and girls." I'd been subconsciously avoiding these classrooms, and my checklist made me think about why—and ensured that I visited those teachers and gave them feedback.

What I found hardest as I walked into a classroom for a mini-observation was slowing down, getting other thoughts out of my head, and smelling the roses. This meant being sharp and fresh—yet another reason for getting enough sleep, exercise, and downtime. When I was "in the zone," I could see a huge amount in a few minutes.

With each cycle, I got better at observing and sharing one interesting insight with the teacher when we talked later on. Some of the follow-up conversations were short and awkward. On a few occasions, I was rushed and gave the impression that I was talking to teachers to check them off my list rather than to impart an interesting insight on their teaching or hear what they had to say. This happened most often when I got behind and was trying to visit too many teachers a day.

After a few months, teachers and students got so accustomed to seeing me in classrooms that they barely looked up when I entered and made no effort to behave differently.

I found that the key was slowing down and doing just four or five teachers a day on a consistent basis—and, like a good politician, focusing on the person I was with and getting other to-dos out of my head. When I did this, conversations were more likely to go into depth about a particular teaching moment, the goal of the lesson, how their kids were doing, and teachers' fears and dreams. After a few months, teachers and students got so accustomed to seeing me in classrooms that they barely looked up when I entered and made no effort to behave differently.

Keeping It Up

Even as I began to hit my stride, I felt the tug of HSPS and it took discipline to stick with the program. At several points that year, crises struck or deadlines loomed and I went for one or two days without doing a single mini-observation. When this happened, it was hard to get back into the groove. So deeply ingrained were my old habits that I quickly slid into madly rushing around, and the force field around classrooms slid up again.

Each time, I had to rally my willpower to get the routine going again. This made me realize just how important it was to have a target number of classrooms to see each day. Visiting forty-two people felt like an impossible challenge, but visiting four or five a day was doable, and I knew that if I kept up the pace steadily, I would get to everyone in about two weeks.

It terms of time management, it was most efficient to fit in my brief visits between other errands and expeditions around the school. *I'm up on the third floor, so let me see Joyce, and maybe I'll have time to see Alan, too, before the fifth-grade team meeting.* Sometimes I was successful in blocking out a whole period for classroom visits, but that amount of time rarely went by without something else coming up. Mostly I squeezed my visits in when there were fifteen or twenty minutes of "open" time.

There was no external pressure to keep up this crazy plan. The Boston evaluation process didn't demand it. My superiors never bought into it, even after I published an article in *Phi Delta Kappan* describing mini-observations. Teachers, despite the fact that they appreciated the substantive conversations we were having, were not clamoring for it. The union reps were basically indifferent, as long as I wasn't using the visits inappropriately.

The only thing pushing me to keep it up was my own belief that this would make a difference in teachers' morale and effectiveness with students. Lacking any external motivation, I had some very shaky moments during the winter and spring, times when I was sorely tempted to return to my old ways. But I kept at it.

One important source of support in this formative period was reading Stephen Covey's (1989) book *The Seven Habits of Highly Effective People*, in which he describes "Quadrant II" activities: those that are important but not urgent, and tend to get pushed aside by activities that are urgent and important, and also by those that are urgent and not important. (Covey popularized an idea first put forward by President Dwight D. Eisenhower.) The concept works for schools, too, as shown in this adaptation:

	Must do right now	**Don't have to do right now**
Important to student achievement	I	II
Not Important to student achievement	III	IV

It struck me that my five-minute visits were a perfect example of a Quadrant II activity. There is no immediate consequence for letting it slide, but in the long run, I theorized, not doing mini-observations would seriously undermine my instructional leadership.

I was also encouraged that teachers were responding well to my comments, and that motivated me to get out of my office and into classrooms. In most cases, I was the only person giving them professional feedback, and as it became clear that most of what I said was going to be positive and specific, my comments were often greeted with smiles and animated discussions about other things that were going on with students.

After a solid day with four or five visits and follow-ups with teachers, I felt like a real principal: we were talking about teaching and learning.

There were other rewards as well. After a solid day with four or five visits and follow-ups with teachers, I felt like a real principal: we were talking about teaching and learning. I was an extra set of eyes helping teachers see things about their work that could help them improve. I was deepening and enriching collegial relationships. I was creating an opportunity for them to talk to me about what they were trying to do in their classrooms—opportunities that had been virtually absent before.

I was also seeing students in a positive setting (which wasn't the case when I was dealing with discipline referrals, stopping students from running in the halls, and supervising the cafeteria). Conversely, on days when I made no visits, I felt superficial and insubstantial, not really earning my pay. On those days, I was very busy. I was working hard. I was coming in contact with a large number of people and solving a lot of problems. But I wasn't dealing with the heart of the matter.

The insights I gained from mini-observations also made me a much more knowledgeable participant when I met with grade-level teams, the parent group, and the School-Site Council. I felt increasingly authoritative talking about instruction; I was the only person in the school who had this combination of broad perspective and detailed knowledge.

All this fueled my willpower and kept me on task, and I was able to maintain the pace, sometimes slower, sometimes faster, through the difficult middle portion of the year.

Closing the Loop with Teachers

Face-to-face feedback was an essential component of the mini-observations. I found that it usually fell into one or two of these categories:

- **Praise.** For example, commenting on some amazing writing in third-grade students' weekly picture books, or on the way a bilingual class was combining with a monolingual class for a lesson, or on the way a teacher called on and drew out a shy student in the middle of a forest of eager hands. I tried to curb the tendency to preface my positive comments with "I liked . . .," talking instead about the impact a particular practice seemed to be having on students. I didn't want to reinforce the typical supervisor-teacher dynamic in which the goal is pleasing the boss rather than thinking together about what's working for kids.

- **Reinforcement.** For example, commenting on a teacher's animated modeling of a textbook passage as contrasted to the halting round-robin reading I'd criticized in a previous visit.

- **Suggestions.** For example, sharing ideas about how to convey specific concepts. On one occasion, after watching fourth graders struggling with how to remember the < (smaller than) and > (greater than) signs, I recommended that the teacher ask students to visualize a dwarf standing beside the small end and a giant standing beside the larger end. With a teacher who was covering the four traditional food groups, I suggested she use the new food pyramid that was just beginning to appear on cereal boxes (since replaced by the FDA's circular food plate).

- **Criticism.** For example, I came down on a teacher for correcting papers while her students watched a movie that most had seen at home, and with another, I expressed strong concern about the way she "dissed" a student in front of classmates.

It was always difficult to give critical feedback, even in brief, informal conversations. On several occasions I pulled my punches, fearful that teachers wouldn't be able to handle the criticism and put it to constructive use. Each situation was a judgment call, and I often erred on the side of caution. On several occasions, I asked myself if I had been cowardly—or done the smart thing by avoiding a defensive and angry reaction.

When I did give critical feedback, I found it was helpful to confess making the same mistake when I was a teacher; this increased the likelihood that the teacher would accept my comments. I always tried to offer a suggestion that the teacher could easily put into practice.

On a few occasions, especially when I was unclear about what I'd observed, I used the time-honored supervisory ploy of leading off the feedback conversation by asking, "Well, how did you feel the lesson was going?" Some teachers showed real annoyance at this approach, not quite putting into words what they were thinking: *You get paid the big bucks to tell me what you think!*

I also realized that leading off with an open-ended question was a trap for teachers: if they said that everything was great and I didn't think so, I was in the awkward position of telling

> *When I did give critical feedback, I found it was helpful to confess making the same mistake when I was a teacher; this increased the likelihood that the teacher would accept my comments.*

them they were wrong and here's my criticism. I therefore began to lead off every follow-up conversation with a declarative statement about what I'd seen and what struck me, trying to be as concrete and descriptive as possible. Then the teacher could react, disagree, or ponder the point.

What happened with increasing frequency was that after I shared my observations, the teacher and I would get into a longer discussion. They often gave me some background on what had been going on before I came in or what happened after I left. This gave me a sense of where the lesson fit into the overall curriculum and their classroom goals for the year.

There was also an increasing amount of give-and-take in these follow-up conversations. What started as a criticism might become a compliment when I learned more about what the teacher was trying to do, and what started as a compliment might evolve into a suggestion on how to handle the situation differently next time.

On a number of occasions, teachers and I debated the value of a particular approach. Round-robin reading came up several times. Whenever I saw teachers having students read one at a time in an all-class setting, I criticized what I believed to be an inefficient and ineffective approach to teaching reading. One teacher responded that her students enjoyed reading out loud, but she added, a little defensively, that she rarely used that approach.

With another teacher who was using round-robin reading, I shared a copy of an article describing a different approach. The teacher read the piece and proceeded to put it into action, and it made a big difference. She had each student rehearse a page of a high-interest book with her or her paraprofessional and then read their pages into a tape recorder. At the end of the lesson, the whole class could listen triumphantly to their well-read, coherent cooperative chapter.

Conversations like these were strikingly different from the stilted, wary interactions that had previously taken place during evaluation time. What made the difference was that comments after a mini-observation didn't carry a judgmental, superior–subordinate tone and instead became part of an ongoing dialogue about teaching and learning. These were conversations between professional colleagues, and I was convinced that teachers and I were both able to learn a great deal more in this low-stakes climate.

How did all this relate to the formal evaluation process I was required to submit at the end of the school year? Although the mini-observations were supervision, not evaluation, they helped me form an overall impression of each teacher and provided background for my formal evaluations. They also helped my assistant principal (AP) and me zero in on teachers who needed support. In several cases, mini-observations identified teachers who had not been on our radar, leading to more detailed suggestions and evaluations. The AP and I decided to target four teachers for additional help and spent more time with them in the formal process.

So Far, So Good

Despite some slow patches, I was able to keep the mini-observations going for all of that first year, and by the end of June, I had completed eleven cycles of the staff. The time for each cycle ranged from two weeks to six weeks, averaging about three weeks. This meant that I'd made only eleven visits per staff member, not nineteen, as I had originally planned.

But "only" eleven per teacher added up to 460 mini-observations for the year, and that was 460 more than I had ever made before. Most important, almost all were high-quality observations followed up by good feedback conversations. This was a quantum leap, and I was elated.

Most important, my frequent unannounced visits gave me an excellent grasp of what was going on in classrooms. Comparing the system to what I had used before—one formal observation a year—mini-observations provided a systematic sampling that gave me a far more representative sense of each teacher's performance.

Most important, my frequent unannounced visits gave me an excellent grasp of what was going on in classrooms.

How did teachers respond? In my end-of-year questionnaire (which most staff members filled out anonymously), I asked teachers to circle any adjectives that applied to my comments after five-minute visits. The most frequent comments were the following:

- Perceptive
- Honest
- Sparked discussion
- Gave me insights
- Affirmed my teaching
- Helped me improve

Only a few teachers had negative comments. One came from a teacher who apparently missed my beginning-of-the-year explanation of mini-observations and expressed distrust for the whole process. But a strong majority said they liked the prompt feedback and wanted me to get around more frequently.

What about teachers' morale and sense that their work was appreciated? These, after all, were the concerns that sparked the idea of mini-observations in the first place. I believe that my detailed, specific feedback contributed to a sense that I was saying what I really believed about people's classrooms. The frequent compliments and occasional criticisms struck teachers as authentic and helpful. All this built trust and improved positive feelings. The staff questionnaire recorded our biggest improvement in morale in years.

But we were still not a truly happy school. To reach that exalted state, we needed to bring about major improvements in our students' achievement, and that hadn't happened. Were mini-observations moving us toward that goal? I believe they were, but at this point, the links between curriculum and tests were still so tenuous that teaching-learning gains were hard to pin down. All that lay in the future.

For the next eight years, I kept up a steady pace of short classroom visits, averaging three or four a day, totaling about five hundred each year. In my best year, I completed fourteen cycles, totaling 630 mini-observations, each with a follow-up chat. In my worst year, because of the challenges of breaking in a new assistant principal and being required to attend a lot of out-of-the-building meetings, I did only seven cycles.

After a few years, the staff became so comfortable with mini-observations that almost everyone allowed me to use my brief observations to write their official performance evaluations (the union reps organized a formal sign-off process). Dog-and-pony shows—contrived, unrepresentative, nervous-making lessons solely for my benefit—were largely a thing of the past. I simply stopped doing formal, announced observations except in a rare instance where a teacher specifically requested one or a teacher was in danger of being rated Unsatisfactory.

A Postscript

When I first launched mini-observations, I had a very capable assistant principal and it would have been logical to split the forty-two-person faculty with her. But she was new to the school and the job and hesitant to take on mini-observations. In retrospect, after a year of confidence-building, I should have insisted on splitting the staff and coached her becoming proficient at mini-observations. Each of us would then have worked with twenty-one professionals.

As it was, this AP did terrific work on school culture, curriculum, parent relations, and discipline in the six years we worked together, playing a key role in my being able to get into classrooms and follow up with teachers as much as I did. We were an excellent team!

As the years passed, mini-observations became the core of my identity as a principal. I began to give workshops to graduate school classes and groups of principals and published a series of articles (see www.marshallmemo.com, Kim's Writing, for free access to all of them) and then the first edition of this book. Speaking, writing, and reading about mini-observations helped me articulate the essential elements, address a number of challenges, and make an increasingly convincing argument for the system.

Chapter Three goes into more detail about problems with traditional teacher evaluations, providing more ammunition for debates with those who want to continue an ineffective process. If you're already persuaded and want to get into the specifics of mini-observations, you'll want to skip ahead to Chapters Four, Five, Six, Seven, and Eight, which present a detailed analysis of how mini-observations can work and how to avoid some common pitfalls.

While my Mather colleagues and I were implementing mini-observations, other educators were also moving away from traditional teacher evaluations and advocating for frequent, short classroom visits and less-formal ways of giving feedback to teachers. Here are six books, each with a different approach to the same basic idea:

- *The Three-Minute Classroom Walkthrough* by Carolyn Downey et al. (Corwin Press, 2004)
- *Leverage Leadership 2.0* by Paul Bambrick-Santoyo (Jossey-Bass, 2018)
- *Now We're Talking* by Justin Baeder (Solution Tree, 2018)
- *The Coach Approach to School Leadership* by Jessica Johnson et al. (ASCD, 2018)
- *Trust-Based Observations* by Craig Randall (Rowman & Littlefield, 2020)
- *Building Teachers' Capacity for Success* by Pete Hall and Alisa Simeral (ASCD, 2008)

Questions to Consider

- *What has been your experience with traditional teacher evaluations?*
- *How do you think teachers in your school would react to the idea of mini-observations?*
- *What is the ideal number of mini-observations per year?*

3

Design Flaws in the Traditional Teacher Evaluation Process

In many schools and districts, teacher evaluation has become simply a matter of numbers, ratings, and rankings.

—Charlotte Danielson

Late one May evening during my Boston principalship, I was sitting at my home computer writing yet another end-of-year teacher evaluation. It was a real struggle to come up with thoughtful comments in each of the categories of the district's evaluation form (Planning, Classroom Management, and the rest). Even though I had spent quite a lot of time in the teacher's classroom with my mini-observations I'd seen less than 1 percent of her teaching, knew very little about her dealings with parents and colleagues, and had no data on how much her students were learning. Suddenly my hands froze on the keyboard. "I'm faking it!" I said out loud. "This is nonsense!" (Or words to that effect.)

It was a defining moment. My accumulating doubts about teacher evaluation crystallized into a depressing train of logic:

- My verbiage wasn't giving teachers clear feedback on how they were doing in most of the evaluation criteria—and how they might improve.

51

- The excellent/satisfactory/unsatisfactory rating scale didn't allow me to make important distinctions on different levels of proficiency.
- My evaluations were mostly superficial and often missed the target.
- It was no wonder teachers often ignored them and rarely changed anything they did in their classrooms based on what I wrote.
- Spending hours and hours on this process was not a good use of my time.

As these realizations hit home, I became a cynic on doing these write-ups. In my remaining years as a principal, I did my them as quickly and as close to the deadline as possible, sometimes with the help of a good stiff drink (don't worry; I was working at home). This was not a productive dynamic—for me or for the teachers I evaluated.

Fellow principals with whom I shared these subversive thoughts often agreed. We ruefully concluded that our annual summative evaluations were an elaborate and largely empty ritual. We observed teachers at work. We did our write-ups and filled out the evaluation forms. Teachers signed them, sometimes with pro forma objections, usually with no comments at all. Occasionally we used evaluations to make a serious criticism, which might or might not be heeded. Very occasionally we used them to make the case for dismissing a persistently ineffective teacher. But most of the time, our evaluations were accepted with a shrug and had virtually no impact.

We can't avoid the conclusion that if our approach to end-of-year teacher evaluation is chewing up large amounts of time and rarely producing improvement, it needs to be changed.

In a more benign era, this ritual didn't attract much attention. Some teachers might have appreciated the fact that it tied supervisors up in paperwork and kept us out of their classrooms (one teacher gave her principal what she considered the highest compliment: "He leaves us alone."). But now the stakes are higher. Educators are being held accountable for the achievement of every single child. We can't avoid the conclusion that if our approach to end-of-year teacher evaluation is chewing up large amounts of time and rarely producing improvement, it needs to be changed. But how?

In most jobs, it goes without saying that supervision and evaluation are key levers for improving performance. The boss inspects and the workers shape up—or ship out. In education, that's been the conventional wisdom as well, with supervisors' classroom visits and year-end evaluations serving as the main vehicles for holding teachers accountable and helping them improve. But how well is this working in schools? Consider the following scenarios:

- A principal boasts that he spends two hours a day in classrooms—and it's true: he really does visit his school's seventeen teachers daily, chatting with students and occasionally chiming in during a lesson. But when teachers are asked what kind of feedback they get, they say the principal rarely talks to them about what he thinks after he pops in.

- An assistant principal (AP) receives several parent complaints about discipline problems in a history teacher's classroom but is so busy that she rarely observes his teaching. When it's time for the annual formal observation, this teacher stages a carefully planned lesson featuring elaborate PowerPoint slides and well-behaved students. The AP believes she has no choice but to do a positive write-up of what she saw and give the teacher a satisfactory rating.

- A principal spends four entire weekends in April and May laboring over teacher evaluations. He puts them in teachers' mailboxes just before the deadline with a cover note: "Let me know if you have any concerns and would like to talk. Otherwise, please sign and return by tomorrow so I can get them downtown by the deadline." All the teachers sign, nobody requests a meeting, and there is no further discussion.

- A well-regarded veteran teacher says she hasn't been evaluated in five years and her supervisor is almost never in her classroom. She takes this as a compliment—her teaching must be "okay"—and yet she feels lonely and isolated with her students and wishes there could be an occasional visit and some feedback.

- A sixth-grade teacher has good classroom management and is well liked by students and parents, but his students do poorly on standardized tests. The new AP mentions the scores and the teacher launches into a litany of complaints about how he always gets the "bad class"; most of his students come from dysfunctional, single-parent families; and he's tired of being asked to "teach to the test." Later that day, the union representative officiously reminds the administrator that it's not permissible to mention test results in a teacher's evaluation.

- A principal observes an elaborate hands-on math lesson in a well-regarded teacher's classroom and notices that the teacher is confusing the terms *mean, median*, and *mode*. The principal notes this error in his mostly positive write-up, and in the post-observation conference, the teacher begins to cry. Ten years later, at the principal's retirement party, he reminds the teacher of this incident (she remembers it vividly) and asks what lessons she took away from it. "Never to take a risk," she says.

Stories like these raise serious doubts about whether supervision (i.e., observation and coaching of teachers during the year) and evaluation (summative end-of-year judgments for teachers' personnel files) can ever make a difference. The emerging consensus is captured by Mike Schmoker (1992): "Evaluation has become a polite, if near-meaningless matter between a beleaguered principal and a nervous teacher. Research has finally told us what many of us suspected all along: that conventional evaluation, the kind the overwhelming majority of

American teachers undergo, does not have any measurable impact on the quality of student learning. In most cases, it is a waste of time."

Here's a poll from one of my workshops of school leaders' anonymous opinions about how their teacher evaluation process is working:

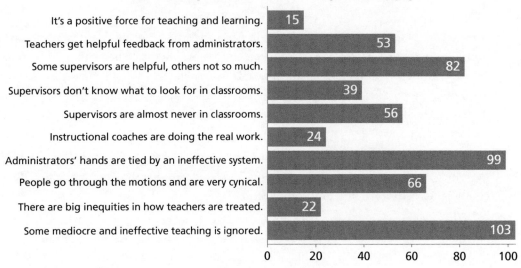

Your candid assessment of your teacher-evaluation process? Check any that apply:

It's a positive force for teaching and learning.	15
Teachers get helpful feedback from administrators.	53
Some supervisors are helpful, others not so much.	82
Supervisors don't know what to look for in classrooms.	39
Supervisors are almost never in classrooms.	56
Instructional coaches are doing the real work.	24
Administrators' hands are tied by an ineffective system.	99
People go through the motions and are very cynical.	66
There are big inequities in how teachers are treated.	22
Some mediocre and ineffective teaching is ignored.	103

This is a mixed bag, to say the least. The most troubling response is the last one; it's common knowledge that some students are being shortchanged by an evaluation process that leaves so much to the good fortune of having the "right" teachers.

Some say we should trust teachers and leave them alone unless there are signs of trouble in a classroom. But anyone who spends time in schools knows that this leaves far too much to chance. Most teachers do the right thing most of the time, but here are some less-effective practices I've seen over the years:

- The teacher lecturing with half of students tuned out and some having side conversations
- The COPWAKTA syndrome—calling on people who already know the answer—that is, the eager students whose hands are waving in the air answer the teacher's questions while the others engage in school prayer: "Please, God, don't let her call on me"
- A pile of uncorrected student papers on the teacher's desk from a week ago
- A teacher jumping up from behind his desk when visitors walk in; he was catching up on email
- Teachers using sarcasm, thinking they're funny—but students wince

- Teachers displaying cultural insensitivity and unconscious bias, struggling with the basics of relating to diverse students
- Teachers closing their classroom doors and working in isolation, cut off from helpful colleagues and up-to-date methods and technology
- Teachers ignoring parts of the required curriculum and freelancing on "some of my favorite things"

Again, most teachers are teaching well most of the time, but when teachers are left alone, mediocrity happens—sometimes worse—and as I argued in the Introduction, the students who suffer the most are those who walk into school with any kind of disadvantage.

What can schools do to counteract these tendencies? First, principals need to hire well. The more intrinsically motivated, hard-working, talented team players, the more likely it is that good teaching will happen day by day.

Second, schools need to pay teachers well and give them the respect and professional support they deserve. In Japan, people literally bow to teachers and the profession is among the most respected in Japanese society with pay comparable to other jobs with similar levels of education.

Third, a school's leadership team needs to create working conditions that support good teaching. Those include a positive school culture, a clear vision and mission, curriculum clarity, high-quality classroom materials, technology, and assessments, time for teacher teamwork, a workable schedule, and smooth operations—including the absolute minimum of classroom interruptions.

But there's something else principals can do: supervise, coach, and evaluate more effectively. That's what this book is all about. I firmly believe that, done right, this troika can be a major player in improving the quality of teaching and learning. At its best, the process enables supervisors to perform these core functions:

1. **Quality assurance.** Being able to honestly tell parents and other stakeholders that all students are taught well virtually all the time. That, of course, includes a clear definition of what "taught well" means.
2. **Feedback.** Communicating appreciation for effective teaching and coaching to improve less-than-effective practices.
3. **Motivation.** Teachers bring their A game every day and strive to continuously improve.
4. **Good personnel decisions.** Making the right calls for teacher awards, tenure, retention, and dismissal.

Note what's implicit in the first item: quality assurance is only possible when supervisors are in classrooms enough to know what's really going on. And this is closely tied to the other three:

Vulnerable students depend on good teaching to overcome their challenges, so a broken teacher evaluation process widens America's proficiency gaps.

good teaching is appreciated, mediocre practices are improved, teachers are invested in self-improvement, and persistently ineffective teachers are shown the door.

When it's designed to fulfill these functions, supervision, coaching, and evaluation can be a powerful player in improving teaching and learning. If we continue with the traditional process, we under-challenge effective teachers and allow mediocre and ineffective practices to continue year after year. Vulnerable students depend on good teaching to overcome their challenges, so a broken teacher evaluation process widens America's proficiency gaps.

So schools have a choice. Will they take the left fork and spend time on a bureaucratic system focusing on evidence, documentation, inspection, judging, and compliance? Or will they find a way to fulfill contractual and legal obligations *and* actually improve teaching and learning?

Can evaluation be a player?

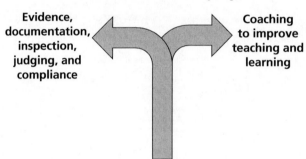

Evidence, documentation, inspection, judging, and compliance

Coaching to improve teaching and learning

Why is teacher appraisal so out of kilter? I believe it's because of seven design flaws in the model we've been using:

- Not enough observations to get an accurate picture
- The dog-and-pony show—glamorized lessons for the evaluator
- Problems with narrative evaluations
- The opportunity cost—time taken from more-effective work
- Power and passivity—an unfortunate dynamic between teacher and supervisor
- Unhelpful to teacher teamwork
- Not linked to student learning

Let's take a closer look at each of these and begin to think about how the system could be fixed.

Not Enough Observations

Most teachers plan and teach about nine hundred lessons each school year (five a day $\times$ 180 days), and supervisors typically observe one or two. The following grid shows what this looks like—two boxes out of nine hundred, or about 0.2 percent of the lessons taught. The remaining 99.8 percent of the time, teachers are essentially on their own with students.

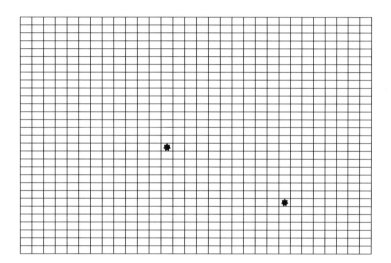

How can anyone, no matter how brilliant, accurately appraise, let alone change, a teacher's performance with so little time in the classroom? And yet this is what we've been asking supervisors to do.

Of course, some teachers get more intensive supervision—rookies and teachers on improvement plans—and many administrators make brief, informal visits to classrooms for other purposes—getting things signed, delivering supplies, wishing students or teachers a happy birthday, or just "managing by walking around." But formal evaluation visits are few and far between.

Hey, no problem! some teachers might say. *Fewer snoopervision visits, less stress. I can close my door and teach.* But for teachers, there's also a downside to being judged on the basis of one or two lessons a year. What if I'm having a bad day? What if I get nervous and teach a mediocre lesson? What if some kids act up?

For administrators, inadequate sampling of those 900 lessons is a huge problem. For end-of-year evaluations to be accurate and helpful, school leaders must have a way of knowing what teachers are doing *day by day*. With the overwhelming number of responsibilities they must attend to every day, how is this possible?

The Dog-and-Pony Show

"Hey, Sean, I see you're being observed today!" a teacher might say to a colleague dressed in a three-piece suit instead of his usual polo shirt and jeans. In many schools, evaluation visits are announced in advance (sometimes because that's required by the collective bargaining agreement, sometimes by tradition), and teachers want to showcase their best work. If the supervisor conducts a pre-observation conference, the teacher has an additional opportunity to fine-tune the lesson plan.

Every teacher's worst fear is being judged on a bad moment or being taken out of context, so the desire to have more control over evaluation visits is quite understandable.

Every teacher's worst fear is being judged on a bad moment or being taken out of context, so the desire to have more control over evaluation visits is quite understandable. But the downside is obvious: the supervisor might not be seeing the kind of teaching students are getting on a daily basis, making the appraisal inaccurate. Two stories illustrate the point.

> In preparation for an evaluation visit by a new principal, an elementary teacher distributes a special handout to her class. At the last minute, the school secretary comes on the intercom and says the principal had an emergency and needs to reschedule the observation. The teacher collects the handout and proceeds with "normal" instruction. A few days later, the principal evaluates the lesson and is quite critical. The teacher is irate, saying, "The last three principals liked that lesson!"

> An administrator walks into a high school history classroom for a scheduled evaluation visit and begins to take notes. When the teacher asks a question, every hand in the room is eagerly waving in the air, and each time he calls on a student, the answer is articulate, high level, and correct. The administrator is impressed and gives the teacher a glowing evaluation. Only later does he find out that students had very specific instructions for what to do when a "suit" is in the class taking notes: when the teacher asks a question, raise your hand; if you're sure you know the answer, raise your right hand; if you're not sure, raise your left hand.

Stories like these are part of the folklore of schools—everybody knows the game. A school leader might even be flattered by a jazzed-up lesson—*Gee, you put this on for me!* But supervisors aren't clueless. They know that many of the lessons they're observing aren't typical—not a "day in the life" glimpse of the teacher's performance. They also know that students tend to act a little better when there's an administrator in the room, which also works in the teacher's favor.

This dynamic might seem benign and unavoidable, especially given the difficulty and complexity of teaching, but it has serious consequences. If evaluations don't accurately appraise day-to-day classroom performance, nothing else works: effective teachers don't get authentic praise and encouragement; subpar teachers don't get targeted feedback, coaching, and support; and more than a few ineffective teachers remain in classrooms, harming their students' futures—especially those who, through no fault of their own, walk into school with disadvantages.

> *To put it bluntly, an evaluation process that relies on announced visits is inaccurate, dishonest, and ineffective.*

In legal parlance, this is a collusive deal: *I'll pretend this is the way you teach all the time and write it up, you'll pretend that's true and sign it, and we'll put it in your file and move on.* To put it bluntly, an evaluation process that relies on announced visits is inaccurate, dishonest, and ineffective.

There's more. When a principal plays along and accepts a glamorized lesson, writes it up, and makes it the most important comment on a teacher's work for the year, it tells the teacher, *You can put on a special show for me and that's what counts.* And that thought has a sibling: *it's OK to do something less special the other 99.8 percent of the time, when only students are present.*

When I make these points to groups of educators, a few rise up to defend announced observations and pre-observation conferences:

- *I want to see what she's capable of,* said a former superintendent. Fine, but it's essential to see whether students are getting that kind of teaching week after week.

- *I can see right through the dog-and-pony show,* said a seasoned middle school principal. Perhaps, but can you document that in a credible way? A hunch will not stand up in an arbitration hearing.

- *I need that pre-conference for feedback on my lesson planning,* said a teacher. But how helpful is discussing a single lesson plan once a year—especially if it's atypical?

Sometimes an attempt to put on a glamorized lesson flops because the teacher and students are thrown off by the high stakes. In this case the evaluation *underestimates* typical performance. But in my experience in a wide variety of schools, the dog-and-pony show almost always succeeds and the supervisor walks away with an impression of competent teaching. The result: a lot of mediocre teaching flies under the radar. Surely, announced observations are a major reason for the egregious grade inflation documented in *The Widget Effect* study of 2009 by Weisberg et al.

Why are so many educators willing to give credence to observations that don't give a true sense of teachers' performance? Perhaps it's because we see teacher evaluation as similar to what we do when we invite guests for dinner—we vacuum, scrub the toilet, and tidy up the living room. Perhaps it's empathy for how difficult teachers' jobs are and how embattled they feel these days—let's cut them some slack. Perhaps it's avoidance: seeing a plausible lesson enables administrators to sidestep difficult conversations about mediocre and ineffective teaching and the arduous work of documenting it.

The fundamental attribution error is also involved: seeing a single lesson makes us feel like we know the teacher, and we believe that they are like that all the time.

Most supervisors have little choice but to go by the book and use the information from formal evaluation visits, even when they know they're not representative of everyday reality.

Whatever the reason, most districts, even without union insistence, accept the idea of administrators scheduling their formal observations in advance, knowing that it's very likely that the teacher will take it up a notch.

True, supervisors get glimpses of reality in informal drop-ins, fleeting impressions of teachers' interactions with students, student and parent comments (praise and criticism), colleagues' off-the-record statements (*This conversation never took place . . .*), and of course, gossip. But these time-honored sources of information can't be included in official evaluations. Most supervisors have little choice but to go by the book and use the information from formal evaluation visits, even when they know they're not representative of everyday reality.

The worst consequence of the glamorized lesson tradition is the way it enables administrators who would rather not confront bad teaching. Dismissing a persistently ineffective teacher is a gut-wrenching, incredibly time-consuming process that often provokes a sympathetic circling of the wagons by other teachers, even if they're well aware that the teacher in question is not performing well. Knowing the unpleasantness and morale problems that holding these teachers accountable can cause, a supervisor might rationalize: the announced evaluation was plausible, the teacher is going to retire in a couple of years, so why jeopardize other initiatives that depend on cooperation and goodwill?

In addition, some teachers who use mediocre or ineffective classroom practices also have scary personalities. One of my favorite cartoons shows a deranged individual using a chain saw to cut the principal's desk in two. "Good idea, Sam," says the principal. "We can finish your evaluation tomorrow."

Very funny. But the price of this kind of avoidance is steep. Michael Fullan said it best (2003, p. 78):

Nothing undermines the motivation of hard-working teachers more than poor performance in other teachers being ignored over long periods of time. Not only do poor-performing teachers negatively affect the students in their classes, but they also have a spillover effect by poisoning the overall climate of the school.

Here's a related quote from Hollie Pettersson and Kerri Briggs (2019):

Teaching is a collective effort, and the most powerful predictor of a student's performance in a subject in any given year is what they learned in the previous grade. What any one teacher or school can achieve with students is critically dependent on the teaching quality of their colleagues.

Most teachers want their colleagues to be effective, but it's not their job to supervise and evaluate the teacher next door. That's administrators' job, and they need to step up.

Most teachers want their colleagues to be effective, but it's not their job to supervise and evaluate the teacher next door. That's administrators' job, and they need to step up.

So what is to be done? Let's look at how the challenge of keeping tabs on large amounts of unobserved activity is handled in two other venues: restaurants and coal mines. There are 24,000 eating establishments in New York City, and the Health Department conducts thorough inspections (using a long list of criteria) and requires the posting of a large A, B, or C grade right by the front door. The stakes are high, because anything less than an A discourages potential customers from walking in.

Are the Health Department's visits scheduled in advance? Of course not. The only way the public can trust the letter grades is for the inspections to be unannounced. This way, restaurants have a powerful incentive to be meticulous *all the time*, not just when they know the inspector is coming. It's not surprising that since this policy was introduced in 2010, the rate of foodborne illnesses among the city's restaurant-goers has declined significantly, and more and more restaurants are earning an A.

In coal mines, two of the biggest safety concerns are coal dust, which leads to black lung disease, and methane, which causes deadly explosions. All mines use sensors to measure coal dust and methane levels to ensure safe working conditions for miners. But media reports (NPR, 2012; Smith, 2012) showed that some mine operators were misleading federal monitors by sending in false data or by giving miners advance warning of inspection visits so that violations could be temporarily fixed. The result: a continuing stream of miners with black lung disease and a 2010 explosion in the Upper Big Branch mine in West Virginia that killed twenty-nine miners.

The key factor in restaurants and coal mines? Unannounced visits to see what's really happening on a day-to-day basis and to motivate constant adherence to good practices. Does this apply to schools? Absolutely. Children's futures are at stake.

Don't get me wrong: I'm not saying we should post teachers' A B C D F "grades" outside their classroom doors or publish them online. We just need teachers to know that what they do with students on a daily basis is what really matters, that supervisors will be dropping in frequently, and that effective performance on a daily basis is a core professional responsibility.

The vast majority of teachers do the right thing most of the time, but this cannot be left to chance. Unannounced visits are the key.

If you're still not convinced, imagine this conversation between the principal of a local public school and a parent thinking of enrolling a child in the school. The parent is trying to decide whether homeschooling, a charter school, or a parochial school is a better option.

Parent: I've looked at your website, but tell me honestly, how's the teaching in this school?

Principal: It's terrific. We have a great staff.

Parent: I'm glad to hear that. Can I ask how you know that?

Principal: I visit classrooms. I've been in this business for twenty-three years, and I can tell you these are great teachers. In fact, I've hired more than half of them.

Parent: OK, I don't want to sound rude, but I've heard about union contracts that prevent principals from making surprise visits to classrooms. What's the policy in this district?

Principal: I can see you've done your homework. Our contract says that official evaluation visits must be scheduled, and I'm required to have a pre-observation conference with each teacher to look over the lesson plan.

Parent: But don't teachers put on an especially good lesson when they know you're coming?

Principal: Sure, they do, but I make allowances for that. And I'm in classrooms informally a lot.

Parent: Excellent. But can you use the informal visits in your official evaluation?

Principal: Actually, no. The contract is pretty explicit about that.

Parent: That troubles me. So how often do you make official evaluation visits?

Principal: Well, the whole process is pretty time-consuming, so it's usually once a year for tenured teachers.

Parent: You mean to tell me that teachers get evaluated only once a year and have a chance to prepare a special lesson for you and nothing else counts?

Principal: That's true, but I'm in and out of classrooms all the time.

Parent: But you can't use what you see in those visits.

Principal: Yeah, that's true. But these are great teachers.

Parent: I know you're a good person and probably a good principal, but I don't trust this system. I think my husband and I are going to look elsewhere.

Principal: (*sotto voce*) Good riddance!

Problems with Narrative Evaluations

Many districts require supervisors to script detailed narratives of each lesson they observe, with an emphasis on capturing everything that's happening in the classroom minute by minute. This is an important skill, especially when administrators need to make the case for dismissing a persistently ineffective teacher. But doing this kind of micro-evaluation on a regular basis has several built-in shortcomings.

First, if supervisors are typing furiously throughout the lesson, they miss a lot. To get a true picture of instruction, they need to walk around, see what students are being asked to do, look at their work, chat with a couple of students, look at what's on the classroom walls, and carefully observe teacher-student and student-student dynamics. It's impossible to see, hear, and feel all this while sitting in one place and writing nonstop.

A second problem with detailed write-ups is that one lesson, however carefully scrutinized, is just a glimpse of the overall quality of a teacher's work. Although a lesson is the fundamental building block of instruction, it's only a part of a teacher's effort to inspire students and convey knowledge and skills. To get the bigger picture, a supervisor needs to know more: What curriculum unit is this lesson part of? What are the unit's big ideas and essential questions? How does this unit align with standards? How will students be assessed? And most important, did students learn what was taught? Supervisors can try to ferret out these missing pieces by asking for lesson plans and conducting pre- and post-conferences, but evaluations usually focus on teacher and student actions during the observed lesson.

Although a lesson is the fundamental building block of instruction, it's only a part of a teacher's effort to inspire students and convey knowledge and skills.

Third, it's impossible to teach most standards in a single lesson; it's a huge leap from big-picture goals like "understanding number sense" to planning a single lesson. Unit plans, which describe a teacher's game plan for teaching skills and concepts over a three- to five-week period, tell far more about whether instruction is coherent, appropriately rigorous, and aligned with standards. Curriculum unit plans help put each lesson in perspective—but supervisors rarely see them—or the tests that teachers give or how well students do on them. We'll address these underemphasized dimensions of supervision and evaluation in Chapters Eleven and Twelve. Suffice it to say that evaluating a teacher's yearlong performance on one lesson is crazy.

A fourth problem with detailed write-ups, especially if they're limited to "low-inference" observations, is that they often avoid answering the big-picture question on every teacher's mind after an observation: *How am I doing?* In my early years as a principal, I wrote hundreds of narrative evaluations, giving detailed descriptions of the dialogue and dynamics of a class.

I commented on the finer points of the lesson, but I rarely stepped back and gave a clear, overall judgment of the teacher's performance. In a narrative-focused evaluation process, the verbiage often obscures this message. This approach also allows the supervisor to avoid making overall judgments that might be difficult to back up.

A final problem with detailed write-ups is that they're difficult to do well. It takes experience and savvy for supervisors to grasp the subtleties of a lesson, it's even more challenging for them to capture those details in writing, and it's *really* hard to criticize performance in a way that will be heard. Some supervisors have had the benefit of excellent training in observing classrooms and writing up what they see, and some, even without training, are fluent writers and gifted "naturalists" (Howard Gardner's eighth intelligence) who can capture classroom nuances and convey them in lucid prose. Teachers fortunate enough to be evaluated by these principals can learn a lot.

But the majority of supervisors aren't operating at this level. Their write-ups might be guilty of these problems:

- **Overload.** Some detailed narratives also provide several evaluative comments and recommendations. This seems like the ideal combination, and with once-a-year evaluations, putting all the cards on the table feels like the right thing to do. When else will the supervisor make these points? But the danger is teachers being overwhelmed and not knowing where to begin. Most people can handle only one or two criticisms at a time; getting too many causes them to shut down or become defensive. If that happens, a lot of the administrator's writing will be wasted.

- **Boilerplate.** Word processing is a godsend to busy supervisors, but it can get them in trouble. When two Boston-area teachers compared their evaluations a few years ago, they found that the principal had pasted in exactly the same paragraphs, changing only the names. Another teacher joined the conversation and said the principal had used the same language in her evaluation—but had forgotten to substitute her name, which provoked great hilarity.

- **Outsourcing.** Principals have been known to ask teachers to write their own evaluations and then quickly review and sign them. This has the virtue of getting teachers to self-assess, but it's a cop-out—a lazy abdication of one of the principal's most important responsibilities.

- **Artificial intelligence.** Some cutting-edge supervisors have tried feeding basic information on teachers into ChatGPT and asking it to write evaluations, and they say it does a plausible job. Yikes!

Isn't the answer to all these unproductive practices to organize more and better training for principals? Or bring in expert third-party evaluators from outside? The sheer expense makes this impossible in most districts, but even if a city had plenty of money, is doubling down on an ineffective system the answer? Expert evaluators would still be dealing with the killer problems of infrequency, glamorized lessons, overwhelming teachers, and the skill required to do good narrative evaluations. It's not a training problem; it's a system problem.

In a 2009 article, Richard DuFour and Robert Marzano said it well: detailed written feedback on full-lesson observations is a "weak lever" for improving teacher performance (DuFour & Marzano, 2009). Jon Saphier, who has trained thousands of administrators (I'm one of them) in the fine art of narrative write-ups, once said that they are a "weak to medium lever" for teacher development (personal communication, 2010). I agree. There are far more productive ways for districts to spend scarce resources—and for supervisors to spend their precious time.

What I'm calling into question is whether this brand of supervision and evaluation actually improves the quality of instruction. In their report, Toch and Rothman (2008) argued that expert observations of teaching can accurately *describe* the classroom practices linked to high test scores. Perhaps, but does the process of observing and evaluating teachers actually *improve* teaching that's not already effective?

This is where the research is ambiguous. I would argue that the first three design flaws in the clinical supervision-evaluation model shown in the following figure—announced observations, once or twice a year, and full-lesson write-ups—form an unholy trinity, each reinforcing the others and preventing the process from playing a constructive role in schools.

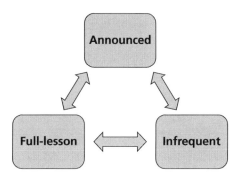

Four additional flaws deepen the problem.

Opportunity Cost

Union contracts don't stipulate that teacher evaluation write-ups must be two or three pages long, but that's the norm in many districts. Principals sometimes push themselves to keep up with (or surpass) prolix colleagues, and the expected page count edges up. As I argued previously, long evaluations with multiple suggestions are overwhelming and counterproductive for teachers, and there's a serious consequence for supervisors: chewing up enormous amounts of time and preventing more-productive instructional work. A New York principal said, "Every evaluation takes me out of the game for four hours."

Supervisors fall into three types: saints, cynics, and sinners.

Supervisors fall into three types: saints, cynics, and sinners. The saints go by the book, and evaluations consume their lives for weeks at a time. Principals who choose to commit serious time to write-ups (or are required to do so by their superiors) have no choice but to close their office doors for days at a time—or spend evenings, weekends, and vacations at their computers. "Like a little term paper every Saturday," said a Boston principal.

The cynics heave a sigh, sit down at the computer, and bang out the required evaluations as quickly as possible. Administrators in this category have lost faith in the evaluation process and don't believe their write-ups will produce any improvements in teaching and learning—but they do their duty.

The sinners are the most daring; they simply *don't do* most evaluations, writing up only the most egregiously ineffective teachers. The proof that there are sinners out there lies in the number of teachers who say that they haven't been evaluated in years. The sinners are audacious scofflaws, thumbing their noses at system requirements and daring higher-ups to catch them. Teachers don't complain because evaluation is as appealing as a root canal. And supervisors' superiors are often none the wiser—or choose to wink at these omissions.

When I present the saint/cynic/sinner model to audiences of principals and ask them to tell me by a show of hands which of the three categories best describes them, a few confess to being sinners, and there are usually significantly more cynics than saints. Then I ask the "money question": Are the saints more effective at improving teaching and learning in their schools than the cynics and the sinners? Principals are quick to say that the answer is no: the saints are no more likely to get high achievement than the other two. At this point, my audience gets a sinking feeling that they might not have been spending their time well.

We'll return to this question in Chapter Thirteen, but three things are clear so far: (1) teacher evaluation is a major time management hurdle for supervisors; (2) the more wedded an administrator is to the conventional model, the more challenging it is to get into all classrooms on a regular basis; and (3) many supervisors have begun to doubt that spending serious time on conventional evaluation has an instructional payoff; it's just one more thing they have to get done and send in to the central office. Some, possibly a subset of the sinners, are mavericks, trying other approaches.

Jon Saphier (1993) has suggested spreading out evaluation work to reduce supervisors' annual burden. He proposed a four-year evaluation cycle in which each teacher rotates through peer evaluation, a study group, self-assessment, and a formal evaluation. This approach sounds like it should work: the supervisor evaluates only a quarter of the staff each year and can spend more time visiting classrooms, doing thorough write-ups, and giving feedback to teachers whose year it is.

But there are problems with this approach: (1) the rate of teacher turnover these days means that many schools have a higher proportion of nontenured teachers (who must be evaluated every year), so supervisors end up evaluating significantly more than 25 percent of their teachers every year; (2) the focus is still on micro-evaluation of lessons, which, I've argued, is not the best way to improve teaching and learning; (3) a four-year cycle gives most teachers a "pass" three-quarters of the time, which could result in supervisors losing the pulse of a significant portion of the school and not tuning in on mediocre or more serious teaching practices; and (4) most states now require annual or biannual evaluation of all teachers.

Power and Passivity

Evaluations are often a one-way street from administrator to teacher, with the boss doing almost all of the work—checking out the lesson plan, observing, the write-up, presenting feedback, and submitting the final evaluation. Charlotte Danielson (2009) says this goes against everything we know about how adults learn. For teachers to get anything out of the process, they must be active, reflective participants.

But in most evaluations, that's not the case. There's also a top-down, paternalistic, distrustful dynamic, as contrasted to an approach that aims to foster employee involvement in improving results. In a classic work published in 1960, MIT professor Douglas McGregor called the top-down approach Theory X and the worker-empowering approach Theory Y. Researchers have found that Theory X management doesn't improve performance beyond reluctant minimal compliance.

Given that the frontline workers in schools are on their own 99.8 percent of the time, it's especially important that supervisors use Theory Y to get teachers invested in the mission and constantly working to improve their craft. Most of the time, there's no one standing over them making them do it (and that wouldn't work anyway).

So the challenge in supervision and evaluation is to activate (or amplify) a supervisory voice inside each teacher's head that guides them as they work with students: *Check for understanding. Ask a higher-order thinking question. Call on the introverts.* One-on-one feedback from an administrator based on actual classroom performance is a golden opportunity for this kind of contextual, individualized professional development, potentially getting teachers to take ownership for a process of continuous improvement.

But conventional supervision and evaluation rarely work this way. In fact, the exact opposite is often true, with teachers waiting anxiously for their boss to judge them and reacting defensively if there's criticism—or just brushing off the whole process.

Why does this happen? Although most teachers don't respect the evaluation process, it still makes them nervous. Collective bargaining agreements provide job protection, but even the best teachers harbor irrational fears. A veteran middle school social studies teacher once said to me, "Every time an administrator steps into my classroom, I feel like my job is on the line."

Although most teachers don't respect the evaluation process, it still makes them nervous.

These fears make it difficult for teachers to open up, admit errors, and talk honestly about things that need to improve. In all too many evaluative interactions, teachers put on their game face and get through it with as little authentic interaction as possible. The supervisor owns the feedback, not them.

Some common interpersonal dynamics can also prevent teachers from learning from critical feedback. A young teacher might see a middle-aged administrator as a parent figure, triggering latent adolescent rebellious feelings. A veteran teacher might resent criticism from a twenty-something administrator. *(I was teaching before this kid was born!)* To some teachers, criticism feels like a power trip on the boss's part. And there's almost always a reason to push back: *You haven't taught in years. You only taught sixth graders. You don't have children of your own. All right, you do have children, but they're in preschool. Why should I listen to you? You don't understand my world.*

The result of vibes like these is that teachers reject or ignore a lot of feedback from supervisors. There's a certain emptiness in the professional relationship between school leaders and teachers, with very few professional conversations about the daily struggles of teaching and learning. And if principals aren't setting the tone, it's less likely that APs, team leaders, and department heads will engage in rich discourse with teachers.

Unhelpful with Teacher Teamwork

Although evaluations are private and confidential, teachers often compare notes. This can lead to bad feelings when one person feels the boss was more generous to someone considered to be less competent. Nothing is more poisonous in a school than the perception of favoritism; at the Mather, teachers were so sensitive to the slightest hint of extra attention to others that I became convinced that half of them had grown up in families where the parents played favorites among the children.

The fact that teacher evaluations go from the supervisor to individual teachers also cuts the process off from teacher collaboration, which has tremendous potential for improving teaching and learning. In schools where same-grade and same-subject teachers don't work together, the evaluation process reinforces this isolation and doesn't serve as a vehicle for getting teachers to talk about curriculum or pedagogy.

This detracts from teachers' sense of responsibility to their grade-level or department team, fails to exploit the potential synergy of collaboration, and means that teachers are often reinventing the wheel in their classrooms—an unfortunate dynamic. In schools like this, teacher meetings tend to be dominated by nonschool topics, gossip, funny stories about kids, and not-so-funny stories about kids. This is not the way to boost achievement.

Of course, accurate appraisal of teachers' overall performance is only the first step of supervision and evaluation. For professionals who are on their own virtually all the time, ensuring intrinsic motivation to continuously improve is just as important. Many teachers possess this inner drive from the moment they enter the classroom, but some lose it as the years roll by, and others never had it—the TGIF set.

Infrequent supervision and evaluation hasn't been effective at building intrinsic motivation, which is why most teachers (as we saw in the poll graph in the Introduction) point to other sources when asked what inspired and helped them become more effective in the classroom—help from colleagues, visiting colleagues' classrooms, workshops and courses outside the school, and feedback from their students.

Not Linked to Student Learning

When evaluation time rolls around, most teachers are happy if they get a good rating—or at least a satisfactory one. It's all about pleasing, impressing, charming, satisfying, or "getting one over" on the supervisor based on the lessons they observe. Whether students are learning is rarely discussed; teachers are being evaluated on the *process*, not the outcome. This is true because in virtually all school districts, teacher unions have been successful in preventing teachers from being evaluated on their students' test scores and other evidence of learning.

Can't supervisors can get a sense of student learning by visiting classrooms, looking over students' shoulders, and asking them questions? Sure, but there are problems with this approach. Many administrators are too busy scripting the lesson to get up and check on learning. Even if they're able to chat with a few students during classroom visits, it's hard to tell whether the whole class understands what's being taught—let alone whether students will remember a few weeks later. Finally, even if supervisors check on downstream learning by looking at unit test and interim assessment results, they are contractually forbidden from using the data to evaluate teachers.

So supervisors have little choice but to focus on teaching inputs versus learning outcomes, on chalkboard razzle-dazzle versus deep

Squeezed by the evaluation process, supervisors are stuck with overmanaging lessons and undermanaging the bigger picture of whether teachers are truly making a difference.

understanding, on pretty bulletin boards versus student proficiency. Squeezed by the evaluation process, supervisors are stuck with overmanaging lessons and undermanaging the bigger picture of whether teachers are truly making a difference.

And because evaluation doesn't focus on student learning, supervisors are rarely able to help teachers emerge from their classroom isolation and reflect with colleagues on what needs to change so that more students succeed. Without a push in this direction, all too many teachers gravitate toward an unfortunate but common default setting: assuming that if something is taught (explained or demonstrated), it is automatically learned (Nuthall, 2004)—and if it isn't learned, teachers have done their part.

So why *not* use test scores to evaluate teachers? Because student learning is the "bottom line" of schools, this idea sounds eminently reasonable, and it's gained high-level support starting in 2009, when the Obama administration made it a key part of the Race to the Top legislation. Advocates contended that "incentivizing" teachers on achievement can be a major force for improving what happens in classrooms. We'll look at the details of this ill-fated initiative in Chapter Eight.

The Imperative for Change

The seven design flaws explain why conventional teacher evaluation has such a disappointing track record for improving teaching and learning—not to mention the time it wastes and the cynicism it engenders among many educators. And yet this process remains firmly entrenched in the majority of schools, and few researchers and reformers challenge its basic components. Why, given the obvious problems? Here are some possible reasons:

- **Old habits.** This is the way we do things around here.
- **Contracts.** Union agreements based on mistrust of administrators require certain components, especially pre- and post-observation conferences and announced classroom visits.
- **Sunk costs.** A lot of money has been poured into training supervisors and we can't just throw it away.
- **Vendors.** Schools have invested in technology aligned with the evaluation process.
- **Power trip.** Some supervisors like the dynamic of nervous teachers striving to impress them.
- **Masochism.** Supervising teachers this way feels like real *work*; it's difficult and time-consuming, but it feels virtuous.

- **Conspiracy theory.** The system is designed to keep supervisors tied up with paperwork so they'll leave teachers alone.
- **No alternative.** Other approaches have even more problems.

None of these are good reasons, especially the last one. There *is* an alternative—we could see its contours as we examined the design flaws of traditional supervision and evaluation. Flipping the negatives to positives, here's a model of how supervision and evaluation *should* work:

- Supervisors and teachers have a shared understanding of good teaching.
- Supervisors are in classrooms a lot and see everyday teaching in action.
- Supervisors are knowledgeable and perceptive observers.
- Teachers get frequent appreciation and coaching.
- Teachers trust the process and engage with the feedback, not just individually but as part of their teams.
- Supervisors address mediocre and ineffective teaching.
- Student learning is central to the process.

Does this sound idealistic? No question. But I hope the subsequent chapters will convince you that it can become a reality in any school.

Questions to Consider

- *Can teacher evaluation be a player in improving teaching and learning?*
- *What are the essential elements of an effective evaluation process?*
- *If your school is still using the traditional teacher evaluation process, why?*

4

Mini–Observations 1

Sampling Daily Reality

> *Trust but verify.*
> —Ronald Reagan

To have a positive impact on teaching and learning, an evaluation system must provide a structure that supports supervisors in three essential parts of their job: sampling daily classroom reality; perceptively observing teaching; and affirming, coaching, and evaluating teachers. Here is the outline of the nuts and bolts of mini–observations, with details under each of those three areas:

MINI-OBSERVATIONS

Sampling daily reality:
1. Frequent and short
2. Systematic
3. Unannounced

Observing perceptively:
4. Humble, curious, and low-tech
5. Observant, a leverage point
6. The bigger picture

Affirming, coaching, and evaluating:
7. Face-to-face conversations
8. Brief follow-up summaries
9. Courage
10. Rubric scoring the year

In this chapter we'll focus on sampling daily reality; in Chapter Five we'll cover observing perceptively; in Chapter Six, affirming and coaching; in Chapter Seven, evaluating; and in Chapter Eight, making student learning central to the process.

Frequent and Short

By making multiple visits, supervisors can get a representative sampling of classroom reality, normalize their presence, reduce teachers' anxiety, minimize disruption, and ultimately convince teachers to trust the fairness of the system.

How frequent is frequent enough? Surprisingly, there are no high-quality studies on this question. Researchers seem to have uncritically accepted the traditional model of full-lesson teacher evaluations and haven't explored the efficacy of more-frequent visits, leaving us to figure out this important question on our own.

From my own experience at the Mather and two decades of school visits since, I've concluded that when teachers are observed about once a month, or ten times a year, supervisors can put together a surprisingly accurate picture of overall performance. Making ten observations per teacher strikes most supervisors as very challenging, but that's because they're used to writing up a full-lesson observation each time. What if the visits are short—mini-observations? Wouldn't that be more manageable? Most supervisors who've tried it agree.

Is there research on how long a mini-observation should be? Very little, but there is one intriguing study. In 1993, Nalini Ambady and Robert Rosenthal found that college students, after viewing thirty-second video "slices" of professors in action, *without audio*, were able to make virtually the same assessment as other students who sat through classes for a full semester. "That's the power of our adaptive unconscious," says Malcolm Gladwell, commenting on this study in his best-selling book *Blink* (2005, p. 13). An instructor's body language, gestures, and the level of confidence communicate a great deal in very little time, even without hearing their voice.

Ambady and Rosenthal's study is striking, but if short visits are going to be part of K–12 teachers' evaluations, there's no way thirty seconds would be seen as fair. Have there been other studies of longer visits? In my extensive reading in journals and magazines, I haven't seen any good research on this very important question. Once again, we're on our own.

How long a supervisor needs to stay in a classroom depends on the purpose. If it's to show the flag *(Good morning, scholars)*, five seconds is plenty—a quick in-and-out. If it's to check on

How long a supervisor needs to stay in a classroom depends on the purpose.

a substitute teacher, six seconds will do *(Thank goodness, the kids seem to be working quietly)*. If the purpose is in-depth professional development, an instructional coach needs to stay the whole period. And if the goal is dismissing a persistently ineffective teacher, there need to be multiple full-period visits, each followed up with a specific improvement plan and a chance for redemption.

But if the goal is to sample the quality of instruction, I've found that ten to fifteen minutes is enough to gather insights on a lesson—provided that there are frequent visits, the observer has a good eye for instruction, there's a face-to-face conversation after each visit, and documentation is very short.

In workshops and webinars, I've found surprising agreement on this amount of time. Here are the results to a recent poll of educators from around the US and several other countries:

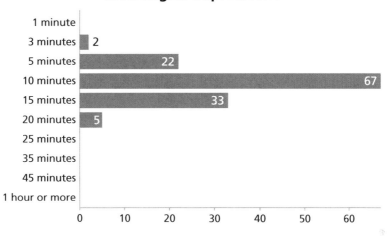

How short? The minimum time for a meaningful impression?

This poll shows that many supervisors don't need much convincing on the efficacy of short visits. One principal told me that when she does her "formals," she usually knows within the first ten minutes what she needs to say to the teacher, and the rest of the period is a waste of time. I predict that when good research is done on the optimal amount of time in a classroom, ten to fifteen minutes will emerge as the Goldilocks length.

Okay, short visits make sense, but is it possible to fit ten for every teacher into a very busy year? Let's do the math. At the Mather, I was responsible for forty-two teachers. Multiplying out, that's 420 mini-observations a year—a big number. I'm exhausted just looking at it. But dividing by 180 (the number of days in the Boston school year), that's only 2.3 mini-observations a day. A lot more manageable.

I predict that when good research is done on the optimal amount of time in a classroom, ten to fifteen minutes will emerge as the Goldilocks length.

But there are days when I didn't get into a single classroom: kid after kid is sent to the office, a student had a medical emergency, angry parents or unexpected visitors commandeered my time, or the superintendent pulled me out of the building for a meeting. I needed some grace—a "stretch" goal of three minis a week. With that target, allowing for occasional "bad" days, I could hit the goal of ten per teacher per year. And in fact, in the nine years I did mini-observations at the Mather, I reached or exceeded that goal in all but one year. But my mini-observations were only five minutes long, reflecting my challenging caseload and other demands on my time.

Forty-two evaluatees is more than most supervisors have on their plate. The average supervisory caseload for US principals is twenty to twenty-five teachers, and as the following chart shows, with that caseload, principals and other supervisors need to average only two mini-observations a day—or ten a week—to hit the target of ten a year.

Number of Teachers	Minis for Year	Number per Day	Stretch Goal per Day
60	600	3.3	4
50	500	2.7	3
40	400	2.2	3
30	300	1.7	2
20	200	1.1	2
10	100	.6	1

Hold on. Implicit in these calculations is that supervisors start mini-observations on the first day of school and keep going to the last day in the spring. Impossible, say some administrators and teachers. Classroom observations can't be done in the super-busy opening and closing days of the school year, the weeks around Christmas, during standardized testing, and in the weeks just before summer vacation.

I push back. The first month of school is crucial for seeing if classroom management is off to a good start, especially for rookie teachers. Testing weeks are a perfect time to focus on art, computer, music, library, and physical education teachers and check in with school counselors. Late December is an emotionally fraught time for many students, and classrooms need especially close monitoring. And during the final days of each school year, supervisors want to make sure parents are getting their money's worth right up to the last bell. Administrators' presence in classrooms throughout the year is possible and *really matters*.

Is there such a thing as too many mini-observations? Absolutely. At the Mather, when I was able to squeeze in more than five in a day, I found that my memory of what happened in classrooms was taxed and the quality and timeliness of feedback suffered. In addition, teachers can feel overmanaged and smothered; they need space to do their work—accountable, of course, for quality and results. Being mini-observed about once a month felt right for the teachers I worked with.

Being mini-observed about once a month felt right for the teachers I worked with.

Deciding on a specific daily or weekly mini-observation goal and tracking the data are important for time management and motivation. A fuzzy goal—*I'm going to get into more class-rooms this month*—won't work. I tracked how long each one of my mini-observation cycles was taking, and that helped get me out of my office and into a classroom when I didn't really feel like doing it. It's like exercise: without a measurable target (three vigorous twenty-minute workouts a week is what most doctors recommend), we won't keep it up.

Here's another way to make this point. When an observer walks into a classroom, there are two possible learning curves. In the first, new insights increase with every minute that passes:

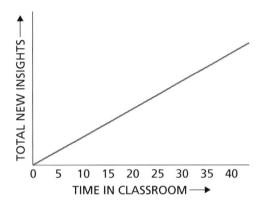

If this theory is true, the observer needs to stay the whole period to grasp what's going on. But there's a second possibility:

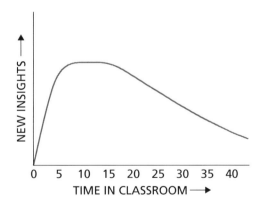

In this scenario, the moment the observer enters, there's a flood of information on classroom climate, the physical characteristics of the room, and what the teacher and students are doing. This mirrors the Ambady-Rosenthal finding on how quickly we take in key details of a classroom.

After five or ten minutes, the number of new insights levels off and then gradually declines for the remainder of the class.

In most cases, the second figure shows what happens during a mini-observation. This suggests that for a very busy supervisor (and what supervisor isn't?), staying beyond a certain point has diminishing returns and is a relatively inefficient use of time (in business jargon, it has a high opportunity cost). For administrators who want to be in classrooms a lot, short observations get the maximum amount of information in the least amount of time. Mini-observations are also much easier than traditional evaluations to fit into the nooks and crannies of a busy day.

At the Mather, I found that if I stayed less than five minutes, my impressions were superficial and I was unable to give teachers feedback that was credible or helpful. If I stayed longer than ten minutes, I couldn't see teachers as often and the insights I picked up in the incremental minutes didn't compensate for the loss of frequency. Five minutes worked for me, yielding surprisingly rich and plentiful information on each classroom.

But in retrospect, I was trying to supervise too many teachers. If I had split the faculty with my assistant principal, each of us would have needed only about two mini-observations a day and could have stayed longer—about ten minutes—which I've come to believe is a better amount of time. The key for supervisors is to get to a manageable caseload so the number of observations a day and the length of each classroom visit reaches an optimal level.

The big takeaway: there's an inverse relationship between the length of each visit and the number of classrooms administrators will be able to visit on a regular basis. The shorter each visit, the more can be squeezed into each day; the longer each visit, the fewer classrooms will be seen. I recommend that supervisors do the math as described, settle on a daily target, and estimate the visit length that makes it possible to keep up that frequency. Explain the rationale to teachers, and then plunge in and start observing, making adjustments as needed.

In some districts, teachers ask that supervisors stay *no less* than a particular amount of time (ten minutes, for example). I think it's diplomatically wise to make this concession, but supervisors should maintain the right to stay *beyond* the minimum. There might be a particularly effective piece of teaching going on, or the administrator might be curious about what will happen next, wonder if the "do now" will ever get wrapped up, or worry about how the teacher will handle a challenging situation. There should be no ceiling on the length of mini-observations; it's a good area for differentiation.

> *There should be no ceiling on the length of mini-observations; it's a good area for differentiation.*

Pre-Observation Conferences

What about commonly required pre-observation conferences, in which the supervisor goes over the lesson plan with the teacher prior to an observation? There are several reasons why these are incompatible with mini-observations. First, talking about a specific lesson often means the teacher knows when the supervisor will observe, meaning that the lesson and lesson plan could be specially amped up—in other words, unrepresentative of what students are getting day to day.

Second, the administrator is looking closely at one lesson plan but not seeing the plans teachers use over time. Third, pre-observation conferences are simply not practical with frequent, short classroom visits. And fourth, they're time-consuming, which will bog down the pace of observations.

That's why Madeline Hunter, in a 1986 article in *Educational Leadership*, said that pre-observation conferences are not a good use of time for supervisors or teachers. In addition, she said, teachers feel locked into the lesson plan they know will be observed and are therefore less agile and adaptable as they teach it. Better to focus on the post-lesson conversation and what can be gleaned from what actually happened.

As I'll argue in Chapter Eleven, the best way for principals to supervise lesson and curriculum quality is to orchestrate effective *unit* planning by teacher teams, review the plans they produce, and spot-check lesson plans during mini-observations.

Situations When Full-Lesson Observations Are Appropriate

Mini-observations are designed to allow supervisors to accurately monitor daily instruction and have an ongoing dialogue with teachers about what's working and what can be improved, culminating in accurate end-of-year rubric evaluations. Minis are the best way to affirm and fine-tune teaching through the year if they are frequent, short, systematic, and always followed up with face-to-face conversations.

But there are two situations when administrators should stay the whole lesson. The first is with teachers who are on improvement plans; there's a gear-shift and it's necessary to do full-lesson observations with detailed suggestions and feedback. If progress is not being made after a reasonable amount of time, these observations can provide evidence for dismissal.

The second is when a teacher invites a supervisor to observe a lesson. In this case, it's courteous and respectful for the visitor to stay till the end, unless called away for an emergency. Follow-up conversations should happen soon afterward and a formal write-up isn't necessary.

Other than these two situations, supervisors should focus on getting into a regular rhythm of mini-observations, in most cases about two a day, and keep that up throughout the year. Implemented this way, minis can completely replace annual, formal, full-lesson observations (why do them unless a teacher is having major problems?), providing much better information for the end-of-year summative evaluation.

What about classroom visits conducted by instructional coaches, peer observers, and teacher teams doing Lesson Study? Wouldn't it make sense for them to stay for the whole lesson? Yes, indeed. Let's look at the details for each one, and viewing videos of lessons:

- **Instructional coaches** are becoming increasingly common in schools. With their experience and pedagogical content knowledge (usually in literacy or math), they are ideal observers of lessons in their area. Feedback from a coach or teacher leader is less threatening and more palatable to teachers because they are usually in the same bargaining unit and are not acting as evaluators. Coaches also have more time than harried principals for full-lesson observations and longer follow-up conversations.

- **Peer observations** can be very helpful, and some districts—notably Toledo, Ohio, and Montgomery County, Maryland—have developed thoughtful protocols for experienced teacher leaders to observe their colleagues. The PAR (Peer Assistance and Review) model has spread to a number of districts around the country (more details on that later).

  Brand-new teachers are especially likely to benefit from a non-administrator watching the lesson from beginning to end and talking it through right afterward—with no write-up and a clear understanding that it's low stakes. Ideally the observer has deep knowledge and experience in that particular subject or grade level—for example, a science department head or a lead second-grade teacher. The principal's role is to organize coverage.

  One concern with peer observations is the "culture of nice." It's hard for teachers to give critical comments to people they eat lunch with every day. Colleagues might say they want honest feedback but turn chilly when they get it, which hurts relationships that are important to a congenial workplace. Training and clear protocols are needed to make peer observations effective.

- **In Lesson Study,** teacher teams develop, pilot, observe, and polish individual lessons designed to address specific student needs. Japanese schools have developed this protocol to a high level in recent decades (see *The Teaching Gap* by James Stigler and James Hiebert, 1999), and it's been implemented in a number of US schools. Lesson Study is one of the most sophisticated and demanding formats for observing and giving feedback, and it definitely requires watching whole lessons.

- **Lesson videos** enable teachers to examine every detail and talk through the finer points of instruction. Watching a videotape of one's own teaching is a powerful way to see flaws and appreciate strengths. With cellphone cameras, making a video of a lesson requires much less skill than writing up an observation, and the interpersonal challenges of giving critical feedback are virtually eliminated; the tape speaks for itself, holding up a mirror to the teacher's practice. A teacher watching a lesson video alone can feel self-indulgent and lead to focusing on small details (*Why do I keep scratching my nose?!*). Teachers learn most when they watch with a critical friend who can help them see beyond the quirks and really analyze the lesson.

> *Watching a videotape of one's own teaching is a powerful way to see flaws and appreciate strengths.*

Stigler and Hiebert have suggested that US schools adapt Lesson Study by using videos of lessons as discussion tools. In schools where teachers craft effective lessons and evaluate their impact, the quality of instruction can improve by leaps and bounds. In addition, teachers' sense of efficacy and professionalism—the deepest kind of morale—will benefit from this kind of detailed, solution-oriented focus on individual lessons. Principals can be members of Lesson Study teams or drop in occasionally, getting insights on the curriculum and the best teaching practices.

Systematic

Supervisors won't get an accurate sampling of each teacher's work unless they're methodical about seeing the following:

- Beginning, middle, and end of lessons
- Morning, mid-day, and afternoon mini-observations
- With elementary teachers, math, reading, science, and social studies
- With middle and high-school teachers, several of the groups they teach

It's also important to spread mini-observations out over the whole school year.

To systematically sample all these dimensions of teaching, supervisors need to keep track of visits with an efficient, user-friendly record-keeping system. Ideally this is a spreadsheet or an electronic product with pull-down menus of teachers and date stamps for when observations and follow-up conversations take place.

Should some teachers have more mini-observations than others? This seems logical because rookie teachers usually need more help than seasoned veterans. Many administrators follow this logic, which is why one teacher in Brookline, Massachusetts, told me she hadn't been observed in seventeen years. Clearly, her principal thought she was doing fine!

Logical as this kind of differentiation might seem, I believe all teachers should get the same number of mini-observations. Why? Teachers talk among themselves, and notice if some are getting more minis than others. Is that a commentary on teaching skill? they wonder. Does the principal like to visit your classroom more than mine? Is favoritism involved?

Teachers talk among themselves, and notice if some are getting more minis than others.

Equity is the best approach. The principal should be able to tell faculty members that by the end of the school year, everyone will have the same number of mini-observations. Novice teachers might have longer debrief conversations and additional help from an instructional coach or peer observer. Veteran teachers might have shorter conversations—but also might be encouraged to spread effective practices to peers or write online articles.

For supervisors, there's great benefit to keeping up a steady rhythm of mini-observations. Not only does it keep them well-informed about instruction, build relationships, and provide frequent opportunities for coaching but also it brings joy: seeing great teaching and *aha!* moments for students can make a supervisor's day. One more thing: supervisors can cross-pollinate, opening classroom doors and spreading effective practices around the school through professional development sessions or a regular newsletter.

A few years ago, I was coaching a middle-school principal in New York City who believed she'd found an efficient way to manage mini-observations. She would go for almost two weeks without visiting classrooms and then, in effect, binge, observing all classrooms in two days. Here's what her pattern looked like:

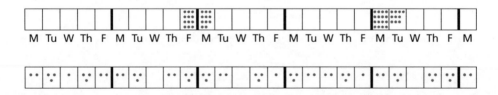

I pointed out several problems with this approach. First, there were stretches of time when she was not out and about and missed a lot of what was happening in classrooms. Second, teachers could let each other know when she was on one of her hyper-observation days and up their game. And third, it was impossible for her to have prompt feedback conversations to so many teachers in one day. I convinced her to spread her mini-observations out, and the second row in the diagram shows a much-improved schedule (with occasional days when she wasn't able do any mini-observations).

Unannounced

As I argued in Chapter Three, pre-announced observations are one of the design flaws of the traditional evaluation process, especially when yoked to two others: observing teachers only once or twice a year and relying on full-lesson write-ups. I was recently on a Zoom webinar about mini-observations with a group of educators in Connecticut, and a high-school math teacher said that in his twenty-one years in the classroom, he'd always hated the annual evaluations. Why didn't evaluators pop in frequently and get a statistical sampling of his teaching?

I believe that being unannounced is a natural and logical feature of mini-observations—if done with fairness and integrity. It opens the door to the following:

- Getting an accurate picture of how teachers are performing on a daily basis
- Delivering believable praise and helpful coaching
- Making good decisions on professional development
- Being vigilant for troubling practices that can be nipped in the bud
- Giving teachers fair and accurate end-of-year evaluations

But unannounced visits make some teachers nervous—especially in schools where everyone is accustomed to knowing in advance when they'll be evaluated and able to showcase their very best lessons. The implicit message is that good teaching should be happening any time a supervisor walks in—an exacting expectation. It's not irrational for teachers to worry about being caught at a bad moment—and in classrooms, everyone has bad moments.

One approach to calming teachers' jitters is citing Ronald Reagan's credo (quoted at the beginning of this chapter) when he was negotiating with the Soviet Union on nuclear missiles. We trust you—after all, you're certified, we hired you, and you're teaching without supervision about 98 percent of the time. But to give credible quality assurance to stakeholders, mini-observations need to be unannounced.

That might reassure some teachers, but I've found the best ways to lower teachers' anxiety is for unannounced visits to be frequent, short, systematic, and *always* followed up with a face-to-face conversation. The implementation details matter, as we'll see in the chapters that follow.

Questions to Consider

- *How many mini-observations do you think each teacher should have a year?*
- *What's the optimal amount of time for supervisors to be in the classroom for a mini-observation?*
- *Should some teachers have more minis than others?*

5 | Mini-Observations 2

Observing Perceptively

> *You can observe a lot just by watching.*
> —Yogi Berra

Here's our outline:

> **MINI-OBSERVATIONS**
> **Sampling daily reality:**
> 1. Frequent and short
> 2. Systematic
> 3. Unannounced
> **Observing perceptively:**
> 4. Humble, curious, and low-tech
> 5. Observant, a leverage point
> 6. The bigger picture
> **Affirming, coaching, and evaluating:**
> 7. Face-to-face conversations
> 8. Brief follow-up summaries
> 9. Courage
> 10. Rubric scoring the year

This chapter focuses on the second section, observing perceptively:

Humble and Curious

Even if supervisors make frequent classroom visits, they're seeing less than 1 percent of teachers' work with students. Each time they walk into a classroom for a mini-observation, a supervisor probably doesn't know any of these aspects of the classroom:

- What went well yesterday, and not so well
- The teacher's insights about student understanding
- Which students are doing well and which are having a bad day
- How this lesson fits into the unit plan
- What's going on in the teacher's life outside school (Brad Morgan, personal communication, 2021)

For those reasons and more, mini-observers should enter classrooms with humility and an open and attentive expression on their face. Genuine curiosity about what's going on in different classrooms is one of the most appealing supervisor qualities for teachers.

Coaching administrators in a wide variety of schools, I've noted some things teachers find distracting and annoying when visitors are in their classrooms:

- Sneaking in a side door and startling the teacher
- Taking copious notes (*What are they writing?*)
- Scowling or yawning
- Whispering to another visitor
- Talking to students while the teacher is addressing the class
- Sitting in the teacher's chair (invading their private space, symbolically taking over)

Mini-observers need to be sensitive as they visit teachers' "homes," observing some basic protocols so their presence will be as neutral as possible.

Protocols

On one of my early mini-observations at the Mather, I sat down next to a second grader and he said, "So, Mr. Marshall, when you don't have anything else to do, you visit classrooms?" This was an amusing question, but it showed that I hadn't done a good job explaining to students what I was up to. Principals might announce at a beginning-of-the-year assembly: "This year I'm going to visit your classroom quite often. I'm doing this because I love to watch you learning. Please go about your business; I'm a fly on the wall. What does that expression mean?"

Similarly, teachers and supervisors should agree on some basic protocols. I've noticed that when I do co-observations with principals, some teachers don't look at us when we walk in—a clear sign that they're nervous. Students who are attuned to adult power dynamics might notice this and be distracted (*Is my teacher in trouble?*). I suggest that schools agree that there should be a quick nonverbal greeting when a mini-observer walks in. This normalizes the process for students and might also lower the teacher's blood pressure a bit.

Teachers should also be discouraged from making a big deal of the supervisor's presence ("Say good morning to Mr. Marshall, boys and girls.") or stopping to explain what the class is working on. Business as usual is the goal, and most teachers appreciate being able to continue without interruption. Most important, they should know there will be a face-to-face conversation after the observation, giving them a chance to explain the context and fill in what the supervisor might not have noticed.

Some schools have a "wave-off" signal—an agreed-on gesture (for example, tugging on an earlobe) telling the supervisor that it's not a good time for a mini-observation—a transition, snack time, or a difficult moment. Another practice I've seen in schools is supervisors showing something (for example, a blue notecard) signaling that the visit is a mini-observation (versus a daily building tour). Both of these are attempts by teachers to have a little more control over the mini-observation process. Not all educators agree on the need for these signals. Here are poll responses from one of my recent in-person workshops:

In your school, should there be a...

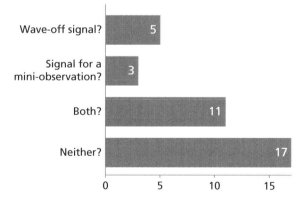

The informal nature of mini-observations makes it possible for supervisors to get involved in a lesson—for example, chiming in with insights or asking for clarification if students seem confused. Whether or not to depart from the *I'm a fly on the wall* protocol is an important question, and we'll address it in some detail in Chapter Nine.

If mini-observations are handled well, they're usually well-received by teachers, but there can always be glitches and misunderstandings. It's very helpful to do anonymous polls to check in with teachers on how things are going—perhaps a couple of times during the first year, annually after that. Here are some possible questions:

> *If mini-observations are handled well, they're usually well-received by teachers, but there can always be glitches and misunderstandings.*

- How often does your supervisor visit your classroom?
- How long do they usually stay?
- Are students distracted? Are you?
- What method of note-taking, if any, do they use?
- Are you getting feedback after each mini-observation?
- What form does it take?
- Are your conversations with your supervisor a two-way street?
- Are mini-observations helpful? How so?
- If there's more than one supervisor, is their feedback coordinated?

Low-Tech

Mini-observers worry they'll forget what they saw during a classroom visit, so naturally they want to take notes. What method works best for administrators—and teachers? I give polls on this question during my presentations, and here's what a group of educators said about which note-taking method they, as a teacher, would prefer their supervisor to use:

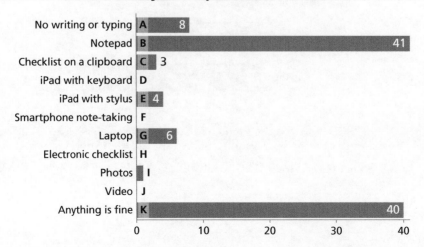

Note-taking: As a teacher, what would you want your supervisor to use?

Option		Value
No writing or typing	A	8
Notepad	B	41
Checklist on a clipboard	C	3
iPad with keyboard	D	
iPad with stylus	E	4
Smartphone note-taking	F	
Laptop	G	6
Electronic checklist	H	
Photos	I	
Video	J	
Anything is fine	K	40

This is a typical range of responses, from "no writing or typing" to "anything is fine," but note the strong preference for lower-tech approaches, with very few preferring laptops or iPads.

Those are teachers' preferences, but what about administrators' convenience? Taking notes on a laptop or tablet is faster and saves the step of transcribing handwritten notes later on. To make note-taking even easier, a number of companies are marketing digital platforms that allow supervisors to record classroom impressions on their smartphones, tablets, and laptops. This technology has undeniable appeal for busy supervisors—"Point, Click, Done" boasts one advertisement.

But this approach has some serious disadvantages. First, the supervisor is tied to a checklist that can't possibly capture the subtleties of a classroom, or has to type observation notes. Second, data entry takes a lot of mental bandwidth. And third, to a teacher, having someone tap-tapping on an electronic device at the back of the classroom is bound to be disconcerting.

That's why I believe note-taking should be minimal and low-tech—a small pad or note card with the teacher's name, the day and date, the period visited, the content, and a possible coaching point. This frees up the supervisor to walk around, look over students' shoulders at the work they're doing, check out anchor charts and displays, and (when the teacher isn't addressing the class) chat with a couple of students. Some good questions: *What are you learning? Why is it important? How will your teacher know when you understand?* Mini-observations work better—and adult learning is more likely to take place—when visits are informal and low stakes and teachers don't feel they're under pressure.

> *Mini-observations work better—and adult learning is more likely to take place—when visits are informal and low stakes and teachers don't feel they're under pressure.*

Whatever method is used—low-tech or high-tech—the most important things are (1) maintaining a nonbureaucratic, attentive posture during each mini-observation; (2) being a focused, thoughtful observer; (3) capturing a few key points for the conversation with the teacher; (4) recording the dates of each mini-observation and follow-up conversation; and (5) keeping track of which teachers have been visited in each cycle. This points to a streamlined, user-friendly electronic platform that's not used during actual classroom visits.

Observant

To make a positive difference to teaching and learning, mini-observers need to be good observers—but what does that mean? In a 2014 article in *Connected Principals*, Shawn Blankenship described what two supervisors saw as they observed the same lesson:

One stood at the back scanning the room and noted the following:

- The learning goal is posted at the front of the room.
- The lesson plan meets district criteria, including differentiation.

- The teacher is moving around and seems to have a good rapport with students.
- Students are well-behaved and seem engaged.
- Students who are called on answer questions correctly.
- The class seems to have mastered the goal.

The other supervisor moved around the class and noted these observations:

- Students with different needs are doing the same work.
- Four students got the first few problems wrong.

The clear takeaway: supervisors need to move around the room, look over kids' shoulders at the instructional task and how they are doing, and check in with several students.

- Two students with unfinished work are reading novels, one is doodling.
- When asked privately, only two of eight students could recall the lesson goal.
- The same three students raised their hands and answered the teacher's questions.

This was the same lesson in the same classroom! The clear takeaway: supervisors need to move around the room, look over kids' shoulders at the instructional task and how they are doing, and check in with several students. But what should mini-observers look for?

Checklists

Education experts have developed a variety of checklists to help classroom observers zero in on what's important—and make sure they don't miss anything. Here's a list of ideal lesson components from Achievement First, a network of charter schools in Connecticut and New York (reprinted with permission, with minor word changes):

- **Great aims.** Rigorous, bite-sized, measurable, standards-based goals are on the board and drive the lesson.
- **Assessment of student mastery.** Learning of the aims is systematically and diagnostically assessed at the end of the lesson.
- **Content-specific knowledge and strategy.** The teacher knows the content cold and uses a highly effective and efficient strategy to guide students to mastery.
- **Modeling and guided practice.** The lesson includes a clear "think-aloud," explicit modeling, and a heavily guided mini-lesson that's captured in a display available to students.

- **Sustained, successful independent practice.** Students have plenty of high-success "at bats" to practice, with the teacher moving around to support them.

- **Classroom culture.** Behavior expectations are crystal clear (for example, being attentive, no calling out, no laughing at classmates' mistakes), and there is a positive, energetic, joyful tone with a high ratio of positive to corrective comments.

- **Academic rigor.** Students do most of the heavy lifting, the teacher uses a good mix of higher-order questions and content, and the teacher refuses to accept low-quality student responses (requiring acceptable grammar, complete sentences, appropriate vocabulary, and understanding) or let students opt out.

- **Student engagement.** High-involvement strategies keep all students on task and accountable (no desk potatoes!), and there is an accountability mechanism to get all students to complete top-quality work.

- **Cumulative review.** In the lesson and homework, students get fast, fun opportunities to systematically review and practice skills already mastered.

- **Differentiation.** The teacher sees that all students' needs are met by providing extra support (especially during independent practice) and varying the volume, rate, and complexity of work.

This is a comprehensive list and has been used to train teachers and administrators in Achievement First schools. But it's geared to full-lesson observations and is clearly too detailed for mini-observations. Doug Lemov's book, *Teach Like a Champion*, now in its third edition, has sixty-three high-leverage teaching strategies—an excellent repertoire for teachers to work toward, but again, too much for one mini-observation.

Here's a somewhat shorter checklist created by WestEd/Teach4Success:

Appendix D. T4S Classroom Observation Instrument

Classroom: _____ **School:** _____ **School:** _____ **District:** _____

Start Time: _____ **End Time:** _____ **Date:** _____ **Observer:** _____

(O = Observed N = Not Observed)

O	N	
		Instructional Practices to Support All Learners
		Communicate Selected Standards or Objectives to All Students
		Make Learning Relevant
		Emphasize Key Vocabulary
		Provide Instructional Scaffolding to Assist and Support Student Understanding
		Provide Verbal Scaffolding to Assist and Support Student Use of Academic Language
		Facilitate Student Interactions or Discussions Related to the Learning
		Provide Specific and Immediate Feedback to Students
		Relate Teacher Actions to Standards or Objectives
O	N	**Student Engagement**
		The teacher demonstrates all of the following attributes:
		_____ Directs students to be engaged in the academic learning
		_____ Directs 85 percent or more of the students to participate in the academic learning at the same time
		_____ Makes student engagement mandatory by ensuring that 85 percent or more of the students are engaged throughout the academic learning
O	N	**Selected Student Engagement Techniques**
		Check the following techniques observed:
		_____ Identifying Similarities or Differences _____ Summarizing
		_____ Note Taking _____ Nonlinguistic Representation
		_____ Advance Organizer
O	N	**Assessment Practices**
		Use Summative Assessment
		Use Formative Assessment to Determine Instructional Needs of All Students
		Monitor and Make Individual or Collective Adjustments

Cognitive Level of Questions and Activities

Remember	Understand	Apply	Analyze — Evaluate — Create

O	N	
		Instructional Approaches
		Facilitate Student-led Learning
		Provide Teacher-led Instruction in a Whole Group Setting
		Provide Teacher-led Instruction in a Small Group Setting
		Provide Student Seatwork or Centers with Teacher Interaction
		Student Seatwork or Centers without Teacher Interaction
		Non-Academic Interaction
O	N	**Learning Environment**
		Foster a Climate of Fairness, Caring, and Respect
		Maintain Standards for Behavior, Routines, and Transitions
		Reinforce Effort of Students or Provide Recognition
		Establish a Literacy-Rich Environment

Here is an even shorter checklist focusing on seven core instructional activities. Every ten seconds, the supervisor notes which of those the teacher is exhibiting by checking the appropriate box (this is an actual record of a classroom in Connecticut several years ago):

UNCA[...] [SH]ORT VISIT PROTOCOL

9/2010

TEACHER DATA — INTERVAL: 10 SECONDS (columns 1–30, TOTAL)

2010 CCT	Adult Actions	Bloom's Revised Tax	Examples of Adult Actions
DIRECT INSTRUCTION			
2.1 3.2	Establishes Learning Focus, Purpose, or Teaching point		states or restates learning objective or lesson expectation; states purpose, relevance, or importance; links the teaching objective to previous learning
1.1 3.3 3.6 3.9	Preview Explicit Instruction		explains and models the learning objective; outlines procedure for achieving the objective; provides guided reading or writing mini lesson; connection to previous work/lesson
INTERACTIVE			
3.3 4.5 4.6	Checks for Understanding	1 Recall, 2 Under-stand	clarifies student understanding by monitoring; asks questions; elicits sample, signal, or choral responses; has students restate; incorporates echo or choral reading/responses; uses assessment strategies, technological and/or digital resources
3.3 3.8 3.9 4.6	Extends Student Understanding	3 Apply, 4 Analyze	elicits answers to higher level questions; uses Think-Pair-Share, Think Alouds, role play techniques, Choice Boards, surveys, TTQA, Jigsaw, non-linguistic tools; Literacy Circles, technological and/or digital resources; teacher confers with student; makes real-world, career or global connections
teacher FACILITATES ONLY — 3.3 4.9 4.6	Supports Reflection, Collaboration & Independent Work/Study	5 Evaluate, 6 Create	students question teacher and peers; students summarize, present, and lead class; students assess progress, students use exit slips & learning logs; students confer with teacher
teacher REINFORCES LEARNING — 4.7 5.5 5.6	Reinforces Effort & Providing Recognition (ETS Marzano)		gives specific and personal feedback; recognizes specific examples of student success or achievement that supports student learning
non-instructional time — 2.1 2.2 2.4 2.7	Manages Classroom		reminds and redirects students; makes transitions

(Left-hand vertical grouping label: **ACTIVE STUDENT ENGAGEMENT**)

Grade:	Group:	Teacher Name:	Time:
Form to teacher:	Content Area:	Coder Initials:	Date:
Task:			

Other:

Tally for teacher using praise such as "good job": _____ Other: _____

2019 CCT Domain 6.
Professional Responsibilities and Teacher Leadership
6.1 6.2 6.3 6.4 6.5

Feedback varies widely. To be helpful, it should be PERSONAL, POSITIVE, AND SPECIFIC; RELATED TO SIP GOAL; STUDENT ENGAGEMENT; DESCRIPTIVE and MEASURABLE; NOT SUBJECTIVE; SHARED AT BOTH INDIVIDUAL & GROUP LEVELS

Harvard professor Ronald Ferguson and his Tripod Project colleagues (2012) created a similarly compact list of key characteristics of effective teaching—the Seven Cs:

> *My concern is that supervisors will have their heads down, focused on fitting what's going on in the classroom into the boxes, and not be present and attentive to the complex human dynamic unfolding around them.*

- Caring about students
- Controlling behavior so students stay on task
- Clarifying lessons so knowledge seems feasible
- Challenging students to achieve
- Captivating students by showing learning is relevant
- Conferring with students to show their ideas are welcome and respected
- Consolidating knowledge so lessons are connected and integrated

Checklists like these are clever and well-intentioned. My concern is that supervisors will have their heads down, focused on fitting what's going on in the classroom into the boxes, and not be *present* and attentive to the complex human dynamic unfolding around them. Can an observer recording data on a clipboard or tablet take in myriad events in a busy classroom: what the teacher is doing, how students are responding to the teacher, what students are working on, the vibe in the classroom, and more?

A broad checklist might be helpful for a tour of a school, recording key data from multiple classrooms. Here's an actual data report from a tour of a K–12 school:

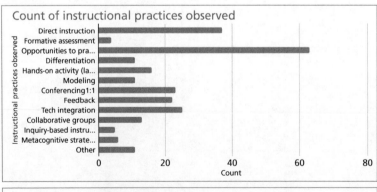

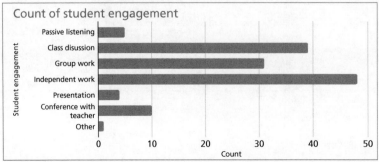

This helped the school's leadership team give general feedback to teachers and spark faculty discussion about classroom techniques and schoolwide trends.

But with mini-observations, where the goal is to have coaching conversations with individual teachers throughout the year, I believe detailed checklists are not the right medium. They will take too much of the supervisor's bandwidth recording data, resulting in less-perceptive observations and superficial feedback that won't be taken seriously by the teacher. Even Robert Marzano, who's developed a list or two in his day, says that using checklists during brief classroom visits is inappropriate (2007).

> *I suggest a "free-range" approach, walking into classrooms head up and mind open, looking for the most important events taking place in* that *classroom.*

So what's best for mini-observations? I suggest a "free-range" approach, walking into classrooms head up and mind open, looking for the most important events taking place in *that* classroom. Mini-observers who take this approach are not imposing a checklist on a fluid, highly complex situation that requires fully focused powers of observation. Supervisors can also walk around the classroom, unencumbered by laptops and tablets, differentiating for each teacher's background and unique classroom setup, confident that they'll see one or two things worth bringing up with the teacher afterward.

Does the free-range approach make quality mini-observations too dependent on superb instincts and extensive subject-area expertise? Might some administrators veer away from the most important issues, going with their pet peeves and personal instructional preferences? Do administrators need extensive training to be good free-range observers?

These are important questions, and addressing them is a key responsibility for superintendents and heads of school. I don't think extensive training is necessary, but doing co-observations with follow-up discussions comparing notes, practicing, and getting feedback are key ingredients. It's also important for districts to think about a shorter list of classroom desiderata that supervisors can keep in their heads.

A Short Mental Checklist

Fortunately, a number of educators have taken on this challenge. In an article in *Journal of Education for Students Placed at Risk* (Johnson et al., 2011), researchers reported on a multiyear study of principals in high-performing, nonselective urban schools. The authors found that the most effective principals looked for these key elements in their formal and informal classroom visits:

- **Student engagement, learning, and understanding.** Were students participating, learning, thinking, making sense, and understanding the skills and concepts being taught?

- **Climate, tone, and atmosphere.** Was the classroom warm, nurturing, calm, relaxed, respectful, flexible, organized, and neat?

- **Effective teacher actions.** Did teachers have clear objectives, lucid explanations, probing questions; perform modeling and check for understanding; and get students to explain their thinking?

Here's an even shorter checklist developed by a New York City principal who says she's able to keep these questions in her head as she does mini-observations:

- Are students clear about what they need to learn in this lesson?
- Does the teacher have a good method for teaching it?
- Does the teacher have a way of seeing if students have, in fact, learned it by the end of the lesson?

Peter Liljedahl, in his book *Building Thinking Classrooms in Mathematics* (Corwin, 2021), urges teachers and supervisors to focus on one big issue: How many students are *thinking* in this class?

But are these lists comprehensive enough?

A few years ago, I challenged a graduate class of aspiring principals to come up with a short, comprehensive, and easy-to-remember acronym summarizing the irreducible elements of effective teaching. What would we want to see every day in our own children's or beloved nieces' and nephews' classrooms, kindergarten through twelfth grade? After a lot of discussion and debate, we came up with SOTEL:

- **Safety.** The class is running smoothly, and students can focus on learning—they feel physically and psychologically safe and are willing to take intellectual risks.
- **Objectives.** It's clear where the lesson is going and the rigor and standards alignment are appropriate; at the highest level, the teacher has the unit's essential questions on the wall.
- **Teaching.** Learning experiences are being skillfully orchestrated; the teacher is using a repertoire of well-chosen instructional strategies to teach the material to all students.
- **Engagement.** Students are "minds-on" involved in the lesson and taking some responsibility for their own learning; the teacher isn't doing all the work.
- **Learning.** There's evidence (via checks for understanding, exit tickets, and other assessments) that what's being taught is being learned by all students.

What would we want to see every day in our own children's or beloved nieces' and nephews' classrooms, kindergarten through twelfth grade?

Some schools heard about SOTEL and began using it for classroom observations. One district in Oregon thought something important was missing. They added an H at the beginning and moved the S to the end, spelling HOTELS (the H stood for *hospitality*; the classroom has a warm and welcoming environment for teaching and learning).

But six look-fors in classrooms struck me as too many—and then I heard that a Massachusetts district was using SOTEL as an observation checklist. Although each of the letters stands for something important, I worried that feedback to teachers after mini-observations would feel compliance-driven to administrators and overwhelming to teachers. For a school with serious problems, this might be a good all-purpose template for classroom observations, but for most schools, I think less is more.

This led me to a shorter mental checklist, boiled down to three questions to keep in mind during a mini-observation:

- **Content.** Is this the right material and rigor for this grade and subject?
- **Pedagogy.** Is this the most effective way to teach the content?
- **Learning.** Are all students on track to mastering the content?

These focus on what's most important, are easy to keep in mind without a checklist, and enable the mini-observer to cast a wide net and think about the most important positive attributes and possible coaching points in each observation. Of course if there are safety issues, the objectives of the lesson aren't clear, or something else comes up, the observer can address them, but those are the core issues.

Whatever a district or school comes up with, it's important to share it with teachers so they know what observers are looking for and can focus their lesson planning on those key elements. A short list can be a helpful bridge between a detailed rubric (we'll discuss this in Chapter Seven) and what good instruction looks like in a single lesson.

Another advantage of the content/pedagogy/learning look-fors is that each element speaks to the all-important issue of equity. The *content* should be appropriate to all students getting standards-based curriculum that's not watered down. The *pedagogy* should follow the principles of Universal Design for Learning: it's culturally sensitive and provides on-ramps for students with learning differences. And the teacher's focus is ensuring that all students are *learning* and on track for mastery.

A Leverage Point

There's still the challenge of not overloading the teacher with too much feedback in the post-mini debrief. I've become convinced that Paul Bambrick-Santoyo is right that supervisors should focus on just one "leverage point" after each classroom visit—the single most important point to discuss with the teacher that has the highest probability to improve teaching and learning. The late Grant Wiggins (2012) recommended a similar approach for soccer coaching:

Expert coaches uniformly avoid overloading performers with too much technical information. They tell performers one important thing they noticed that, if changed, will likely yield immediate and noticeable improvement.

With this in mind, it's helpful to have jotted down a tentative idea for the leverage point. This might change in the conversation with the teacher, but having one or two in mind is a helpful start.

Here are some examples of leverage points that Julie Jackson decided on for three different teachers when she was an elementary principal in Newark, New Jersey (from *Leverage Leadership* by Paul Bambrick-Santoyo, p. 76):

- Increase your radar: when you are engaging with one student, deliberately scan the room to make sure all students are on task.
- During the turn-and-talk, try to listen in so you can select a group that had a good discussion and an answer that you want to be heard by everyone.
- Do not engage. Just give the consequence with your teacher "look" and refrain from getting into the details of why (which interrupts the flow of your lesson). You can go into the *why* once the rest of the group is working.

Here's another example:

- A Boston principal observes a first-grade guided reading group. A student reads *trouble* when the correct word is *danger*, and reads *teeth* instead of *tongue* (the story was about a snake). Both are "good" errors in the sense that they don't interfere with meaning, but they must be corrected as part of improving the student's decoding skills. The teacher puts her finger on each incorrectly read word and prompts the student. The principal thinks this is too much support. His coaching point: make the child do more of the work.

The Bigger Picture

So far we've focused on teachers' pedagogical moves and aspects of classroom culture that mini-observers see when they're in a classroom. But being a good observer also involves pulling back and getting a broader perspective. Supervisors can see more in a classroom when they're aware of a wider scope:

- The teacher's goals for the year
- The curriculum unit this lesson is part of
- Recently implemented curriculum materials and programs
- How students did on a recent assessment

- What the teacher's team has been discussing
- The leverage point in the previous mini–observation
- The teacher's life outside school: family matters they've shared and so on

Here's a diagram of the bigger picture of instruction for a sixth-grade math teacher, showing how the lesson being observed fits into the unit, the game plan for the year, the end-of-year objectives, and the K–12 plan for the school district:

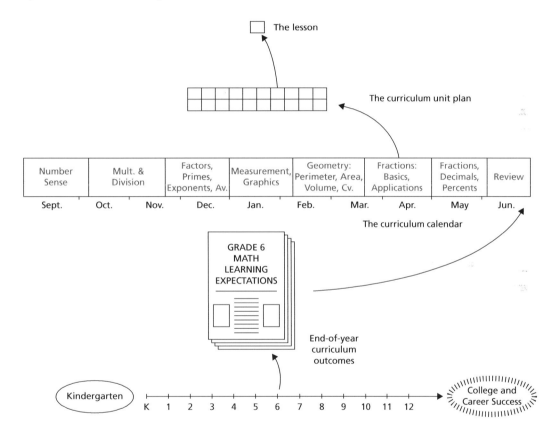

The more a mini-observer knows about the context of a lesson, the better the conversation with the teacher will go afterward.

Perhaps the teacher has the sequence of curriculum units on a bulletin board, like this middle-school math classroom on Long Island:

The more a mini-observer knows about the context of a lesson, the better the conversation with the teacher will go afterward.

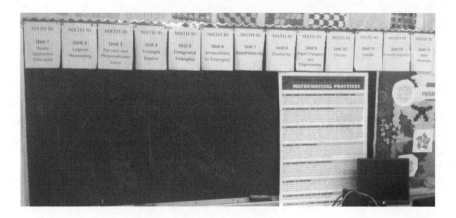

Or perhaps the teacher has essential questions for the unit, helping students (and visitors) think about the provocative issues the unit is addressing. Here are the questions in a New York City high school classroom studying *King Lear*:

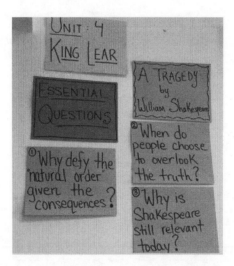

Then there's the teacher's professional activities outside the classroom, for example, interactions with parents, tutoring, a critical friends group, extracurricular activities they supervise, union activity, student clubs, the school newspaper, and curriculum work. All this plays a part in what the mini-observer sees in a classroom and what will be discussed afterward.

Questions to Consider

- *What are your main look-fors visiting a classroom?*
- *What kind of checklist, if any, do you think is necessary?*
- *What's your view on using a laptop or tablet to take notes during a mini-observation?*

6 | Mini-Observations 3

Affirming and Coaching

Remember: it's not your fault that things are the way they are, but it is your responsibility to do something about them.

—Elena Aguilar

MINI-OBSERVATIONS

Sampling daily reality:

1. Frequent and short
2. Systematic
3. Unannounced

Observing perceptively:

4. Humble, curious, and low-tech
5. Observant, a leverage point
6. The bigger picture

Affirming, coaching, and evaluating:

7. Face-to-face conversations
8. Brief follow-up summaries
9. Courage
10. Rubric scoring the year

This chapter will focus on face-to-face conversations, brief follow-up summaries, and courage.

Options for Giving Mini-Observation Feedback

What is the best way to affirm and coach teaching after a mini-observation? Some supervisors think it's efficient to share their impressions with teachers before leaving the classroom, while students are working independently or in groups (I sometimes did this as principal at the Mather). But this has several disadvantages: it's too soon to know how the lesson turned out, there isn't time for a meaningful discussion with the teacher, and criticism is pretty much out of the question because students might overhear.

How about immediate written feedback? Some supervisors leave a sticky note on the teacher's desk with a short overall comment—*Go Tiger! Great lesson!*—or write comments in a two-column format—one for *Wows,* another for *Wonders*—and email it while they're in the classroom or shortly afterward. Another approach is sending notes on what was observed and asking the teacher if they want to meet.

All of these seem efficient: supervisors have checked feedback off their to-do list and put the ball in the teacher's court, and many teachers appreciate knowing right away what supervisors thought. Waiting for hours after a mini-observation can be nerve-racking, especially for the most conscientious teachers, who worry about every detail.

But off-the-cuff written appraisals of mini-observations have no fewer than six disadvantages. First, supervisors don't know what happened before and after their visit, as well as important background information about the curriculum, the students, and the teacher's state of mind. Unless the administrator is super-perceptive and has very good intel, the feedback that's sent will lack context and could be superficial and unhelpful.

Second, if the feedback contains criticism, there's the risk of getting it wrong. Here's an example: a few years ago, a Boston administrator sat in a classroom typing feedback, noting (among other things) that the teacher didn't have an anchor chart for the skill being taught. When the teacher read the email, she was furious: her beautifully crafted anchor chart was right behind the supervisor's head.

Even if a critical comment is on target, putting it in writing is tricky; we don't always know how others will read our emails.

Another story. A Connecticut administrator did a mini-observation in the middle of a class and emailed comments, including a suggestion about handling lesson closure. "But you left!" said the teacher when they talked. "Everyone needs help with closure," replied the supervisor.

Third, the fear of making blunders like these might incline supervisors to take the path of least resistance, giving bland, descriptive comments and not addressing mediocre and ineffective practices.

Even if a critical comment is on target, putting it in writing is tricky; we don't always know how others will read our emails.

Fourth, when teachers receive written or electronic comments, it signals that the administrator's mind is made up. Even if the message concludes with the words, *Let me know if you'd like to talk*, a conversation is unlikely to happen. The feedback is already in writing, so why bother?

Fifth, it takes ten to fifteen minutes to compose and proofread a thoughtful written message (not the sticky note approach, of course). If the comments are pro forma, evasive, or annoying to the teacher, the time spent writing it was not spent well. Immediate written feedback seems like good time management for the supervisor, but in terms of the bigger purpose of mini-observations—having an authentic dialogue about teaching and learning—it's a false efficiency.

Finally, the paperwork involved in sending this kind of feedback can feel burdensome to supervisors, especially if they suspect it's not making a difference. That will be one more reason to avoid doing mini-observations; other activities will elbow them aside.

Face-to-Face Debriefs

So how *should* supervisors follow up after a mini-observation? I believe the most effective approach—and also the most efficient—is catching the teacher as soon as possible for a short informal, face-to-face debrief, using a few hand-jotted notes to start the conversation. Handled this way, the probability of positive impact is much higher than with written feedback. Here's why:

- In-person feedback feels less bureaucratic and evaluative, making it more likely that teachers will lower their guard and engage in non-defensive reflection.

- Teachers have a chance to quickly fill the administrator in on the broader context of the lesson, including what happened before and after the visit.

- Teachers can correct something the supervisor missed or misunderstood (like the anchor chart in the story), quickly dealing with an ill-informed criticism and moving on to something more important.

- The teacher can describe important details about the curriculum and materials being used.

- The teacher can show samples of students' work, talk about evidence of learning, and discuss difficulties students might be having.

- Supervisors can make an on-the-spot decision to shift to a different coaching point; the teacher's body language gives important clues about how much criticism they're ready to handle.

- Face-to-face conversations are a chance for teachers to talk about what's on their minds—perhaps staff dynamics or a personal issue outside of school.

In short, these conversations widen administrators' observational window, open the door for ongoing dialogues about pedagogy and results, and help teachers trust the process. Steven Levy (2007) said it well:

I am more likely to learn from someone in a conversation than in an e-mail exchange, which simply does not allow for the serendipity, intensity and give-and-take of real-time interaction.

Ideally, teachers walk away from feedback conversations feeling that their work is understood and appreciated, and with specific ideas for improving practice.

This is especially true of conversations about K–12 classrooms, with all their complexity and ups and downs. Ideally, teachers walk away from feedback conversations feeling that their work is understood and appreciated, and with specific ideas for improving practice.

These seem like compelling reasons to have face-to-face conversations after each mini-observation, but every time I propose the idea, there's pushback. How can debriefs be fitted into a busy school day? Won't teachers see this as an intrusion on their time? Do very effective teachers need verbal feedback? Don't these debriefs require a lot of skill on the part of supervisors? Won't there be too much to cover in a short conversation? Why does there always need to be criticism? Isn't being summoned to the office intimidating for teachers? How to bring closure? And what about regular check-in meetings instead? Let's look at each of these concerns.

Fitting Them In

I constantly wrestled with this when I was a principal—and things haven't gotten any less hectic since then. Here are some strategies for dealing with the time management challenge, from macro to micro:

- Have a manageable number of teachers per supervisor (twenty-five or fewer), which means adequate administrative staffing and delegation to all possible mini-observers in the school and from the central office.
- Have a daily goal (usually two debriefs a day or ten a week) and keep track.
- Buffer email with an "I'm in classrooms" message during the school day so it's possible to get out of the office (more about that in Chapter Thirteen).
- See teachers as soon as possible after each mini-observation so insights are recent and fresh.

- Be strategic about catching teachers at a good time. I always had a small laminated schedule in my pocket so I knew teachers' planning and lunch periods.
- Keep debrief conversations short and informal (five to ten minutes is usually enough).
- Limit suggestions to one leverage point.

Who takes responsibility for scheduling the debrief conversations? At the Mather, I was the one who tracked teachers down; most teachers played it cool and waited for me to find them. There are better options! The supervisor can leave a sticky note on the teacher's desk on the way out or send a text or email, suggesting a time to meet. There might be times blocked out in the supervisor's schedule reserved for mini-debriefs, with teachers texting or emailing to reserve one of them. Or there might be a standing agreement to meet during the next planning period in the teacher's schedule.

Large schools with more than one hundred teachers are a challenge, but principals don't have to do this work alone. Assistant principals (APs), department heads, deans, and others can divvy up the work. In one Massachusetts high school, the principal and AP split the staff in half. In another New York City school, administrators did mini-observations in tandem, comparing notes after they left each classroom (people sometimes see different things in the same visit, and this is a great way to hone observation skills).

Large schools with more than one hundred teachers are a challenge, but principals don't have to do this work alone.

Other teams prefer having all administrators see all classrooms, comparing notes in weekly meetings on what they're observing and which teachers need support. Some principals do mini-observations with an instructional coach; coaches have deeper pedagogical content knowledge than principals so they can "tutor" the boss on the finer points of lessons in their area after each visit—while getting schooled on more-generic pedagogical issues. Some leadership teams compare their visit frequency and challenge each other to keep up the pace.

One shortcut on the time management challenge is having face-to-face debriefs only with teachers where criticism is warranted, while others get feedback via email. But there's a problem with this approach: teachers realize that if they're having an in-person conversation with their supervisor, something was wrong with the lesson—a reason to dread in-person talks. That's why doing face-to-face conversations with everyone is the best approach.

Contractual Pushback

Some teachers refuse to have feedback conversations during their planning periods, and with some collective bargaining agreements, that's their right. It's wise to accommodate these teachers, providing coverage for their classes for mini-observation debriefs. But I've found that there are usually only one or two teachers in a school with this mindset—often the union representative who feels obligated to abide by the letter of the contract. Here's a recent poll of school leaders:

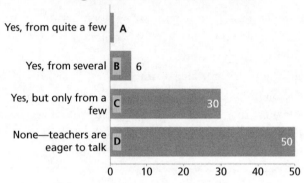

Do you anticipate teacher push-back on having face-to-face debriefs?

Most faculty members are curious to hear their supervisors' reactions, interested in feedback, and eager to talk about their students and the curriculum.

Most faculty members are curious to hear their supervisors' reactions, interested in feedback, and eager to talk about their students and the curriculum. Teachers spend most of their working days with kids and want to know what other adults think—especially the boss. If feedback conversations are short, authentic, affirming, and helpful, the vast majority of teachers are happy to give up a little of their planning time—or meet before school, during lunch, or after dismissal.

Do Great Teachers Need Debriefs?

It's easy to rationalize not doing mini-observations and debriefs for teachers who are performing well. Administrators hear good things about them from students, colleagues, and parents, and can see just by walking past their classrooms that things are going well. Closely supervising high-performing teachers doesn't seem like a good use of time. Here are some counterarguments.

First, excellent teachers are often using pedagogy and materials that will benefit their colleagues, but they are shy about seeming to toot their own horn. Spotting these in frequent visits to their classrooms, supervisors can encourage them to share ideas in their grade or subject team meetings or with the whole faculty. Administrators can also suggest that other teachers visit exemplary classrooms and try out those practices.

Second, strong teachers might be lonely, with nobody in the school to talk to about their work and a spouse who couldn't be less interested in Algebra II. Faculty lounge conversations are often about other subjects, which is fine—everyone needs a break. Having an intelligent educator make frequent visits and chat afterward is a balm for great teachers, encouraging them to reflect on what they're doing—and maybe think about ways to do even better.

> *Having an intelligent educator make frequent visits and chat afterward is a balm for great teachers, encouraging them to reflect on what they're doing—and maybe think about ways to do even better.*

Third, teachers chat among themselves about mini-observations, and if they notice that some colleagues are getting more visits than others, invidious conclusions might be drawn. Are teachers who get more mini-observations less effective? The only way to prevent this morale-busting dynamic is equity; principals should be able to assure teachers that everyone is getting the same number of observations and debriefs.

Finally, a true story. I was walking around a Maryland school with the principal, and this subject came up. The principal said with great assurance that some teachers really didn't need mini-observations. We were walking by a seventh-grade classroom, and the principal said this teacher was a perfect example: she was fine and didn't need to have conversations about her work. *Okay*, I said. *Let's drop in to see some great teaching.*

As we entered the classroom, students were at their desks with a novel open in front of them, and an audio device was playing a recording of the book being read aloud. A quick scan of the room revealed that several students were not reading along, and two kids' heads were down on their desks. Where was the teacher? She was at her desk on email, but quickly got up when she spotted us. The principal was irate—and quite embarrassed—and the point was made.

Launching and Structuring Debriefs

Most administrators haven't had training on in-person debriefs right after classroom observations, and it strikes some as quite challenging. But when I show a short classroom video and ask groups of supervisors to pair up and do a role-play, they don't find it that difficult and are usually done in five minutes.

That said, there are some less-than-effective approaches to avoid, starting with the way the supervisor kicks off the conversation:

Thanks for having me in your class. The teacher's silent rejoinder might be, *Actually, you're my boss and I have no choice.* A seemingly polite opener can get the conversation off on the wrong foot.

How's it going? This rather global question could be taken as an invitation to share something unrelated to the mini-observation—perhaps a family emergency—taking the conversation away from what happened during the lesson.

How did you feel the lesson went? This seems like a good way to get the teacher's perspective, but what if the supervisor saw a significant problem and the teacher says the lesson was great? Then the administrator is in the awkward position of contradicting the teacher right up front—or holding off on an important coaching point.

Being disingenuous—Most teachers are self-aware enough to see if a supervisor is being superficial and pulling punches. If there's an important concern about what happened during the mini-observation, it needs to be named—with tact and sensitivity.

I liked the way you did that. . . I just loved it when you. . . These feel like warm, personal compliments, but by stating them in terms of subjective approval, the unintended message is that the teacher's job is making the administrator happy. Better to praise effective practices in terms of their impact on student engagement and learning.

The feedback sandwich—First there's a compliment, then a suggested improvement, then another compliment. This very common approach has built-in problems: the two positive slices can lead the teacher to ignore the criticism, or the criticism looms large and the compliments feel insincere. "When people hear praise during a feedback conversation," said Adam Grant in a 2016 article, "they brace themselves."

So what is the best way to kick off a mini-debrief? Here's an adaptation of the feedback sandwich, combining it with the widely used "four squares" approach (Glow, Grow, Suggestion, How Can I Help?):

Structuring Feedback Chats

1. Appreciate something that went well, with details.	2. Get the teacher talking about the lesson with a good prompt.
3. Decide on a leverage point and talk about it.	4. Agree on an actionable next step and offer support.

A closer: What was your big takeaway?

With the lead-off compliment, it's helpful to get the teacher explaining how the effective practice came about—for example, "Can you tell me how you got students to take turns speaking without raising their hands?" This encourages teachers to narrate the positive, basically complimenting themselves.

Here are some ways to get teachers talking that I've picked up in school visits. Which one to use (or a good opener that's not on this list) depends on what happened during the mini-observation, the supervisor's relationship with the teacher, and the teacher's level of confidence and proficiency:

- Tell me what happened before I came in. After I left?
- When do you think the most learning was taking place?
- Did something happen that you didn't expect?
- Did you get your intended results? What worked?
- On a scale of one to ten, how close was this lesson to your ideal? What would you tweak?
- Tell me something you hoped I would notice.
- Is there something you'd especially like feedback on?
- Are there students this lesson didn't work for?
- Can you walk me through your thinking on this segment?
- I saw that Helene was really buckling down. What changed?
- Can we look through the exit tickets?
- You're a great teacher. That lesson wasn't great. Let's talk.

The last one came from a New Jersey AP who vividly remembered his boss kicking off a blunt feedback talk with those exact words.

Here's a different approach to structuring post–mini-conversations—the US Army's "after-action review" (described in Daniel Coyle's 2009 book, *The Culture Code*):

- What were our intended results?
- What were our actual results?
- What caused those results?
- What will we do the same next time?
- What will we do differently?

One Leverage Point

There are usually four or five potential coaching points in a mini-observation, and sharing them all will overload the teacher.

There are usually four or five potential coaching points in a mini-observation, and sharing them all will overload the teacher.

Deciding on one leverage point for each debrief is much more likely to result in productive follow-up—and it keeps the conversation short. The fact that there will be as many as ten mini-observations over the school year gives the supervisor opportunities to get to other possible feedback.

An exception to the one-leverage-point approach is when there's a major meltdown in a classroom; the administrator needs to shift gears and help the teacher think through a new approach to classroom management.

In Chapter Five, we saw supervisors deciding on leverage points. Here are several more examples showing how the supervisor sometimes needs to be nimble in a face-to-face conversation:

- During a mini-observation, a principal notices that a fifth-grade special education teacher is mispronouncing a word—in fact, she says it incorrectly three times. As the debrief begins later that day, the principal is about to bring this up, but something tells him to go with Plan B, and he compliments the teacher on a thoughtful comment she made to a student. The teacher thanks the principal and says her daughter had an asthma attack the night before and after a visit to the hospital (*Thank God, she's okay*), nobody in the family got any sleep. The principal made the right call—but should watch for another opportunity to correct the mispronunciation.

- A New York City ninth-grade ELA class, predominantly students with special needs, is reading *Catcher in the Rye*. The class is not going well, but it's not clear why. Is it the relevance of the book to students' lives? Is the Lexile level of the book too high? Is it the desk configuration, with students facing different directions (and why is one boy sitting alone over by the window)? Is it the fact that students with reading difficulties are being asked to read aloud? Could the second teacher be used more effectively? In the debrief, the principal has an open-ended discussion with the teachers, genuinely not knowing the best leverage point.

- During a mid-lesson mini-observation of a Grades 3–4 gifted class, the principal comes in just as the teacher finishes reading from a novel and witnesses a lively discussion about racial prejudice and bullying in an urban neighborhood. It's a remarkably high-level discussion with the teacher saying nothing as students respond to each other, refer to the text, share poignant stories, and take turns without raising their hands. In the debrief, the principal comments on this but wonders how this fitted into the social studies curriculum. He is surprised when the teacher says that this was an impromptu lesson following up with her students' mean behavior toward a substitute teacher when the teacher was out sick the day before.

- After a mini-observation, an AP is mildly critical of a middle-school music teacher because the boys playing the drums were fidgety and kept moving around while the teacher explained something to the class. The teacher's reply: "That's why they're drummers." *Interesting*, thought the administrator, seeing the boys' behavior in a different light. But she persisted: *Shouldn't the fidgety drummers be calm and attentive when the teacher was talking? Were the teacher's expectations high enough? In a middle-school music class, how much calm attention was appropriate?* The AP and teacher have a lively discussion about this, without clear resolution.

These vignettes make several points. First, mini-observation debriefs should be organic, open to the possibility that they might go in unexpected directions as the teacher responds. Administrators can't come across as all-knowing after only a few minutes in a classroom. Second, each debrief doesn't have to resolve the issue; the coaching point can be part of an ongoing dialogue—or put off for a future visit. Third, the beauty of mini-observations is that supervisors will have multiple at bats and can decide which possible coaching point to discuss each time, engaging in an ongoing dialogue about teaching and learning.

Must There Always Be a Criticism?

It really annoys teachers when supervisors nit-pick and find fault with lessons no matter how brilliant they were. It's also burdensome for administrators as they struggle to find a "grow" in an excellent lesson and feel foolish sharing it. *There doesn't always have to be a leverage point!* Sometimes a lesson sparkles, and the feedback should be totally appreciative—with plenty of detail from the supervisor—perhaps followed up by encouragement to share the practice and materials with colleagues or the wider world.

The goal of mini-debriefs is not providing formulaic glow/grow feedback but creating a climate where it's okay for the teacher to be vulnerable and explore better ways to reach all students.

The goal of mini- debriefs is not providing formulaic glow/grow feedback but creating a climate where it's okay for the teacher to be vulnerable and explore better ways to reach all students. Teachers should feel comfortable saying, "My team just spent two weeks teaching quadratic equations and my kids bombed in the test. Can you help us figure out what happened?"

Teachers need to know that their boss is keenly interested in how well students are learning (not just on high-stakes state tests, but on their assignments, projects, and classrooms tests) and feel able to reach out for support. The essence of these conversations should be an ongoing, collegial exploration of what's working in each classroom and what's required to take teaching to the next level and reach all students.

Location, Location

Being summoned to "the office" can be triggering for teachers because of the principal's role as student disciplinarian. Colleagues might ask with mock concern: *Ooh, I saw you were in with the principal. Is everything okay?* Cognizant of this trope, many supervisors choose other locations for debriefs. Here are the responses to a poll I recently gave to group of teachers and administrators asking which of a number of possible locations would be best for mini-observation debriefs (one was tongue-in-cheek):

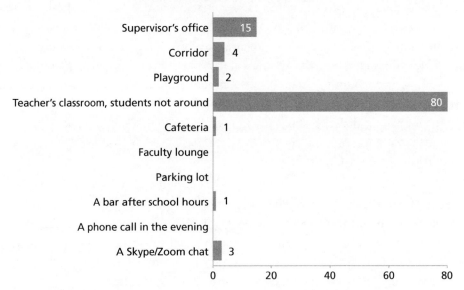

Best venue for feedback?

Asked why so many chose the fourth option, people gave these reasons:

- The power dynamic is different; supervisors make a humble gesture when they take the time to go to a teacher's classroom.
- On their home turf, teachers are more likely to talk frankly about the ups and downs of a lesson.
- In a classroom, the supervisors can remember details about what happened during the mini-observation, including what individual students said.
- Teachers and supervisors have ready access to student work, curriculum artifacts, and material on the walls.
- There are fewer interruptions than is often the case in the main office.

- Conversations in classrooms are usually informal and conducted standing up, which keeps them short.
- It's easier for supervisors to wrap up after a few minutes and make their exit, compared with the difficulty of bringing closure to a sit-down conversation in an office with comfortable chairs and a supply of candy.

On their home turf, teachers are more likely to talk frankly about the ups and downs of a lesson.

Of course, it's not always possible to debrief in the classroom where the mini-observation took place; another teacher could be using the room or students might be doing catch-up work. In that case, supervisors need to choose one of the other options, with an eye to informality and privacy (but probably not the bar).

In some cases, especially with district supervisors who drive from school to school to visit teachers—fine arts, music, science, physical education—it's challenging to schedule face-to-face debriefs within twenty-four hours of mini-observations. When the time lag is going to be too long, a Zoom call is a good second choice, a phone call a third choice. But I always urge itinerant supervisors to keep trying for face-to-face chats, which add another dimension to communication, trust, and pedagogical substance.

Closure

As noted in the four quadrants protocol, an effective way for supervisors to end a debrief is with a simple, low-key question to the teacher: "What's your big takeaway from our chat?" This encourages the teacher to summarize and consolidate the leverage point, and helps the supervisor to see if the point connected and will result in follow-up. Here's an example of this closure question providing an important insight:

A high school principal spoke quite critically to a teacher about lesson planning and preparation. When she asked the teacher for his main takeaway, he said, "That you want me to do lesson plans because the Department of Education requires them." The principal realized that she needed to try again, more clearly this time, to explain the critical importance of thinking through a lesson beforehand.

Check-In Meetings

Another way to handle mini-debriefs is regular, scheduled check-in meetings. In a Bronx high school, the two APs divided up the teachers (each had sixteen) and had short meetings on Thursday or Friday (they dubbed them TFMs—Thursday-Friday meetings). The administrators found TFMs were an ideal opportunity to give feedback on mini-observations and discuss other artifacts teachers brought with them—samples of student work, grade books, unit plans, interim assessment results. They believe TFMs were one of the biggest reasons the school had a trusting, high-achieving professional climate.

There is one disadvantage of using regular check-in meetings for mini-observation debriefs. Because it's good to debrief with teachers within twenty-four hours of a mini-observation, visits need to happen the day before, which limits the days that the administrator can visit the teacher's classroom. That's a reason to do mini-debriefs separately from check-in meetings.

How do mini-observations and debriefs work with school counselors, social workers, and psychologists? Clearly, supervisors can't observe their confidential meetings with students. For this category of staff members, regular check-in meetings are best, discussing their overall case-load, general trends, and students who merit a detailed discussion.

Summing Up the Case for Face-to-Face Debriefs

Is doing in-person mini-observation debriefs too difficult for the average principal? I hope I've convinced you they are doable. Is it sometimes difficult to find time for the debriefs? Yes. Do supervisors occasionally handle a conversation ineptly? I certainly did. Is this hard work? Definitely. Is it challenging to fit these pieces into busy school days? Always. Will there be crazy days with no classroom visits and follow-ups? Of course.

But this is the work. Every administrator's priority management challenge is getting to it almost every day, amidst all the other stuff, and keeping up the pace. That's how they'll make a difference. These design features of mini-observations make them practical and effective in most schools:

- Informal
- Frequent
- Medium stakes
- Often on teachers' home turf
- Focused on one coaching point at a time

Teachers appreciate the individual attention and having a chance to talk about what's going on in their classrooms.

That's why I believe debrief conversations can be handled well by almost all school administrators almost all of the time. This structure brings out the best in supervisors, and as I'll argue in Chapter Fourteen, the skill set is eminently coachable by superintendents.

Teachers appreciate the individual attention and having a chance to talk about what's going on in their classrooms. Because of that, they're willing to give administrators some grace for awkward moments and misunderstandings. That's what Mather teachers did with me; they helped me get better at the conversations over time.

Several people have suggested to me that this style of informal, frequent coaching is an especially good match for Generation Z teachers. People in this age group are eager for feedback and ready to put it to work.

The ultimate goal of feedback, whether it's a supervisor's mini-observation feedback or a full-lesson visit by an instructional coach or peer observer, is to nurture a supervisory voice in teachers' heads and foster an acute consciousness of whether students are learning what's being taught. Achievement will soar when individual teachers and teacher teams are constantly puzzling, theorizing, and debating about how students are responding and how teaching can be improved.

Supervisors who frequently and systematically visit all classrooms have a unique schoolwide perspective and are constantly seeing ideas that can be leveraged to improve teaching and learning in other classrooms. They can be *cross-pollinators*, spreading good ideas to individual teachers or teams and getting people to observe colleagues in other parts of the school. Supervisors can also pass along insights to instructional coaches and arrange for training in specific areas of need, drawing on expertise from within the building or from outside consultants.

Brief Follow-Up Summaries

In the nine years I did mini-observations at the Mather, I didn't give teachers anything in writing after our follow-up chats. This was partly because of PTSD from the grievance I'd lost my first year about detailed note-taking during observations. I wanted to keep the optics of the minis as unofficial and non-evaluative as possible. Another reason was that I was observing forty-two teachers and didn't have time.

A few years after I left the Mather, I was coaching Alex Estrella, a middle-school principal in New York City. She quickly picked up the idea of mini-observations and was adept at getting into classrooms and giving face-to-face feedback. But it seemed to her that something was missing. A few teachers were not taking her suggestions to heart, and the district superintendent was skeptical about this unconventional approach to supervision.

Estrella decided to start sending a brief email to each teacher after the face-to-face chat summarizing what they'd talked about. She told me this was helpful because it left no ambiguity about what had been discussed, while giving the teacher an opportunity to push back if they thought the summary wasn't accurate. She noticed that teachers put positive emails on their bulletin boards and brooded about those that were critical. Another advantage of written summaries: having a track record of what was happening in the mini-observations won her superintendent's support for mini-observations.

I was persuaded! Giving teachers a written summary after each mini-observation debrief adds an important component to the system. But there are two caveats. First, supervisors need to have a manageable caseload of teachers—ideally no more than twenty-five. Second, the summaries need to be *short*. Administrators trained in the traditional evaluation process can easily write a page and a half after a mini-observation debrief, which will bog the process down in paperwork and undermine the goal of frequent, non-bureaucratic coaching interactions with teachers.

> *Giving teachers a written summary after each mini-observation debrief adds an important component to the system.*

Fortunately, a solution was dreamed up by three Tennessee educators who developed T-EVAL, an evaluation app (www.edusoftllc.com). In T-EVAL, when supervisors type a summary of a mini-observation debrief, they are limited to one thousand characters—about 160 words—and when they reach that ceiling, the software won't let them type another character; they have go back and cut words. It's like a whalebone corset for administrators, constraining them to make their points in as few words as possible.

This is a terrific idea. It gives administrators "permission" to limit the time they spent on evaluation paperwork. Working with administrators who are using this app, I've found that once they get in the groove, it takes only ten to fifteen minutes to write a less-than-one-thousand-character summary. Following are some sample write-ups.

A Kindergarten Reading Lesson

Alexandra,

It was good to see you in action yesterday. *The New You* is a delightful read-aloud, and you read with such expression, especially when you imitated a rock star. There was a priceless eyes-in-the-back-of-the-head teacher moment when you motioned for Rebecca to pay attention without looking at her.

As we discussed, introducing "smart words" helps stretch students' Tier 2 vocabularies, and you gave several examples of what the smart word of the day—*exemplary*—meant, showing an exemplary math paper. The turn-and-talk on what students wanted to be when they grew up went smoothly: students paired up and shared, then quickly came back together when you told them to do so.

As I mentioned, and this is not a major point, my only concern was the choice of *exemplary* as the smart word. Although it appeared in the dedication of *The New You*, it didn't play a part in the story. You agreed that it's a better idea to choose a smart word that is central to the story being read.

Best, Kim

A Fourth-Fifth Grade Gifted Class

Becky,

I'm so glad we talked about my observation. Your students' discussion skills are flourishing: they conducted a high-level conversation on the fraught topic of race without interrupting each other, listening respectfully even when they disagreed, without any direction from you. They didn't even need to raise their hands! Your decision to let the discussion flow seemed wise.

I did wonder how this conversation fit into the curriculum, and you explained that it was an impromptu decision: you read the passage from the novel hoping students would make the connection with their mean behavior with the substitute the day before. That didn't happen while I was there, but after I left, you said you were explicit and students "got it" and were appropriately penitent. We agreed that next time it would be better to make the connection clear up front.

But this was by no means a failed lesson. Bravo for making the attempt, because the discussion was excellent and students learned a lot.

Best, Kim

A Sixth-Grade Math Lesson

Helen,

Thank you for the discussion of yesterday's lesson. Your management is really progressing, especially the *1–2–3 eyes on me* prompt and the choral response, *Yes, Ms. Jones* when you say, *Am I making myself clear?* The lesson was well organized and provisioned.

Calling one group to the front to demonstrate the textbook activity on measuring arms involved those four students. But you said that after I left, replicating the activity didn't go well, especially the group that demonstrated it—they were at loose ends. You said you were not surprised that exit tickets revealed half the class didn't understand the concept of finding the average.

We agreed that the arm-measuring activity was not the most effective way to teach the concept to sixth graders, and you were pleased that I said you are free to depart from the textbook script and invent a more relevant example of finding the mean. I look forward to seeing you implement one of the options you suggested tomorrow.

Best, Kim

A Seventh-Grade Science Lesson

Katie,

I appreciated your openness discussing yesterday's second-period science class. Your positive energy as you walked around checking students' planners was evident ("Happy teacher, happy teacher"), as was your rapport with students (Charlie's chicken-in-mouth question made me laugh out loud). The mnemonics you dreamed up to help students remember eleven human organ systems are great, and your room set-up—skeleton, Einstein poster, quotes, marathon number—speak to your commitment to students.

As we discussed, having students call out answers on major bones was not the most effective way to check for understanding and improve retention. While kids showed a lot of enthusiasm, some of their answers were wrong, and while you repeated the correct answers, I wasn't sure they were heard. You agreed that a better system for checking for understanding is needed, and you're going to experiment with Kahoot to pinpoint misconceptions and help students commit the right answers to memory.

Best, Kim

An Eighth-Grade Math Lesson

Mr. Ormsby,

Thanks for taking time to debrief this morning's lesson with me. At the beginning of the class, students got right to work, you made a classy recovery from the missing instruction about a designated grapher (admitting you were nervous), and you energetically moved around the room helping students, getting right down to their level.

As we discussed, students were not working collaboratively to solve the problems, and most of the help you gave was to individual students, rather than encouraging the group to put their heads together and find a solution. We agreed that when you teach this lesson to a different group tomorrow, you'll take time up front to discuss what collaborative work looks like, have each group designate roles (including the grapher), and when you circulate, if a student has a problem, you'll ask other members of the group for ideas on solving it. I look forward to dropping in tomorrow to see how this goes.

Best, Kim

A Tenth-Grade English Lesson

Maura,

Following up on my visit and our debrief yesterday, here are my thoughts. Your classroom management is much tighter, with strategic wait time, using proximity (you were all over the room), and insisting on attention before you began. You clearly stated the lesson objective, reminded students of what was covered yesterday, and tied the lesson in with the memoir unit objectives. Your poster on the five senses was helpful, and I saw other good visuals around the room. It's clear you're working hard to create a rich learning environment for your students.

As we discussed, the lesson could have gotten off to a brisker start. There were five minutes of getting-ready-to-get-going up front; I think you were too patient with students and did too much shushing and directing as you walked around distributing the handout from *Owl Moon*. You agreed that you will make better use of student helpers (kids are amazingly willing to pitch in for their teachers) and your paraprofessional to get handouts on students' desks and pencils in their hands so the lesson can get started within a minute of the bell.

I look forward to seeing these tweaks in action as an excellent unit unfolds.

Best, Kim

An Eleventh-Grade Biology Lesson

Mara,

Thank you for making time to debrief the Mendel heredity lesson I observed yesterday. As we discussed, describing your family's history of epilepsy made inheritance vivid for students, and mentioning that your husband was adopted showed students that there are families in which tracing inherited traits is complex. Having all students briefly write about inherited characteristics was a good way to activate prior knowledge, then turning and talking, then sharing with the whole class.

But when Cynthia shared with the class that she is showing signs of being bipolar, probably inherited from her father, that was a tricky moment. Although I believe you handled the situation well, you and I wondered if your very personal stories opened the door to oversharing by this student. We agreed that the next time you teach this lesson, it will be wise to share less yourself and limit students' discussions of inherited traits to characteristics that are physical (I liked your suggestion of tongue-rolling). I look forward to hearing how the revised lesson goes tomorrow. And we'll both check in with Cynthia's counselor to make sure she has the support she needs.

Best, Kim

Here are some suggested criteria for this kind of brief summary:

- A personal message to the teacher, not in the third person
- Detailed appreciation of effective teaching strategies and progress being made
- Referring back to the debrief conversation—"As we discussed . . ."
- A direct and specific summary of the leverage point
- A summary of the agreed-on next step
- Any resources and support for the next step

Like other evaluation platforms, T-EVAL has pull-down menus for quick access to each teacher's record, automatic date stamping for classroom visits and follow-up conversations, and the evaluation rubric the school is using. Ideally when the teacher opens the digital message, that constitutes legal proof that it's been received so there's no need to get the teacher's signature. Of course, it's important that everything in the platform is protected as a personnel record from improper or illegal disclosure.

Can mini-observations replace traditional evaluations?

Let's summarize. A mini-observation cycle for one teacher takes about thirty minutes—ten for the mini-observation, ten for the debrief, ten for the written summary. A single traditional evaluation takes four hours, and in most cases is not a productive use of time. In the same four hours, spread over several days, a supervisor can do eight mini-observation cycles:

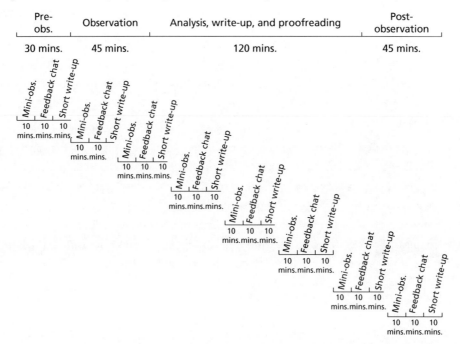

This figure packs a powerful punch. One ineffective, time-consuming evaluation compared to eight classroom visits, eight conversations, relationship and trust building, a substantive dialogue about actual teaching and learning, and documentation—all in the same four hours.

What would it take to convince policymakers to allow mini-observations to officially replace the traditional system? Telling stakeholders about wonderful face-to-face feedback conversations will not suffice. For superintendents, heads of school, board members, and union officials to accept mini-observations, there must be documentation. Short summaries of mini-debriefs, formatted as a letter to the teacher, can close the loop with teachers and provide credible data for the process. Using a confidential data platform pulling all the key information together closes the case.

In Chapter Three, I argued that full-lesson write-ups add almost no value. Frequent mini-observations, face-to-face debriefs, and short write-ups provide enough gravitas to provide a convincing alternative. Are we ready to take this leap of faith? Read on.

Courage

Doing regular mini-observations, administrators see lots of good teaching, but they will inevitably come across mediocre and ineffective practices—a teacher doing personal email during class, students doing inane busywork, a sarcastic comment directed at a student, a homophobic gibe from one student to another left unchallenged, grammatical mistakes on the board. Principals need to say something to these teachers afterward; if they don't, the inescapable message to the teacher is that whatever they were doing or not doing is officially all right. As the old saying goes, *what you permit you promote*. A leader who is silent on ineffective teaching practices speaks loudly.

There are several reasons why principals sometimes fail to confront teachers about less-than-effective practices or fail to follow up when nothing has changed after several rounds of mini-observations and suggestions. One is a simple lack of intestinal fortitude. As Rudi Gatti, a former California superintendent, put it: "The real problem with evaluation is that people are gutless." This is especially likely if a supervisor has reason to expect an angry or defensive reaction from the teacher. And indeed, some teachers have strong personalities. At the Mather, there were several who got my stomach churning when I even considered criticizing them.

No excuses. Supervisors have to step up to the plate and do their jobs. If they don't, who will? The essential elements:

- Frequent unannounced classroom visits

- A belief that good teaching matters, especially for vulnerable students

- A good eye

- A sense of urgency—every minute in classroom counts

- Courage

- Confidence that higher-ups will back them up if a valid criticism is challenged

No excuses. Supervisors have to step up to the plate and do their jobs. If they don't, who will?

A second reason for avoiding difficult conversations is being overly concerned with maintaining harmonious relationships with the staff. Here's what Michael Huberman (1993) had to say:

> Public school principals depend heavily on the cooperation of teachers to get their core administrative, custodial, and political tasks accomplished. Such cooperation is endangered by close supervision. Teachers have thousands of subtle means of retaliation (forgetting requests, over-loading administrators with trivial demands, working to rule, slacking off on monitoring of corridors, feeding parental grievances). And teachers know that the punishment-and-reward system of administrators depends first on the semblance of maintaining control, harmony, and parental inactivity. (p. 41)

In addition, some school leaders have the fatal weakness of wanting to be *liked*. Big mistake. When Harry Truman was in the White House, he said, "If you want a friend in Washington, get a dog." This is good advice, and great for the pet industry.

A third reason for avoidance is that principals haven't talked with their colleagues and reached agreement on classroom red lines—practices that are unacceptable in the school—and mediocre practices—things that are not horrible but really need to be improved. Here's an example: a teacher correcting papers or doing lesson planning while students work at their desks.

My gut feeling when I encountered this at the Mather was that it wasn't an appropriate use of contact time; the teacher should be walking around checking for understanding and giving students real-time coaching, or perhaps calling students up for individual conferences. But because we had never reached consensus on this question, I hesitated to criticize a teacher when

I saw it in a classroom. What seemed obvious to me might not seem obvious to a teacher—so I held back.

A fourth reason for not stepping up to the plate is that many principals haven't had enough practice with difficult conversations. When I became a principal, I had little experience being a boss and was truly a novice when it came to giving critical feedback. I wish I'd been able to role-play with other principals in a "safe space." Giving supervisors this kind of practice responding to real-life case studies is an essential part of the superintendent's and head's job.

But actually, frequent classroom visits and informal, low-stakes feedback chats make the job of criticizing teachers a bit less daunting—not easy, but more manageable. If a principal does only one formal observation a year and comes down hard on a teacher, then 100 percent of that teacher's evaluations will have a negative tone. But if the principal does ten mini-observations and two or three of them are critical, it's much easier for the teacher to accept.

> *If a principal does only one formal observation a year and comes down hard on a teacher, then 100 percent of that teacher's evaluations will have a negative tone.*

What about persistently ineffective teachers? When administrators spot serious problems in mini-observations and things don't improve after suggestions and coaching, it's time to shift gears and launch into a more formal process: full-lesson observations, a second opinion, a detailed diagnosis and improvement plan, lots of support, and repeating the cycle until the teacher either improves or is dismissed. In such cases, smart principals should get advice from their superintendent and the district's legal counsel, and also keep union representatives informed as appropriate.

The free *Best of Marshall Memo* website has a super-curated collection of thirteen article summaries on critical feedback and difficult conversations, available as a PDF or podcast. You can access both at www.bestofmarshallmemo.org.

Questions to Consider

- *Are you convinced of the efficacy of face-to-face debrief conversations?*
- *What's your go-to prompt to get teachers talking during debriefs?*
- *What would it take for mini-observations to replace traditional evaluations in your school?*

7 | Mini-Observations 4

End-of-Year Rubric Evaluation

Today in America the biggest problem with education is not that it is bad. It is that it is variable. In hundreds of thousands of classrooms in America, students are getting an education that is as good as any in the world. But in hundreds of thousands of others, they are not.

—Dylan Wiliam

Here's our outline:

> ### MINI-OBSERVATIONS
> **Sampling daily reality:**
> 1. Frequent and short
> 2. Systematic
> 3. Unannounced
>
> **Observing perceptively:**
> 4. Humble, curious, and low-tech
> 5. Observant, a leverage point
> 6. The bigger picture
>
> **Affirming, coaching, and evaluating:**
> 7. Face-to-face conversations
> 8. Brief follow-up summaries
> 9. Courage
> 10. Rubric scoring the year

In this chapter we'll focus on rubric scoring the year.

In the three previous chapters, I've suggested that supervisors make frequent, short, systematic, unannounced classroom visits; observe perceptively; follow up with face-to-face conversations and brief written summaries; and step up to the plate when they see mediocre or ineffective teaching. But how will all this work be summed up at the end of the school year? What goes in each teacher's personnel file?

Since the mid-2010s, rubrics have emerged as a new model for summative teacher evaluation. Charlotte Danielson paved the way with her 1996 *Framework for Teaching*, which broke instruction into seventy-six separate categories and described four levels of performance: Distinguished, Proficient, Basic, and Unsatisfactory. Originally designed as a coaching tool, Danielson's rubric flew under the radar for years, with some supervisors using its detailed descriptions of instruction to give teachers informal feedback.

Then in 2013, the Measures of Effective Teaching study changed the game. Funded by the Bill and Melinda Gates Foundation, the MET study proposed (among other things) that principals should use rubrics to *evaluate* teachers. The idea swept the nation, and rubrics, Danielson's among them, are now widely used for end-of-year teacher evaluation.

When I initially looked at this new generation of evaluation tools, they seemed like a big improvement over traditional checklists and narratives. Using research on effective teaching, rubrics deconstruct pedagogy, provide detailed descriptions of performance, and enable supervisors to give teachers specific feedback on how they're doing in each area. Most important, rubrics do most of the writing for supervisors, making teacher evaluation less burdensome.

But as I observed how rubrics were being implemented in schools, I saw three problems. First, most rubrics are so long and detailed that they overload administrators' and teachers' brains. Second, although Danielson's framework was originally designed as a coaching tool, in evaluation mode the 4-3-2-1 rating scale makes teachers feel they're being graded like a student.

Trying to give real-time ratings on a multipage rubric is extremely difficult.

Third, some supervisors bring their rubric into classrooms and score individual lessons. This strikes me as an especially bad idea. Rubrics are a comprehensive description of a teacher's yearlong work; they are the wrong "grain size" (Justin Baeder's term) for assessing an individual lesson. Trying to give real-time ratings on a multipage rubric is extremely difficult. In addition, focusing on a rubric distracts supervisors from walking around a classroom, talking with students, and observing what's happening in a thoughtful and open-minded way.

There's a straightforward solution to the third problem: don't use the rubric for classroom visits; instead, use it at the end of the year to sum up all the information gathered from multiple observations and other points of contact with each teacher. This fits well with mini-observations, where supervisors gather lots of authentic information on teachers throughout the year. Here's a graphic showing this and other inputs to the supervisor's overall assessment, making possible fair and accurate rubric scoring at the end of the school year:

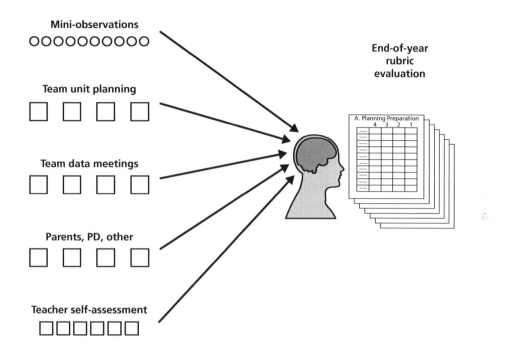

Mini-observations and follow-up conversations and summaries (ideally ten over the course of a year) are a primary source of evaluative information, along with glimpses of teachers at work with their colleagues, parents, outside-the-classroom activities, complemented by each teacher's self-assessment, which helps fill in gaps and gives the teacher's perspective. Putting all this information together can, I believe, produce quite an accurate picture of a teacher's overall performance.

What about my two other concerns about rubrics—too long and too judgmental? To address the first, I wrote a rubric that I believe is more streamlined and user-friendly. On the second, I have suggestions for introducing and implementing any rubric that address this teacher concern.

Building a Better Mousetrap

In 2006, a principal in Newark, New Jersey, asked if I'd be willing to write a teacher rubric for his school. Why didn't they use Danielson's? I asked. The school believed it was too long and detailed. Would the school pay me? Yes, said the principal, and I got right to work.

My raw materials were several published rubrics—Danielson's, Marzano's, and others being used around the US. I also studied *The Skillful Teacher,* Jon Saphier's widely read book, and drew on the best research on what works in classrooms. After multiple drafts and suggestions from a wide range of educators, I produced a new synthesis. Here are the ways my rubric is different from its predecessors (on whose shoulders it stands):

- **More comprehensive.** Other rubrics have important gaps in their descriptions of teachers' classroom work and their broader responsibilities.
- **More succinct.** I used as few words as possible, and tried to keep the headline for each criterion to one word.
- **Descriptive language.** I avoided using stock words or phrases (Always, Mostly, Sometimes, Never) and gave a vivid picture of performance in each cell.
- **Discrete.** Each cell describes one teaching behavior; other rubrics, especially shortened versions (such as Danielson's 22-item edition), combine several items in a single cell.
- **Left-to-right sequence.** Putting effective practices on the left and less-effective on the right creates a more positive tone.
- **Attainable.** The teaching behaviors at the highest level should be possible during the contract day and without extraordinary heroics.
- **One domain per page.** This allows a clear visual picture of a teacher's performance in each area of pedagogy.
- **Minimal paperwork.** Circling or highlighting the chosen levels does the work of describing a teacher's performance. There are only a couple of lines at the bottom of each page for written comments, keeping them to a minimum.
- **Free and open source.** Having been paid by the Newark school, I decided to make the rubric available at no charge, authorizing schools to modify it in any way they see fit.

Creating a new rubric involved a number of key decisions. Here's a brief summary:

What Are the Domains?

With any evaluation instrument, the first decision is the "buckets" for sorting the countless criteria of performance. Danielson's teacher framework has four domains:

- Planning and preparation
- The classroom environment
- Instruction
- Professional responsibilities

This is a solid list, but as I looked at other rubrics, I thought a couple of important elements were buried in the details of Danielson's rubric and needed more prominence. I ended up adding a domain for monitoring, assessment, and follow-up and one for family and community outreach, and made some changes in wording. Here were my six domains:

- Planning and preparation
- Classroom management
- Delivery of instruction
- Monitoring, assessment, and follow-up
- Family and community outreach
- Professional responsibilities

How Many Rating Levels and What to Call Them?

Several rating scales are being used in schools around the US, with anywhere from two to ten levels of teacher performance and a variety of descriptive labels. Here are some examples:

Two levels (New York City until 2010):

- Satisfactory
- Unsatisfactory

Three levels (Boston until 2012):

- Excellent
- Satisfactory
- Unsatisfactory

Four levels (Danielson and others):

1. Distinguished
2. Proficient
3. Basic
4. Unsatisfactory

Five levels (Tennessee)

1. Significantly above expectations
2.

3. At expectations

4.

5. Significantly below expectations

Seven levels (Missouri)

1. Distinguished

2.

3. Proficient

4.

5. Developing

6.

7. Emerging

Note that the Tennessee and Missouri scales don't have labels for the even numbers on their scales, nor do they have descriptive language at those levels. Why? Because (as I've learned from drafting descriptive language for my rubric) when there are more than four levels, it's very difficult to come up with language that teases out the fine distinctions between levels. In Tennessee and Missouri, the rubric designers didn't even try, leaving it up to supervisors to eyeball teachers' ratings in the in-between levels.

> *The philosophical stance of four-point rubrics is that performance at the top two levels is likely to produce good student achievement, the opposite for the bottom two levels.*

As it turns out, rubrics with five or more rating levels are the exception; four-point scales are the choice of the vast majority of schools. Four is a level of detail that strikes most teachers and administrators as manageable, and it's an even number, drawing a bright line between proficient and less-than-proficient performance. The philosophical stance of four-point rubrics is that performance at the top two levels is likely to produce good student achievement, the opposite for the bottom two levels.

How should the levels be labeled? This is an important decision, conveying beliefs about teacher performance and improvement. Here are some examples of rating labels in different evaluation systems:

- **Level 4.** Distinguished, expert, exceeding the standard, exceeds expectations, advanced, innovating, lead, highly effective

- **Level 3.** Proficient, meeting the standard, meets expectations, applying, highly accomplished, effective

- **Level 2.** Basic, needs improvement, developing, emerging, progressing toward the standard, proficient, working toward, beginning, minimally effective
- **Level 1.** Unsatisfactory, beginning, needs improvement, graduate, novice, ineffective

Examining these and other scales helped clarify my thinking about the messages a teacher evaluation rubric should send. I liked the way a four-point scale creates a clear division between the top two levels (excellent and solid teaching) and the bottom two (mediocre and poor), with no rating comparable to "average." I also noticed how rating labels communicate beliefs about what each level represents, which drives the way the criteria are written.

For example, using Novice rather than Unsatisfactory for the lowest level reflects a supportive, "not yet" approach to less-than-proficient performance. Using Innovating rather than Distinguished for the highest level presupposes that the best teachers are creative. Using Effective rather than Proficient puts more emphasis on a teacher's impact on student learning. I wanted my rubric to support improvement, convey a growth mindset about improvement, and send a stern message about mediocre and ineffective teaching.

One of the most important decisions writing a four-level rubric is the difference between teacher performance at the highest level and performance at level 3. Here is what's different about the highest scoring level in these rubrics:

Danielson—Student involvement in instruction
Marzano—Innovation
Massachusetts—Being able to model

I have concerns about each of these. There are areas of teaching where student involvement can't be included, so it's not applicable across the board. Some very effective teachers aren't especially innovative but they get results. And is it fair to evaluate a teacher based on outside-the-classroom modeling? I decided that the descriptors at level 4 in my rubric would take level 3 up a notch in each area, without a rubric-wide theme.

All this translated into the following philosophy for each level:

- **Level 4** is reserved for teachers who are truly exceptional, well above standards, and using methods that research says will maximize student learning. Having the top level be a high bar addresses a perennial problem with teacher evaluation—grade inflation. The clear expectation should be that only teachers who are expert at their craft will attain this level.
- **Level 3** represents solid professional work—the expected norm of performance—without the slightest suggestion of mediocrity. Teachers who are working at level 3 should be able to hold their heads high (while still, perhaps, aspiring to reach the top level).

- **Level 2** is barely passing and should convey the clear message that performance is mediocre and needs to be improved. No teacher should be comfortable with ratings at this level—it's not getting by or getting over. Educators would not want their own children or beloved nieces or nephews to be in the classroom whose teacher is rated at level 2.

- **Level 1** is clearly unsatisfactory, below standards, ineffective with students, unacceptable, and headed straight toward job termination unless improvement happens quickly. Needs Improvement is too soft a label for this level, but the label should avoid sounding terminal and inescapable—such as Ineffective. The rubric has to hold out hope and push for improvement.

To be rated Effective or Highly Effective, you need to prove yourself with student learning results— growth mindset thinking.

Among the options, Effective puts the emphasis on results and student achievement, versus the teacher's professional image. Distinguished and Expert have a fixed mindset tone. When you're rated Distinguished, you have arrived. To be rated Effective or Highly Effective, you need to prove yourself with student learning results— growth mindset thinking.

For level 2, I thought Minimally Effective sounded too positive. The same could be said for Needs Improvement. Abraham Lincoln was an amazing president, but he needed improvement.

Thinking about all the options, here are the labels I decided on:

1. Highly Effective
2. Effective
3. Improvement Necessary
4. Does Not Meet Standards

Drafting the Rubric

I began by writing the Effective level for each domain. It's more efficient to start with level 3—the prime meridian of the rubric—and do all the writing, editing, sorting, synthesizing, sequencing, and getting feedback before teasing the criteria out to the other three levels. If you're thinking about tweaking my rubric, I highly recommend working on the Effective level first. If you try to edit all four levels at once, you'll drive yourself crazy.

Educators and researchers have been trying to identify desirable teacher qualities and bottle the magic from time immemorial, and there are hundreds of criteria out there. I delved into the literature and evaluation instruments from numerous schools, looking for descriptors with the strongest links to student achievement and positive professional culture. I set up six files in my computer, one for each domain, and began loading ideas into them.

The challenge with all this raw material was combining, consolidating, and shuffling within each domain. I wanted lists that were comprehensive and yet short, and individual criteria that were expressive yet compact. Working on my first draft, I made a rule: each descriptor had to fit on one line (12-point type, half-inch margins). If it spilled over, I worked on shortening it. Then I came up with a one-word label for each row (in a few cases hyphenating two words).

When all the combining, synthesizing, and wordsmithing was done, there were exactly ten criteria per domain and each fitted on one page. Amazing! There seemed to be a sonnet-like logic. Did I force the content or leave anything out to have exactly ten per domain? It didn't feel that way.

The next step was taking the Effective language for each cell up a notch to Highly Effective, down a notch to Improvement Necessary, and down another to Does Not Meet Standards. I wrote the descriptors to reflect the philosophy behind the different performance levels, with the Highly Effective items describing truly exceptional performance, Improvement Necessary describing marginal performance that clearly needs to change, and Does Not Meet Standards describing unacceptable performance that will result in job action if it doesn't improve. The goal was vivid, observable descriptions in every cell.

Note that in my rubric, there is a bigger jump from the second to the third levels—from Improvement Necessary to Effective—than between the top two levels (Highly Effective and Effective) and between the bottom two levels (Does Not Meet Standards and Improvement Necessary). That's because the top two describe excellent and solid teaching and the bottom two describe mediocre and below-par teaching. There's no "average" level between them, no "gentleman's C."

The final step was writing a summary page that enables the supervisor to pull together the ratings for the six domains in one place so overall performance can be seen at a glance. There's also space for the supervisor and teacher to write general comments and sign off on the evaluation. At the bottom of this page is the standard disclaimer that the teacher's signature doesn't necessarily denote agreement with the evaluation.

Should supervisors write comments to supplement rubric scores? If there's something to add that isn't captured in the rubric language, absolutely. In a thoughtful 2016 article, Rob Jenkins listed admirable teacher qualities that aren't in any rubric: good-natured, professional without being aloof, a good sense of humor, enjoy what they do, demanding without being unkind, comfortable in their own skin, tremendously creative, making teaching look easy.

The rubric provides detailed descriptions, and any supplementary commendations should be as succinct as possible.

These subjective, ineffable qualities are just the sort that might appear in comments at the bottom of each domain page or in the summative page.

But most of what a supervisor has to say about each teacher's performance should be communicated in what's circled or highlighted on each page. The rubric provides detailed descriptions, and any supplementary commendations should be as succinct as possible. Scoring is easy: principals can use a highlighter or, if the rubric is in electronic form (as they are in T-EVAL, www.edusoftllc.com), click the chosen levels for each teacher.

The Latest Revision

Spurred on by preparing the third edition of this book, I took another look at the teacher rubric I'd last revised in 2014 and got out a file of ideas and suggestions I'd been gathering. This led to a number of wording tweaks, some of them quite important, and two major changes:

- **No more 4-3-2-1.** I've been convinced that numerical scores at the top of each page create the wrong tone, distracting teachers from the detailed descriptions of effective and less-than-effective practices. I hope that taking the numbers off will nudge evaluation conversations toward focusing on substance rather than "grades." Not having numbers might also make it less tempting to give a faux-precise decimal score for each domain.

- **Trimming from sixty to fifty-four evaluation items.** In the interests of making the rubric a little less burdensome, I took a close look at each domain and found that it was possible to cut or consolidate one line on each page without detracting from its analysis of teaching in that area. Is it possible that all the domains went from exactly ten to exactly nine lines and still maintained their integrity? The question is whether anything important is missing on each page—or whether there's any superfluous fluff. You be the judge.

The new edition of the rubric appears on the following pages. As mentioned, this rubric is free and open source (available as a PDF at www.marshallmemo.com, click on Kim's Writing and scroll down) and can be adopted and edited by any school or district. A number of schools and districts have used previous editions of the rubric successfully in recent years, and a number of state have approved them for statewide use. If you want to modify the rubric, email me at kim.marshall48@gmail.com for an Excel version.

This rubric is still a work in progress. It's been through sixteen revisions, and I'm open to further suggestions for improvement.

A. Planning and Preparation for Learning

The teacher:	Highly Effective	Effective	Improvement Necessary	Does Not Meet Standards
a. **Expertise**	Is expert in the subject area and how to relate it to students' developmental and learning needs and cultural heritage.	Knows the subject area and how it can be related to students' developmental and learning needs.	Is somewhat familiar with the subject area and has a few ideas on how it relates to students' developmental and learning needs.	Has little familiarity with the subject area and few ideas on relating it to students' developmental and learning needs.
b. **Goals**	Has a detailed plan for the year geared to explicit, challenging, achievable outcomes for all students, aligned with external standards.	Has explicit, challenging, achievable goals for all students, aligned with external standards.	Plans week by week aiming to cover external standards.	Plans lesson by lesson with little reference to external standards.
c. **Units**	Plans almost all units with big ideas, essential questions, knowledge, skill, transfer, and non-cognitive goals covering most Bloom levels.	Plans most units with big ideas, essential questions, knowledge, skill, and non-cognitive goals.	Plans lessons with some thought to larger goals and objectives and higher-order thinking skills.	Teaches on an *ad hoc* basis with little or no consideration for long-range curriculum goals.
d. **Assessments**	Prepares diagnostic, on-the-spot, interim, and summative assessments to monitor student learning.	Plans on-the-spot and unit assessments to measure student learning.	Drafts unit tests as instruction proceeds.	Writes tests shortly before they are given.
e. **Anticipation**	Anticipates students' likely preconceptions, misconceptions, and confusions and develops strategies to overcome them.	Anticipates misconceptions and confusions students might have and plans to address them.	Has a hunch about one or two ways that students might become confused with the content.	Proceeds without considering misconceptions students might have about the material.
f. **Lessons**	Designs lessons and practice work with clear, measurable, achievable goals aligned with standards and unit outcomes.	Designs lessons and practice work focused on measurable, achievable outcomes aligned with unit goals.	Plans lessons and practice work with some consideration of long-term goals.	Plans lessons and practice aimed primarily at entertaining students or covering textbook chapters.
g. **Materials**	Designs lessons that use an effective mix of high-quality, culturally responsive learning materials and technology.	Designs lessons that use an engaging, culturally responsive mix of materials and technology.	Plans lessons that involve a mixture of good and mediocre learning materials.	Plans lessons that rely mainly on mediocre and low-quality textbooks, workbooks, or worksheets.
h. **Differentiation**	Designs lessons that captivate students across a wide range of differences, with low-floor/high-ceiling activities and productive struggle.	Designs lessons that engage and provide access to students at different levels of achievement and varied interests.	Plans lessons with some thought to engagement and accommodating varied student needs.	Plans lessons with little or no differentiation for varied student needs.
i. **Environment**	Uses room arrangement, materials, and displays to create an inviting climate and maximize student learning.	Organizes classroom furniture, materials, and displays to support unit and lesson goals.	Organizes furniture and materials to support the lesson, with only a few displays.	Has a conventional furniture arrangement, hard-to-access materials, and few displays.

Overall rating:_____ Comments:

B. Classroom Management

The teacher:	Highly Effective	Effective	Improvement Necessary	Does Not Meet Standards
a. Expectations	Is direct, specific, consistent, and tenacious in communicating and enforcing very high expectations.	Clearly communicates and consistently enforces high standards for student behavior.	Announces and posts classroom rules and consequences.	Comes up with *ad hoc* rules and consequences as events unfold during the year.
b. Relationships	Shows warmth, caring, respect, and fairness for all students and builds strong, mutually respectful relationships.	Is fair and respectful toward students and builds positive relationships.	Fairness and respect are uneven and some relationships are negative.	Is sometimes harsh, unfair, and disrespectful with students and/or plays favorites.
c. Social-emotional	Implements a program that successfully fosters positive interactions and builds key social-emotional skills.	Fosters positive interactions among students and teaches useful social skills.	Often lectures students on the need for good behavior, and makes an example of "bad" students.	Publicly berates "bad" students, blaming them for their poor behavior.
d. Routines	Successfully inculcates and maintains class routines to maximize learning time.	Teaches routines and prompts students to maintain them all year.	Tries to train students in class routines but many of the routines are not maintained.	Does not teach routines and is constantly nagging, threatening, and punishing students.
e. Responsibility	Gets virtually all students to be self-disciplined, take responsibility for their actions, and have a strong sense of efficacy.	Develops students' self-discipline and teaches them to take responsibility for their own actions.	Tries to get students to be responsible for their actions, but many lack self-discipline.	Is unsuccessful in fostering self-discipline in students; they are dependent on the teacher to behave.
f. Repertoire	Has a highly effective discipline repertoire, including being able to capture and hold students' attention at will.	Has a repertoire of discipline "moves," including being able to get students' attention when needed.	Has a limited discipline repertoire and some students are not paying attention.	Has few discipline skills and constantly struggles to get students' attention.
g. Efficiency	Skillfully uses coherence, momentum, and transitions so that almost every minute of classroom time produces learning.	Maximizes academic learning time through coherence, lesson momentum, and smooth transitions.	Sometimes loses teaching time due to lack of clarity, interruptions, inefficient transitions, and off-task teacher behavior.	Loses a great deal of instructional time because of confusion, interruptions, ragged transitions, and off-task teacher behavior.
h. Prevention	Is alert, poised, dynamic, and self-assured and has a plan to nip virtually all discipline problems in the bud.	Has a confident, dynamic presence and nips most discipline problems in the bud.	Tries to prevent discipline problems but sometimes little things escalate into big problems.	Is unsuccessful at spotting and preventing discipline problems, and they frequently escalate.
i. Incentives	Gets students to buy into an effective system of incentives linked to intrinsic rewards.	Uses incentives effectively to encourage and reinforce student cooperation.	Depends on extrinsic rewards to get students to cooperate and comply.	Uses low-quality extrinsic rewards (e.g., free time) and doesn't use them to leverage behavior.

Overall rating:_____ Comments:

C. Delivery of Instruction

The teacher:	Highly Effective	Effective	Improvement Necessary	Does Not Meet Standards
a. **Expectations**	Exudes high expectations, urgency, and determination that all students will master the material.	Conveys to students: This is important, you can do it, and I'm not going to give up on you.	Tells students that the subject matter is important and they need to work hard.	Gives up on some students as hopeless.
b. **Mindset**	Actively inculcates a "growth" mindset: take risks, learn from mistakes, through effective effort you can and will achieve at high levels.	Teaches students that effective effort, not innate ability, is the key.	Doesn't counteract students' belief that innate ability is what makes the difference.	Communicates a "fixed" mindset about ability: some students have it, some don't.
c. **Framing**	Highlights lesson goals and unit essential questions up front and has students summarize and internalize key learning at the end.	Highlights lesson goals at the beginning of the lesson and has students sum up what they've learned at the conclusion.	Tells students the main learning objectives of each lesson but doesn't wrap things up at the end.	Begins and ends lessons without giving students a sense of what it's all about.
d. **Connections**	Engages student in each unit's and lesson's content and vocabulary by activating their interests and prior knowledge.	Links newly introduced lesson content and vocabulary to students' interests and prior knowledge.	Is only sometimes successful in making the subject interesting and relating it to things students already know.	Rarely hooks students' interest or makes connections to their lives.
e. **Clarity**	Presents material clearly and explicitly, with well-chosen examples and vivid, appropriate language.	Uses clear explanations, appropriate language, and examples to present material.	Sometimes uses language and explanations that are fuzzy, confusing, or inappropriate.	Often presents material in a confusing way and/or uses language that is inappropriate.
f. **Repertoire**	Uses a wide range of well-chosen, effective strategies, questions, materials, technology, and groupings to accelerate student learning.	Orchestrates effective strategies, questions, materials, technology, and groupings to foster student learning.	Uses a limited range of classroom strategies, questions, materials, and groupings with mixed success.	Uses only one or two teaching strategies and types of materials and fails to reach most students.
g. **Engagement**	Gets virtually all students involved in focused activities, actively learning and problem-solving, losing themselves in the work.	Has students actively think about, discuss, and use the ideas and skills being taught.	Attempts to get students actively involved but some students are disengaged.	Mostly lectures to passive students or has them plod through textbooks and worksheets.
h. **Differentiation**	Successfully reaches virtually all students by skillfully differentiating and scaffolding and using peer and adult helpers.	Scaffolds instruction and uses peer and adult helpers to accommodate most students' learning needs.	Attempts to accommodate lessons to students with learning needs, but with mixed success.	Fails to differentiate instruction for students with learning needs.
i. **Nimbleness**	Deftly adapts lessons and units to exploit teachable moments and correct misunderstandings.	Is flexible about modifying lessons to take advantage of teachable moments.	Sometimes doesn't take advantage of teachable moments.	Is rigid and inflexible with lesson plans and rarely takes advantage of teachable moments.

Overall rating:_____ **Comments:**

D. Monitoring, Assessment, and Follow-Up

The teacher:	Highly Effective	Effective	Improvement Necessary	Does Not Meet Standards
a. **Criteria**	Consistently highlights and reviews clear criteria for good work, with rubrics and exemplars of student work at each level of proficiency.	Highlights criteria for proficiency, including rubrics and exemplars of student work.	Tells students some of the qualities that their finished work should exhibit.	Expects students to know (or figure out) what it takes to get good grades.
b. **Diagnosis**	Gives students a well-constructed diagnostic assessment before each unit and uses the information to shape instruction.	Diagnoses students' knowledge and skills at the beginning of a unit and tweaks lessons based on the data.	Does a quick review before beginning a unit.	Begins instruction without diagnosing students' skills and knowledge.
c. **Goals**	Has students set ambitious goals, continuously self-assess, and take responsibility for improving their work.	Has students self-assess, set goals, and know where they stand academically at all times.	Urges students to look over their work, see where they had trouble, and aim to improve those areas.	Allows students to move on without assessing and improving problems in their work.
d. **Feedback**	Uses a variety of effective methods to check for understanding; immediately unscrambles confusion and clarifies.	Frequently checks for understanding and gives students helpful information if they seem confused.	Uses mediocre methods (e.g., thumbs up, thumbs down) to check for understanding during instruction.	Uses ineffective methods ("Is everyone with me?") to check for understanding.
e. **Recognition**	Frequently displays students' work with rubrics and commentary to celebrate progress and motivate and direct effort.	Regularly displays students' work to make visible their progress with respect to standards.	Displays some 'A' student work as an example to others.	Displays only a few samples of student work or none at all.
f. **Analysis**	Works with colleagues to immediately use assessment data to fine-tune teaching, re-teach, and help students who need support.	Promptly uses data from assessments to adjust teaching, re-teach, and follow up with students who need support.	Records students' assessment grades and notes some general patterns for future reference.	Records students' assessment grades and moves on with the curriculum.
g. **Tenacity**	Relentlessly follows up with struggling students with personal attention so that virtually all reach proficiency.	Takes responsibility for students who are not succeeding and gives them extra help.	Offers students who fail tests some additional time to study and do re-takes.	Tells students that if they fail a test, that's it; the class has to move on to cover the curriculum.
h. **Support**	Makes sure that students who need academic support or services receive appropriate services promptly.	When necessary, refers students for academic support or services.	Sometimes doesn't refer students promptly for support, and/or refers students who don't need it.	Often fails to refer students for support services and/or refers students who do not need them.
i. **Reflection**	Works with colleagues to reflect on and document what worked and what didn't and continuously improve instruction.	Reflects on the effectiveness of lessons and units and continuously works to improve them.	At the end of a teaching unit or semester, thinks about what might have been done better.	Does not draw lessons for the future when teaching is unsuccessful.

Overall rating:_____   Comments:

E. Family and Community Outreach

The teacher:	Highly Effective	Effective	Improvement Necessary	Does Not Meet Standards
a. **Respect**	Shows sensitivity and respect for family culture, values, and beliefs and finds ways to make all feel welcome in the school.	Is respectful with family members, sensitive to different cultures, and welcomes all to the classroom.	Tries to be sensitive to the culture and beliefs of students' families but sometimes shows lack of respect.	Is often insensitive to the culture and beliefs of students' families.
b. **Belief**	Shows each parent an in-depth knowledge of their child and a strong belief that he or she will meet or exceed standards.	Shows parents a genuine interest and belief in each child's ability to reach standards.	Tells parents that he or she cares about their children and wants the best for them.	Does not communicate to parents knowledge of individual children or concern about their future.
c. **Expectations**	Gives parents clear, user-friendly learning and behavior expectations and exemplars of proficient work through the year.	Gives parents clear expectations for student learning and behavior for the year.	Sends home a list of classroom rules and the syllabus for the year.	Doesn't inform parents about learning and behavior expectations.
d. **Communication**	Makes sure parents hear positive news about their children first, and immediately flags any problems.	Promptly informs parents of behavior and learning problems, also updating parents on good news.	Lets parents know about problems their children are having but rarely mentions positive news.	Seldom informs parents of concerns or positive news about their children.
e. **Involving**	Frequently involves parents in supporting and enriching the curriculum for their children as it unfolds.	Plans appropriate ways for family members to be involved in their children's learning.	Sends home occasional suggestions on how parents can help their children with schoolwork.	Rarely if ever communicates with parents on ways to help their children at home.
f. **Responsiveness**	Deals immediately and successfully with parents' concerns.	Responds promptly to parents' concerns.	Is slow to respond to parents' concerns.	Is unresponsive to parents' concerns.
g. Reporting	Uses informal and digital channels and student-led conferences to regularly inform parents on their children's progress.	Uses digital channels and reports to regularly keep parents informed on their children's progress.	Uses parent conferences intermittently to tell parents the areas in which their children need to improve.	Completes reports, not always on time, and expects parents to deal with their children's learning needs.
h. Outreach	Successfully contacts virtually all parents, including those who are hard to reach.	Reaches out to all parents and is tenacious in contacting those who are hard to reach.	Tries to contact all parents, but ends up talking mainly to the parents who tend to be responsive.	Makes little or no effort to contact parents.
i. Resources	Successfully enlists extra resources from homes and the community to enrich the curriculum.	Reaches out to families and community agencies to bring in additional resources.	Asks parents to contribute extra resources.	Does not reach out for extra support from parents or the community.

Overall rating:_____ **Comments:**

F. Professional Responsibilities

The teacher:	Highly Effective	Effective	Improvement Necessary	Does Not Meet Standards
a. **Language**	In professional contexts, speaks and writes correctly, succinctly, and eloquently.	Uses correct grammar, syntax, usage, and spelling in professional contexts.	Periodically makes errors in grammar, syntax, usage and/or spelling in professional contexts.	Frequently makes errors in grammar, syntax, usage, and/or spelling in professional contexts.
b. **Reliability**	Carries out all duties and assignments conscientiously and punctually and keeps meticulous records.	Is punctual and reliable with paperwork, duties, and assignments and keeps accurate records.	Occasionally skips assignments, is late, makes errors in records, or misses paperwork deadlines.	Frequently skips assignments, is late, makes errors in records, or misses paperwork deadlines.
c. **Professionalism**	Presents as a consummate professional and always observes appropriate boundaries.	Demonstrates professional demeanor and attire and maintains appropriate boundaries.	Occasionally acts and/ or dresses in an unprofessional manner and/or violates boundaries.	Frequently acts and/or dresses in an unprofessional manner and violates boundaries.
d. **Judgment**	Is invariably ethical, honest, and forthright, uses impeccable judgment, and respects confidentiality.	Is ethical and forthright, uses good judgment, and maintains confidentiality with student information.	Sometimes uses poor judgment, is less than completely honest, and/or discloses student information.	Is frequently unethical, dishonest, uses poor judgment, and/or discloses student information.
e. **Teamwork**	Is an important member of teacher teams and committees and volunteers for extra activities.	Shares responsibility for grade-level and schoolwide activities and takes part in extra activities.	When asked, will serve on a committee and attend an extra activity.	Declines invitations to serve on committees and attend extra activities.
f. **Leadership**	Frequently contributes valuable ideas and expertise and instills in others a desire to improve student results.	Contributes ideas, expertise, and time to the overall mission of the school.	Occasionally suggests an idea aimed at improving the school.	Rarely if ever contributes ideas that might help improve the school.
g. **Openness**	Actively seeks out feedback and suggestions from students, parents, and colleagues and uses them to improve performance.	Listens thoughtfully to other viewpoints and responds constructively to suggestions and criticism.	Is somewhat defensive but does listen to feedback and suggestions.	Is very defensive about feedback and resistant to changing practices.
h. **Collaboration**	Meets frequently with colleagues to plan units, share ideas, and analyze assessment results.	Collaborates regularly with colleagues to plan units, share teaching ideas, and look at student work.	Meets occasionally with colleagues to share ideas about teaching and students.	Meets infrequently with colleagues, and conversations lack educational substance.
i. **Growth**	Actively reaches out for new ideas and engages in action research with colleagues to figure out what works best.	Seeks out effective teaching ideas from colleagues, workshops, and other sources and implements them well.	Can occasionally be persuaded to try out new classroom practices.	Is not open to ideas for improving teaching and learning and has not implemented suggestions.

Overall rating:_____ **Comments:**

Evaluation Summary Page

Teacher's name: _____ School year: _____

School: _____ Subject area: _____

Evaluator: _____ Position: _____

RATING ON EACH DOMAIN:

A. Planning and Preparation for Learning:

    Highly Effective   Effective   Improvement Necessary   Does Not Meet Standards

B. Classroom Management:

    Highly Effective   Effective   Improvement Necessary   Does Not Meet Standards

C. Delivery of Instruction:

    Highly Effective   Effective   Improvement Necessary   Does Not Meet Standards

D. Monitoring, Assessment, and Follow-Up:

    Highly Effective   Effective   Improvement Necessary   Does Not Meet Standards

E. Family and Community Outreach:

    Highly Effective   Effective   Improvement Necessary   Does Not Meet Standards

F. Professional Responsibilities:

    Highly Effective   Effective   Improvement Necessary   Does Not Meet Standards

OVERALL RATING:

Highly Effective   Effective   Improvement Necessary   Does Not Meet Standards

OVERALL COMMENTS BY EVALUATOR:

OVERALL COMMENTS BY TEACHER:

Evaluator's signature: _____ Date: _____

Teacher's signature: _____ Date: _____

(The teacher's signature indicates that he or she has seen and discussed the evaluation; it does not necessarily denote agreement with the report.)

Reducing Teachers' Anxieties About the Rubric

Even though my rubric is more compact than many others, it can still seem overwhelming to teachers and supervisors when they flip through the pages. *Six pages of fine print! Fifty-four evaluation criteria! Too much!* The initial reaction might be to cut down the number of items and not score teachers on all the details, giving just an overall rating on each of the six domains.

> Some teachers have a negative reaction to being pigeon-holed at four performance levels. "I don't like being put in a box!"

Here are additional concerns I've encountered. Some teachers have a negative reaction to being pigeon-holed at four performance levels. "I don't like being put in a box!" exclaimed a Washington, DC, department head. There are objections to Effective being the expected level of performance; lots of teachers justifiably think of themselves as excellent, and being scored at the next-to-top level feels like getting a B.

As with any evaluation tool, it's essential that at the beginning of the school year, the rubric is presented to teachers for review and sign-off. A rubric is the school's definition of good (and not-so-good) instruction, and ethically and legally, all employees need to have advance notice of the standards on which they'll be evaluated. The way this obligatory exercise is handled makes all the difference.

For school leaders introducing this rubric to colleagues, I recommend using the particular-general-particular strategy—zooming in on specific details and zooming out to the bigger picture. Here is the step-by-step process I've developed as I've introduced the rubric over the years. For this meeting, participants should have a hard copy of the full rubric in their hands, and the presenter should be able to project key slides on a large screen.

1. Start by having people look at the list of six domains on the cover page. Explain how Kim Marshall researched different approaches to divide up teaching and decided on these six buckets.

2. Explain that the rubric sums up each teacher's performance for the year, pulling together information from classroom visits, follow-up conversations, other points of contact, and the teacher's self-assessment.

3. Share the Rob Jenkins list of teacher qualities that are not in the rubric and ask why. People are quick to say that they're desirable but too subjective to include in any rubric. This is an important note of humility about the rubric; it's not all-inclusive and perfect, but it has many important aspects of teaching.

4. Explain the four-level rating scale and the rationale for the labels, emphasizing that the top level is a very high bar and Effective is solid, expected professional performance, nothing to be ashamed of.

5. Describe Kim's rationale for taking the 4-3-2-1 numbers off the top of each domain, saying they were there in earlier editions.

6. Have people turn to one page inside the packet (Monitoring, Assessment, and Follow-up is a good choice) and ask them to silently read just the Effective column from top to bottom. It's helpful if this column is projected on a screen.

7. Pick one item from that column and read it out loud. This drives home the point that Effective is a rigorous yet manageable level of performance, what educators would want to see in their own children's or nieces' and nephews' classrooms.

8. Project that rubric page with all the details and explain how the Effective level—the starting point—was teased out to the other three performance levels and each row was given a one-word label on the left.

9. Pick one horizontal row on that page and read it out loud from right to left, one cell at a time. This shows the gradations of performance from Does Not Meet Standards to Highly Effective.

10. Display that page of the rubric with your own self-assessment when you were a teacher highlighted, humbly displaying a mixture of scores at different levels.

11. "Do the math" on what your score would be as a mixed decimal (for example, 2.6) and ask whether that kind of mathematical precision is a good idea. There's usually clear consensus that it's not, because different criteria have different levels of importance, and for each teacher, some are more important than others. Better to write the level descriptor in the space at the bottom of the page—for example, Effective.

12. Display your self-assessment on all six pages, modeling humility and showing graphically the amount of detailed information about a teacher's work that the rubric pulls together and displays.

13. Show the three improvement goals that you and your supervisor would agree on for the following year, based on your rubric scores (mine were classroom management, better checking for understanding, and working with my grade-level team).

14. Ask people to think about evaluating a teacher they know well (perhaps themselves) on one page (Classroom Management is a good choice). Ask how long would it take to write a narrative evaluation. Most people estimate half an hour.

15. Now ask people to evaluate the teacher using the rubric. Have them read the Effective cell with each row first, then go left or right and circle or highlight the best description of the teacher's performance on that criterion. While people do this, the room usually gets very quiet and they're done in about three minutes.

16. When people have finished, have them give their teacher an overall rating for the page and ask for a show of hands how many scored at the Highly Effective, Effective, Improvement Necessary, and Does Not Meet Standards level, then how many single Highly Effective scores there were.

17. Next, have people flip through each page of the rubric as you read aloud one Effective descriptor for each page. This gives a quick tour of the whole document while zooming in specific criteria.

18. Next, have people discuss in small groups the pros and cons of using a rubric this way.

19. Finally, ask people to share their conclusions, starting with positives and then concerns and questions.

I've found that this process takes thirty to thirty-five minutes and is always effective at demystifying the rubric and making it seem less daunting and more manageable. Here's a poll I use to gauge reactions at this point and responses from a recent workshop:

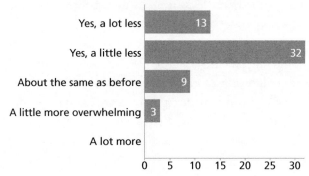

Do the rubrics feel a little less intimidating and overwhelming now?

When groups of educators list positive aspects of the rubric, there's usually consensus on these key advantages for end-of-year evaluations:

- It provides a common language about good and not-so-good teaching.
- Feedback from different supervisors is more objective than using narratives.
- Teachers have the rubric in advance and can self-assess and set goals.

The detailed descriptions in the rubric provide a bridge from the mini-observations and debriefs during the year to a teacher's summative evaluation.

- The detailed descriptions in the rubric provide a bridge from the mini-observations and debriefs during the year to a teacher's summative evaluation.
- The language at successively higher levels of performance provide a ladder for improvement.
- It's easier to accept a few low ratings among the fifty-four criteria.
- It's quick for administrators to fill out.
- Patterns of proficiency on each domain are visually accessible.
- Ratings for staff members can provide valuable data for professional learning experiences.

Asked to list concerns with the rubric, a few worries come up: specific items on the rubric (especially classroom incentive systems on the Classroom Management page); whether the Highly Effective level is achievable in certain areas; whether supervisors will be in classrooms enough to give accurate ratings; whether teachers will have input; whether rubric ratings will be used for salary increases; and, most interestingly, how ten leverage points in the year's mini-observations can translate into fifty-four rubric ratings at the end of the year.

On the last point, the answer is that beyond the leverage points that are shared in face-to-face debriefs, there are the compliments paid to the teacher after each mini-observation; other insights from classroom visits that weren't discussed; insights from visits to teacher team meetings; seeing teachers in action with colleagues, students, and families; and, of course, the teacher's self-assessment. Reading the Effective level of each rubric line, it's amazing how the specific language pulls this information from memory.

On using the rubric for high-stakes decisions, it's important to say that rubric ratings aren't mathematically precise, and teacher pay should not be based on them. But for the purpose for which this process is designed—substantive, detailed, and credible end-of-year feedback on the teacher's job—this process works well.

At this point in the rubric-introduction meeting, it's important to describe how the rubric will be used during the school year and how it meshes with mini-observations: teacher goal setting, teacher input at a midyear check-in and end-of-year rubric conferences. This figure shows the steps:

Faculty Roll-Out

At a beginning-of-the-year faculty introduction to the rubric, the principal might ask teachers to self-assess on the other five pages over the next few days. If the school is using T-EVAL, teachers can anonymously enter their scores online and everyone can look at the composite picture of ratings for the staff. This pinpoints specific areas of strength and areas in which professional development would be helpful. There are likely to be teachers and administrators in the building who are strong in those areas and can lead professional development during the year.

If administrators are being evaluated on my principal evaluation rubric (or another one), it might be a good idea to show teachers that rubric so they understand that their leaders are going through a similar process with their superintendent or head of school (see my principal evaluation rubric in Chapter Fourteen). Brave supervisors might even ask teachers to anonymously rubric-score them.

Teacher Goal Setting

Teachers should use the rubrics to self-assess at the beginning of each school year (or use their ratings from the previous year). Any area at the Improvement Necessary or Does Not Meet Standards level is a target for improvement. These naturally translate into specific, measurable goals for the year—for example:

- Designing and implementing two Understanding by Design curriculum units
- Teaching a social competency curriculum
- Becoming proficient using several new kinds of on-the-spot assessments

Teachers will probably take these goals seriously and monitor them with their principal throughout the year—in marked contrast to the safe, often meaningless goals I have seen teachers setting (*I will improve my bulletin boards*).

Midyear Check-In

Brief midyear conferences with each teacher give them an interim sense (not "counting" yet) of how they are doing on the rubric criteria so far. Teacher and supervisor should both fill out the rubric in pencil before meeting and compare ratings page by page, focusing on those on which they disagree and setting goals for the remainder of the year. This fills in gaps in the supervisor's assessment, gives the teacher a heads-up on any concerns, and avoids unpleasant surprises at the end of the year.

End-of-Year Rubric Evaluation

Shortly before their summative evaluation meeting, teacher and supervisor fill out the rubric with end-of-year status, and then meet to compare ratings page by page, focusing on disagreements. On elements on which they differ, the teacher might be able to fill in gaps in the supervisor's knowledge (especially on parent and community outreach and professional responsibilities). Teachers are sometimes super-critical of themselves, and the supervisor might be in a position to reassure them and show them that they deserve a higher rating. (*Come on, you're being way too hard on yourself there! I've seen you doing that very effectively with your students.*)

In some cases, teachers are overly generous to themselves, and the supervisor will have to gently challenge the score. (*Gee, that's not the impression I've had in my mini-observations. Can you tell me more about what you're doing with your students in that area?*) The teacher might very well persuade the supervisor to move a rating up if there's convincing evidence. Or the supervisor might not be persuaded. Needless to say, supervisors who are giving Improvement Necessary or Does Not Meet Standards ratings to teachers need to have evidence—notes from mini-observations, data reports, and other documentation.

The supervisor is "the decider" on final ratings, but evaluations will be fairer and more credible if teachers have substantive input—and the boss really listens. Teachers and administrators usually agree on 90 percent or more of the rubric items, and those don't need to be discussed. This makes the process quick and efficient—usually about thirty minutes per teacher.

> *The supervisor is "the decider" on final ratings, but evaluations will be fairer and more credible if teachers have substantive input—and the boss really listens.*

How is this process received by initially skeptical administrators and teachers? In this recent poll, educators were surprisingly optimistic about the do-ability of rubric evaluation of teachers:

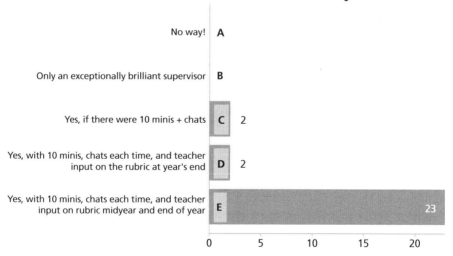

Could a supervisor accurately evaluate a teacher on a rubric at the end of the year?

No way!	**A**
Only an exceptionally brilliant supervisor	**B**
Yes, if there were 10 minis + chats	**C** 2
Yes, with 10 minis, chats each time, and teacher input on the rubric at year's end	**D** 2
Yes, with 10 minis, chats each time, and teacher input on rubric midyear and end of year	**E** 23

Note the elements that almost everyone taking part in this survey believed would be necessary: frequent mini-observations, debrief conversations after each one, and teachers' self-evaluation input on the rubric both at midyear and for the summative evaluation. Those are the essential elements for fair and accurate rubric evaluation of teachers at the end of the school year.

When I was in graduate school in the early 1980s, I remember a professor asserting with great confidence that the supervisor and evaluator can't be the same person—the functions need to be separated. I've come to disagree with that school of thought. Mini-observations are an arena in which the supervisor—the official rating officer—can provide useful supervisory feedback and support to teachers on a day-to-day basis *and* use information gathered to do a formal evaluation at the end of the year.

> *Thinking back to my early years as a principal, I rue the hours I spent on narrative evaluations that rarely made a difference to teaching and learning.*

Thinking back to my early years as a principal, I rue the hours I spent on narrative evaluations that rarely made a difference to teaching and learning. I needed a process that would enable me to give teachers clear, specific, and helpful feedback with as little paperwork as possible. And I needed all the time and energy I was burning up on evaluation write-ups to see what was being taught, how effectively it was being taught, the quality of teacher team meetings, and how teaching could improve. Looking back, I believe well-designed rubrics would have been the answer to my prayers. I envy principals who use them today.

How optimistic are educators about the impact a good rubric can have on teaching and learning? Responses from a recent poll:

What kind of impact might rubric evaluation have on teaching and learning?

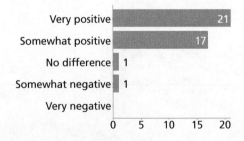

Rounding out this chapter, here are some additional considerations when implementing a rubric: charting all-faculty data; using a different rubric for novice teachers; using different weights for rubric domains and lines; giving teachers numerical rubric ratings; knowing how to handle teachers who are rated Improvement Necessary and Does Not Meet Standards; providing the link to professional learning communities and the Peer Assistance and Review (PAR) program.

Charting All-Faculty Data

Once a leadership team has decided on rubric ratings to an entire faculty, it's possible to create a spreadsheet that can serve as a valuable guide for prioritizing professional development. The following figure shows the domain ratings for a hypothetical staff of eleven teachers. (In Excel, the cells can be color-coded to enhance the impact of the table; for example, blue for Highly Effective ratings, green for Effective, yellow for Improvement Necessary, and red for Does Not Meet Standards. Because the figure is in black and white, it has numbers to show the ratings. In keeping with my new approach of not using 4-3-2-1 ratings in the rubric, I suggest using colors and not numbers in the chart.)

	A. Planning and Preparation	B. Classroom Management	C. Delivery of Instruction	D. Assessment, Monitoring, Follow-Up	E. Parent and Community Outreach	F. Professional Responsibilities
Cynthia	3	3	3	1	3	3
Henry	3	4	3	3	3	3
Belinda	3	3	3	2	3	3
Marcia	4	4	4	4	4	4
Charles	3	3	3	2	3	4
Raymond	3	3	3	1	3	4
Sandy	3	3	3	2	3	3
Mark	4	4	4	4	4	4
Placida	3	3	3	2	3	3
Anne	3	3	3	1	3	3
Richard	2	3	2	1	2	1

Such a chart—which would, of course, be available only to the leadership team—vividly highlights the highest-priority area in a school—in this case, Monitoring, Assessment, and Follow-Up. It also reveals that two teachers—Marcia and Mark—are experts in this area and can be very helpful to their colleagues. The team could further unpack the data, making a spreadsheet of teachers' ratings in the nine areas within Monitoring, Assessment, and Follow-Up (see the second figure), providing even more guidance on what kind of training and support would be most helpful to bring teachers up to speed and which teachers have expertise that could be shared with colleagues.

D. Monitoring, Assessment, and Follow-Up

	a. Criteria	b. Diagnosis	c. Goals	d. Feedback	e. Recognition	f. Analysis	g. Tenacity	h. Support	i. Reflection
Cynthia	3	3	2	2	2	1	2	2	3
Henry	3	3	2	3	3	2	3	3	3
Belinda	2	3	2	2	2	2	3	2	2
Marcia	4	4	2	4	3	2	3	4	4
Charles	2	3	2	2	2	2	2	4	2
Raymond	3	4	2	3	3	2	3	2	3
Sandy	2	3	2	2	3	2	2	3	2
Mark	4	4	2	3	4	2	3	4	4
Placida	3	3	2	2	2	2	3	2	3
Anne	2	3	2	3	2	1	2	2	3
Richard	2	2	1	1	2	1	3	1	2

A Different Rubric for Novice Teachers?

I'm occasionally asked whether it's fair to hold first-year teachers to the same standard as their more-experienced colleagues. Should the Improvement Necessary level be an acceptable score for rookies, or should a different rubric be used, with a narrowed-down list of criteria?

I disagree with using a rubric with lower standards. The kindest and most helpful thing we can do with novice teachers is to give them a clear sense of the school's definition of good and not-so-good teaching and provide lots of feedback and support as their first year unfolds. It's understandable if a beginning teacher has fewer Effective and Highly Effective ratings on the rubric, and receiving honest feedback on rigorous criteria is one of the best ways to get better. Low scores are feedback, and as Ken Blanchard (1982, p. 67) has said, "Feedback is the breakfast of champions."

Different Weighting for the Domains and Lines?

Another rubric implementation question is whether the six domains should be equally weighted when determining teachers' overall performance. Should Classroom Management and Delivery of Instruction, for example, be given more weight than Planning or Family Outreach? The argument could be made that management and instruction are more central to a teacher's effectiveness. But it could also be argued that without good planning, teaching will be ineffective. The same could be said for checking for understanding, parent relations, and professional responsibilities.

I don't think debating different weights for the domains or criteria is a good use of time. Three of the domains cover the time the teacher is with students—Classroom Management, Delivery of Instruction, and Monitoring and Assessment. The other three address outside-the-classroom responsibilities. Everything is important to student learning, with variations from teacher to teacher. For some, classroom management is a critical factor. For others (including me when I was a teacher), checking for understanding is more important. Supervisors should zero in on those areas based on classroom observations, follow-up conversations, and other points of contact and highlight them in the summative evaluation, without getting into different weightings.

Should Teachers Get Numerical Ratings?

For their end-of-year evaluation, all teachers should get domain ratings (e.g., Effective, Improvement Necessary), ratings on all the lines within each domain, and general commendations or suggestions for improvement. This fulfills HR requirements and gives each teacher detailed feedback on their performance.

Some districts and states ask for an overall score for each teacher. If numerical scoring is required, here's something to bear in mind. As described, my rubric is written with a bigger jump from Improvement Necessary to Effective than between the top two levels (Highly Effective and Effective) and between the bottom two levels (Does Not Meet Standards and Improvement Necessary). It's almost as if there is a phantom level in the middle of the four-point scale. For this reason, if numerical ratings are required, I recommend this approach:

- 4 for Highly Effective
- 3 for Effective
- 1 for Improvement Necessary
- 0 for Does Not Meet Standards

It's almost as if there is a phantom level in the middle of the four-point scale.

This reflects the real performance levels in the rubric and gives an appropriate score boost to teachers performing at the top two levels.

A very important point about ratings: superintendents and heads of school should not ask that school leaders grade their teachers on a curve. I've heard of districts where the word from on high is "We don't give Highly Effective to new teachers," or asking that ratings be distributed according to a district-wide formula. This is not an effective or fair process with student grades, and the same is true for rating teachers.

Of course, it's important that all supervisors are well trained, have a good eye for instruction, and that there's a reasonable amount of inter-rater reliability across classrooms and schools. That's why supervisors getting close supervision from the superintendent is so important, as we'll discuss in Chapter Fourteen. But ratings should not be curved according to any preconceived formula.

Teachers Who Are Rated Improvement Necessary

What should supervisors do when a teacher gets an overall score of Improvement Necessary? Performance at this level is mediocre at best, and none of us would want our own children (or beloved nieces and nephews) in a classroom with this kind of teaching. But Improvement Necessary isn't grounds for dismissal. Should these teachers be allowed to skate along with mediocre teaching year after year? Here is a typical poll response when teachers and administrators are asked this question:

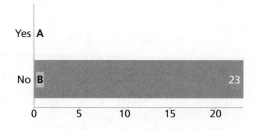

Would it be OK for your own child, or a niece or nephew, to be in a classroom with level 2 teaching?

Obviously, this is not in the best interests of children—or colleagues—and I have a suggestion. The school district negotiates the following clause in the teachers' contract:

An overall rating of Needs Improvement must be followed up immediately by the teacher (setting goals geared to the evaluation), the principal (drafting an individual improvement plan for the teacher), and the leadership team (providing plenty of support tailored to the teacher's needs). A teacher who doesn't pull up the overall rating to Effective or above the following year will face dismissal.

A few years ago, Hillsborough, Florida, implemented this policy with union approval because the union leader, Jean Clemons, was quite blunt in saying that she wouldn't want her own children subjected to mediocre teaching, but she would want to give that teacher a fair chance to improve.

Teachers Performing at the Does Not Meet Standards Level

In a timely fashion, these teachers must get a formal heads-up on the areas that need improvement. This is the one situation where the rubric should be used during the year, following these steps:

1. As soon as a teacher is identified as unsatisfactory by mini-observations or other information, the supervisor does an evaluation using rubric pages in the areas of concern.
2. The supervisor writes a diagnosis and prescription with specific recommendations or mandates for remedial action—for example, attending a workshop on classroom management, visiting an exemplary colleague's classroom, or working with an instructional coach.
3. The supervisor gives the teacher a specified amount of time to improve (usually a month), and then returns for a second interim evaluation.
4. This cycle is repeated with the teacher getting clear direction and support each time.
5. Any teacher who still does not meet standards after a designated number of cycles is subject to dismissal.

Exact procedures and an appeal process need to be worked out with the district's or school's legal counsel, as should the question of whether some of the six domains should carry more weight in dismissal decisions—for example, Classroom Management and Delivery of Instruction.

Providing struggling teachers with a detailed diagnosis and prescription, and a chance to improve, is an important ethical and legal responsibility. It's also time-consuming. Supervisors in this mode have no choice but to spend many hours visiting the teacher's classroom, conferring

*Providing struggling teach-
ers with a detailed diag-
nosis and prescription, and
a chance to improve, is an
important ethical and legal
responsibility.*

and providing support, and writing detailed improvement plans. In situations like this, using the rubric probably won't save the administrator much time compared to conventional evaluation instruments. But for teachers performing at the Highly Effective, Effective, and Improvement Necessary levels, the rubric is much less onerous.

Professional Learning Communities

As I will argue in Chapter Twelve, one of supervisor's most important jobs is getting teacher teams invested in a professional learning community (PLC) process of continuous improvement so that teachers are working collaboratively on planning and assessment and a "supervisory voice" is present inside all teachers' heads, prodding them to think constantly about what students are learning and how teaching can be improved.

Nine of the rubric criteria touch on this area, and they can be used to point teachers in the direction of taking increasing responsibility for improving teaching and learning themselves in the 99.8 percent of the time when their supervisor is not around. Here is a cluster of PLC-related rubric elements (with language from the Highly Effective level):

- **(Ad) Assessments.** Prepares diagnostic, on-the-spot, interim, and summative assessments to monitor student learning.
- **(Df) Analysis.** Works with colleagues to immediately use interim assessments data to fine-tune teaching, reteach, and help students who need support.
- **(Di) Reflection.** Works with colleagues to reflect on what worked and what didn't and continuously improve instruction.
- **(Fh) Collaboration.** Meets frequently with colleagues to plan units, share ideas, and analyze interim assessments.
- **(Fi) Growth.** Actively reaches out for new ideas and engages in action research with colleagues to figure out what works best.

When principals introduce the rubric at the beginning of each year, they might highlight these criteria and stress their importance to professional growth and learning—and offer support to maximize their development in the school.

Peer Assistance and Review

How are unions reacting to teacher evaluation rubrics? There isn't much information so far, but in districts where unions have signed off on rubrics, the key factors are transparency with the criteria, input on choosing and revising a rubric, clear advance notice to all teachers on the process, administrator training, and lots of classroom visits and feedback throughout the year. With those elements in place, there is no reason why rubrics can't be accepted as the new norm for teacher evaluation.

A few US school districts are using PAR, a union-approved process for enlisting top-notch teachers to support and make evaluation recommendations on novice teachers and others who are having difficulty in the classroom. PAR originated in Toledo, Ohio, in 1981, the brainchild of Dal Lawrence, then president of the local American Federation of Teachers (AFT) branch, and spread to a number of other districts, including Cincinnati and Columbus, Ohio; Rochester, New York; and Dade County, Florida.

The basic idea is to free up highly effective educators to act as "consulting teachers" for two or three years and assign them to work with novice teachers or more-experienced teachers who are having difficulty. Consulting teachers help their charges with lesson and unit planning, curriculum materials, observation and feedback, emotional support, and advocacy with the principal.

Consulting teachers report to a districtwide board composed of teachers and administrators, usually cochaired by the union president and the district's director of human resources. At board meetings, members discuss individual cases and share ideas on effective coaching strategies. Each spring, the board makes recommendations on continued employment of certain teachers to the superintendent, who decides which names to pass along to the school board.

Here is how PAR addresses several common issues:

- **Giving teachers feedback.** A well-designed PAR program assigns a caseload of twelve to fifteen teachers to each consulting teacher and ensures that they visit classrooms at least once a week (some are unannounced) and give ongoing feedback. Consulting teachers are also available for consultation in impromptu meetings, phone calls, and emails. Data from PAR districts indicate that this kind of attention and support helps teacher retention. In Columbus, for example, 80 percent of new teachers are still in the district after five years, and in Rochester the retention rate is 85 percent.

- **Linking evaluation to professional development.** Consulting teachers are in and out of classrooms on a regular basis and have an accurate sense of how things are going. They can build trust, give their charges ongoing instructional feedback, create individual assistance plans, and draw on authoritative standards for good teaching.

- **Telling ineffective teachers the truth.** PAR pierces the isolation of many classrooms and gives teachers ongoing, honest feedback on their performance from a peer who speaks from personal knowledge. Equally important, consulting teachers are held accountable for their evaluations (by their review panel) in a way that principals are not. Principals who take part in the PAR process often learn a lot about observation and feedback. Clear standards of effective teaching help everyone get beyond the hackneyed

"I know good teaching when I see it" approach and promote conversations based on real evidence of what's going on in classrooms.

- **Credible evaluations.** Consulting teachers working with principals and their review panels can produce evaluations with much more heft.

> *Principals who take part in the PAR process often learn a lot about observation and feedback.*

- **Firing ineffective teachers.** The joint union-management committee can recommend dismissal based on classroom evidence and bona fide opportunities for underperforming teachers to improve. Consulting teachers, who have double credibility by virtue of their status as teachers and the time they are spending in classrooms, are willing to recommend dismissal when a teacher is not improving despite intensive support.

A California principal said: "I'm working collaboratively with the union. It's a whole different feel and there's a sense that the union and I agree that we need teachers who use best practice, and we're working together to have best practices occur, and we're not opposed in terms of keeping some person in there who is not utilizing best practice. I feel like we're all on the same team and it's about children and the kind of teaching they get."*

PAR programs continue, with disruption in some districts caused by the economic crisis of 2008–2009, Race to the Top's emphasis on value-added measures, and of course the Covid-19 pandemic. There are active programs in these school districts, among others: San Juan, Puerto Rico; Philadelphia; Rochester and North Syracuse, New York; Baltimore and Montgomery County, Maryland; Minneapolis; and Miami-Dade, Florida; and statewide in California and Ohio. Commentary in recent years has been positive, noting beneficial effects of frequent, informative, subject-based support of teachers and a cost-effective way of addressing the needs of struggling teachers. But there's been very little research on the impact of PAR on student achievement.

Questions to Consider

- *How are rubrics being used in your school?*
- *What do you see as the pluses and minuses of the latest edition of the Marshall rubric?*
- *What should go in a teacher's personnel file at the end of a school year?*

---

*The preceding bulleted list through this paragraph are from my *Marshall Memo* summary of a 2008 article by J. Goldstein (2008).

8

Mini-Observations 5

Making Student Learning Central

The more you teach without finding out who understands the information and who doesn't, the greater the likelihood that only already-proficient students will succeed.

—Grant Wiggins

In the early 2000s, a coterie of education experts proposed a new way to improve teaching and learning and address the nation's troubling racial and economic proficiency gaps: *make student learning a major component in teacher evaluation.* The logic seemed unassailable: it's not enough for a teacher to teach; students need to learn—or, to put it more bluntly, if students haven't learned something, teachers haven't taught it. This cartoon captures the idea:

By looking at evidence of student learning, the argument went, we can identify great teachers and reward them, perhaps with merit pay, and pinpoint ineffective teachers and fire them.

But what measures would be used to link teacher performance to their students' learning? Report card grades? Benchmark tests? Student projects and portfolios? None of these are sufficiently reliable for high-stakes teacher accountability. How about traditional teacher evaluations, which involve observing a couple of classroom visits a year? Again, not suitable because they focus on teachers' actions rather than student learning.

Accountability advocates suggested what they believed was a better approach: use students' standardized test scores. If student achievement is measured on a four-point scale, it could be compared with teachers' evaluations, also on a four-point scale, and surely there would be a linear correlation between the two, with the students of effective teachers scoring high, the opposite for students of ineffective teachers. Conceptually, it should look like this:

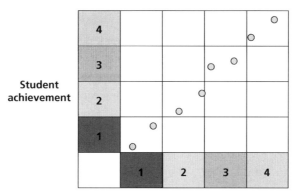

Teacher's evaluation score

By working backward from students' test scores, advocates said it was possible to identify the best and worst teachers and those in between.

Critics immediately attacked the idea, pointing out that there isn't always a straightforward correlation because a number of factors—biased tests, poverty, substandard schools, unfavorable testing conditions, and more—could unfairly pull down the assessment of good teachers.

But William Sanders, an agricultural economist in Tennessee, developed a formula that claimed to take into account the factors not under teachers' control and produce a reliable measurement of each teacher's "value added" to their student's academic achievement (Sanders & Rivers, 1996; Sanders et al., 1997). Here is a value-added model (VAM) formula, similar to Sanders's, used in a one-time evaluation of thousands of New York City teachers under Chancellor Joel Klein:

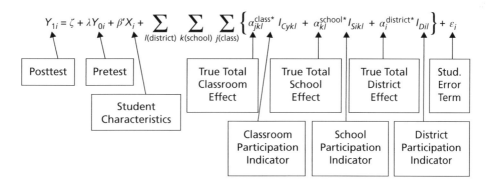

Among the variables the formula took into account to produce a value-added score for each teacher were posttest, pretest, student characteristics, true total classroom effect, true total school effect, true total district effect, classroom participation indicator, school participation indicator, district participation indicator, and student error term.

In a meeting in the Oval Office on January 29, 2009, advocates for teacher accountability persuaded President Barack Obama and his incoming Secretary of Education, Arne Duncan, that formulas like this made it possible to use test scores to hold teachers accountable for their students' learning. Obama was convinced, and the Race to the Top legislation that followed required using test scores as a significant part of teachers' evaluations in order for states to get millions of dollars of federal funding.

Race to the Top made sense to many Americans, and the idea of holding teachers accountable swept the nation, with almost all states getting on board.

Race to the Top made sense to many Americans, and the idea of holding teachers accountable swept the nation, with almost all states getting on board.

A political cartoon about this time showed a teacher behind her desk with an A evaluation while students in front of her are all holding papers with F grades. The message: How on earth can the teacher have a good evaluation when her students are failing?

To most noneducators, especially politicians and people in the business world, it seemed logical that teachers should be judged on their work product—kids' learning—and how else to measure them but test scores? Pressured by public opinion, teacher unions moved away from their long-standing opposition to the idea and agreed (at least in principle) to using student learning as part of teacher evaluation.

But the American Statistical Association, the American Educational Research Association, and other researchers (Darling-Hammond et al., 2012; Johnson, 2012; and others) cautioned against using VAM data for high-stakes decisions on teachers' employment status. Here's a compilation of their arguments:

- Standardized tests are designed to measure the learning of groups of students at one moment in time, not the work of individual teachers over a school year. This has fueled litigation by teachers who suffered negative job consequences based on test score data. In at least fifteen court cases, expert witnesses testified that creating high stakes for teachers was an inappropriate use of these tests, and teachers prevailed.

- There's a problem with the timing of standardized test scores: the results of state tests are usually not published until the very end of the school year or over the summer, but teacher evaluations typically must be completed in May or earlier. This would seem to make it impossible to make test scores part of teacher evaluation until a year later—a significant delay—and by that time teachers have done another year's work with new groups of students.

- VAM formulas purport to isolate the contribution of each teacher from September to June. It turns out that three years of value-added scores are needed to reduce quirky ups and downs in value-added data (Galley, 2011), which introduces an even more significant time lag for intervening with teachers who are identified as ineffective. Students moving from school to school further complicates the ability to gather valid data on individual teachers' impact over time.

- Even with three years of data, there are worrisome imperfections in value-added data. The impressive-looking formula used by New York City has startling inaccuracies at the individual teacher level. It had a confidence interval of 35 percentage points for math and 53 for English language arts; this compares to the confidence interval of a typical Gallup poll of 3 to 4 percentage points. Because of random variations that have nothing to do with the quality of teaching, this year's A teacher can be next year's F teacher.

- There can be collateral damage for individual teachers. When the New York City schools publicly released the VAM scores for thousands of teachers (having previously promised not to do so), the *New York Post* published the name of one teacher, Pascale Mauclair, and said she was the "worst teacher" in New York City (Roberts, 2012). Her VAM score was indeed very low, but when reporters visited the school, they found that she was actually a very good teacher—so said students, colleagues, parents, and her principal. The elaborate formula has simply gotten her wrong.

- State test data that can be used for value-added calculations are available for only 20 to 30 percent of teachers—usually Grades 4 to 8 math and ELA teachers and some in high school. This raises equity concerns about how all the other teachers will be evaluated— kindergarten, first grade, second grade, art, computer, music, library, physical education, and most high-school teachers.

- For teachers whose students don't have standardized test scores, many states have used a version of student learning objectives (SLOs). Teachers use pre- and post-assessments and report student gains, which seems like a logical solution. But with high stakes attached to SLO calculations and a requirement to send data to the state department of education, teachers frequently game the system by setting a low baseline and reporting on a narrow area of learning.

- Using test scores for teacher accountability can prevent teacher teams from functioning effectively. Same-grade and same-subject teamwork has the potential to bring about major improvements in pedagogy, but when individual teachers' evaluations are linked to their students' test scores, the tendency is to focus on boosting one's own stats and not sharing effective practices with colleagues.

- Evaluation consequences from test scores lead some teachers to engage in low-level test prep, which dumbs down the curriculum. Many critics of standardized tests have observed that when teachers focus too much on test preparation and spend their time drilling simpler, easy-to-test skills, students don't get the full college- and career-aligned curriculum to which they're entitled.

- Including student test scores in the teacher evaluation process also increases the possibility that ethically challenged teachers and administrators will cut corners. When students take high-stakes tests, they are usually proctored by their own teachers; most teachers act professionally, but when the heat is turned up, it's inevitable that some (especially those who have the least confidence in their ability to raise achievement) will give inappropriate help to students or even falsify results. This invalidates the assessments and produces deceptively rosy information on students that keeps them from getting the support they need.

  The experience of Atlanta Public Schools from 2009 to 2015, where more than 170 public school teachers and administrators were caught cheating on high-stakes tests, is sobering indeed. This is an example of Campbell's law (Campbell, 1976):

  > The more any quantitative social indicator is used for social decision-making, the more subject it will be to corruption pressures and the more apt it will be to distort and corrupt the social processes it is intended to monitor.

- Publicly praising or criticizing classroom ELA and math teachers for their students' test scores fails to take into account the work done by pullout teachers, specialists, tutors, and teachers in previous grades, all of whom contribute to student success.

This is a deeply troubling list of concerns, and it's hard to avoid the conclusion that this part of the Race to the Top program, well intentioned though it was, ended up producing a contentious labor-management dynamic, fostering resistance and cynicism among teachers, and adding nothing to the quality of teaching and learning. The intuitively appealing linear correlation between student achievement and teacher quality as discussed actually looks more like this:

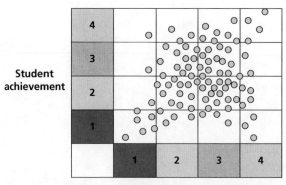

Teacher's evaluation score

Yes, there's a general correlation (the "line of best fit") between good teaching and high student achievement, but because of a variety of real-world factors, there are plenty of outliers. Why?

- A badly designed or culturally biased test that doesn't reflect student learning
- Curriculum misalignment—what's taught is not on the test or vice versa
- Too much pressure on students and teachers (they "grip the bat too hard")
- Unfavorable testing conditions (a dog barking outside the classroom window)
- Heavy test prep
- Cheating
- Good progress, but not enough to move out of the lowest level

Enough said. The attempt to yoke teacher evaluation to student test scores was poorly thought through and has had many negative consequences.

The attempt to yoke teacher evaluation to student test scores was poorly thought through and has had many negative consequences.

Good News—and Ways That Student Learning *Can* Be Used

In 2015, at the very end of the Obama administration, the ESSA (Every Student Succeeds Act) legislation passed, withdrawing the requirement that student test scores and other achievement measures be a significant part of individual teachers' evaluations. This was a helpful pivot in federal educational policy, removing a misguided requirement that had distorted the evaluation process. Not every state has stopped using VAM and SLOs, but in most schools there's been less emphasis on the role of student achievement.

But here's the thing: President Obama was not wrong to link teaching quality with student learning. If students are not learning, something is amiss and it needs to be addressed. Too many students are not attaining a basic level of academic proficiency, and there continue to be troubling class and racial/ethnic proficiency gaps. Shouldn't student learning be part of the teacher evaluation and accountability process?

I believe it can, if teachers and supervisors use *formative* data on student learning *throughout the school year*, not to evaluate teachers but to get them continuously thinking about ways to improve teaching practices and students' learning.

This puts student learning at the center of teacher supervision, coaching, and evaluation without making the mistakes of the VAM and SLO era. Here are seven ways this can happen, all an integral part of frequent classroom visits and face-to-face conversations with teachers and teacher teams:

- Coaching teachers on formative assessments
- Coaching teachers on the retrieval effect
- Coaching teachers on peer instruction
- Focusing on big ideas and essential questions
- Using graphic displays of student learning
- Sharpening PLC work
- Asking for end-of-year value-added reports

Interestingly, teachers and coaches involved in band, drama, debate, and athletics put these strategies to work all the time—the performance or competition is the learning target. Classroom teachers have a lot to learn from them!

Coaching Teachers on Formative Assessments

Dylan Wiliam, the British assessment expert, put his finger on a crucial element of highly effective teaching (2021):

> When a teacher teaches, no matter how well he or she might design a lesson, what a child learns is unpredictable. Children do not always learn what we teach. That is why the most important assessment does not happen at the end of learning—it happens during the learning, when there is still time to do something with the information.

Many teachers know this intuitively, but some are using weak checks for understanding. This should be a prime look-for during mini-observations. Some examples:

- **Gauging students' facial expressions.** Some teachers are confident they can tell if students are with them by looking at their upturned faces.
- **"Is everyone with me? Any questions?"** Many students are embarrassed to admit they don't understand, but teachers take silence as assent and move on.
- **Thumbs-up or thumbs-down.** This time-honored check for understanding is mediocre for two reasons: students might be reluctant to admit they don't understand in such a visible way, or they might *think* they understand when in fact they don't. This kind of public self-report gives the teacher little usable information.

- **Low-level and recall questions.** Some teachers conduct an ongoing catechism of the class, asking true-or-false and yes-or-no questions, or asking about simple recall of facts. It reveals almost nothing about deeper understanding, and maintains a teacher-student-teacher-student interaction pattern that's bound to bore many students.

- **The COPWAKTA syndrome.** All too many teachers are calling on people who already know the answer. There might be a lively discussion with those eager and high-achieving students, but the rest of the class is a passive audience.

- **Quizzes with slow turnaround.** If students don't get rapid feedback on tests, a lot of the learning potential is lost—they look at the grade and file the paper or toss it out.

It's not enough for a teacher to go through the motions of checking for understanding; it has to be done skillfully. Here are some examples of effective on-the-spot assessment:

- **Think-pair-share.** After initial instruction, have students reflect for a moment about a question, talk to an "elbow partner" (the teacher circulates and listens in), and then share thoughts with the whole class.

- **Cold-calling.** By randomizing which students are called on, you can get a better sense of the whole class's level of understanding. One method is writing students' names on popsicle sticks, putting them all in a container, and pulling one out to see which student will answer the next question. Some smartboards have apps that enable the teacher to tap and get a randomly generated name from the class.

- **Quick-writes.** Get students to write quick notes or paragraphs that allow the teacher to look over students' shoulders and get an immediate sense of how well they grasp what's being taught

- **Dry-erase boards.** Have students write answers to questions—for example, what's a fraction between 1/6 and 1/7?—on small individual whiteboards and then have students simultaneously hold up their answers so the teacher can assess how many are on track.

- **Polling.** Use electronic audience response devices that gather instant data on in-class questions and graphically display the number of students choosing each multiple-choice answer, cueing the teacher on next steps.

- **Quick quizzes.** Have students answer a few key questions and immediately score and process the results.

- **Exit tickets.** These gauge student understanding of one or two key points at the end of a lesson and enable immediate follow-up the next day.

It's not enough for a teacher to go through the motions of checking for understanding; it has to be done skillfully.

Author/consultant Mike Rutherford created this graphic to show the role of during-the-lesson checking for understanding and the decision teachers make at that point:

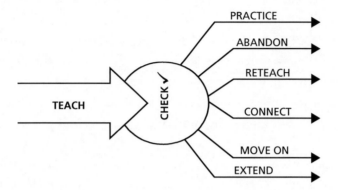

Dylan Wiliam stresses the urgency of putting the assessment information to work immediately to fix learning problems (2007, p. 191):

If students have left the classroom before teachers have made adjustments to their teaching on the basis of what they have learned about the students' achievement, then they are already playing catch-up. If teachers do not make adjustments before students come back the next day, it is probably too late.

Classroom climate is a key element—helping students see errors as a natural part of the learning process.

The research on effective use of formative assessments is rock-solid, and in frequent classroom visits, supervisors can spot ineffective or mediocre practices and coach teachers on strengthening the connection between their teaching and their students' learning. Classroom climate is a key element—helping students see errors as a natural part of the learning process.

With supervisors' help, teachers can raise their consciousness about the critical importance of keeping student learning central throughout every lesson. Another Dylan Wiliam quote (2021):

The fact that students can do something successfully at the end of a lesson does not mean that they will be able to do it in two weeks' time. But if they can't do it at the end of the lesson, it is highly unlikely that they will be able to do it in two weeks' time.

Why do on-the-spot assessments have such a good research track record for improving student achievement? Because, used well, they set up a continuous feedback loop between teaching and learning, producing much better levels of student proficiency.

- **Individual accountability.** When students know that they might be called on at any moment to show whether they understand, they stay on their toes and are thinking through the answer to every question the teacher asks.

- **Live data.** On-the-spot assessments give teachers immediate insights into students' misconceptions and confusions and enable them to clarify and reteach before learning problems compound and widen the achievement gap. As Douglas Fisher and Nancy Frey put it in their 2007 book, these quick assessments "provide a window into the minds of learners by answering the teacher's perpetual question: What is the next instructional move?" (p. 134).

- **Better planning.** If teachers understand why students aren't learning, they can fine-tune future teaching so learning is more efficient next time. For a middle or high school English teacher, this might be as soon as the next teaching period; for an elementary school teacher, it might mean waiting until next year.

- **Growth mindset.** The implicit message to students is that they can get smarter by working at understanding day by day. Carol Dweck, in her book *Mindset* (2006), shows how important the concept of malleable intelligence is to children's intellectual development.

Coaching Teachers on the Retrieval Effect

Many teachers have not been exposed to new insights on how to make information stick in students' minds. They wish all students were like their "best" student—you tell them once and they remember it—not understanding that a lot of what's taught in classrooms doesn't make it into students' long-term memory bank.

Recent brain research is helping us understand the "forgetting curve"—and that the best way to commit new information to long-term memory is *retrieval*: testing ourselves, or being tested, a few minutes after it's been presented ("The best time to remember something is when you have begun to forget it" says Doug Lemov, 2021, p. 84), then retrieving at spaced intervals—an hour later, a day later, a week later, a month later—then interleaving it with other information we want to commit to memory. This figure shows how this might work:

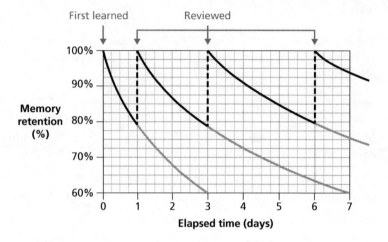

Supervisors need to help teachers understand the science of remembering—that low-stakes quizzes and self-tests are memory modifiers, strengthening neural pathways. Here are three quotes from experts:

> Retrieving a fact is not like opening a computer file. It alters what we remember and changes how we subsequently organize that knowledge in our brain.
>
> Henry Roediger III

> When you retrieve knowledge from your mind over and over again, you know where to find it next time, and you quickly discover where the gaps in your memory are.
>
> Adam Grant

> It's a no-stakes learning opportunity that is flexible and quick, with a huge impact on long-term student achievement.
>
> Pooja Agarwal

Putting these insights to work in classrooms is very different from using standardized test scores to hold teachers accountable—and it's much more effective at improving teaching and learning in real time.

Coaching Teachers on Peer Instruction

Real-time learning data can be used to reveal misunderstandings and get students teaching each other. We frequently see students being asked to "turn and talk," but not all teachers are getting the full potential from this practice.

> *Real-time learning data can be used to reveal misunderstandings and get students teaching each other.*

Eric Mazur is a Harvard physics professor who early in his career stumbled on the power of peer instruction. He now intersperses his fifty-minute classes with carefully chosen conceptual questions that students answer via anonymous polls with students' choices displayed on a screen. When Mazur sees that between 30 and 70 percent of students have answered incorrectly, he says, "Convince your neighbor" and walks around the lecture hall listening to the lively debates. A few minutes later he re-polls the question and the number of correct answers increases significantly; students who understand the concept do a good job persuading their neighbors who do not, multiplying Mazur's power as a teacher.

Using this approach, Mazur's students have brought about major gains in their level of conceptual understanding; he says that peer instruction *triples* student learning gains. Mazur has become an advocate for getting students to play an active part in improving their classmates' learning, influencing the quality of teaching in universities and K–12 settings.

An unanticipated effect of Mazur's adapted pedagogy has been on gender equity. Before he shifted to this approach, young women in his classes had been underachieving and were less likely to continue with STEM classes at Harvard. That dynamic was reversed with peer instruction, probably because female students are more actively engaged in every class and gain confidence in overcoming the stereotype threat beaming in on them from society's erroneous beliefs about female proficiency in math and science.

Focusing on Big Ideas and Essential Questions

When supervisors visit classrooms, they frequently look for lesson objectives on the board or at the beginning of a teacher's PowerPoint presentation. This provides a way of gauging whether the content is appropriate to the grade and course and getting insights—during the mini-observation and in the conversation with the teacher afterward—into how well students are learning. But what about the bigger picture? That's where good unit plans that define big ideas and essential questions come in.

We'll address this in detail in Chapter Eleven, but you can see how this fits in with making student learning central to supervision and coaching of teachers. If teachers—ideally working with their grade-level or course team—have defined the curriculum unit's knowledge and skill goals, big ideas, likely misconceptions, transfer goals, and essential questions, and if the essential questions are posted and woven into lessons, the mini-observer has much greater insight on the lesson, and the debrief with the teacher can focus not only on what students learned in that. lesson but also on how learning is progressing toward bigger-picture learning outcomes.

Using Graphic Displays of Student Learning

Another way to make student learning central is skillfully displaying learning data (being careful to maintain confidentiality). Good graphic displays—encouraged by supervisors who visit classrooms and team meetings—have the following effects:

- Showing student learning in ways that numbers can't (a picture is worth a thousand words)
- Tracking progress toward goals and celebrating success
- Sharpening teacher team discussions by zeroing in on student misconceptions and effective teaching practices
- Spotlighting student learning challenges by name and need
- Identifying weak areas in the curriculum and defective test items
- Highlighting effective and ineffective teaching practices
- Motivating teachers and students

Sharpening PLC Work

We'll do a deep dive into this in Chapter Twelve, but here's a brief preview. Same-grade/same-subject teacher teams have great potential for frank, low-stakes discussions of what's working and what isn't in classrooms. The question that supervisors should be most delighted to hear in team meetings is, "Your kids did better than mine—what did you do?" This is an indication that the team has given a common assessment, looked honestly at learning in all classrooms, and has a culture of humility and trust in which teachers are constantly exploring best practices and learning from one another.

The question that supervisors should be most delighted to hear in team meetings is, "Your kids did better than mine—what did you do?"

The key role of supervisors is making sure that the following elements are in place for each team, because when these aren't present, PLC meetings tend to be low-quality:

- Teaching the same curriculum content at the same time
- Giving common, high-quality assessments
- Prompt scoring and item analysis

- Enough time in the school's schedule to meet and discuss
- Trust among team members, psychological safety
- Student data and actual test items in hand
- Each teacher's results visible to the team
- Frank discussion of what worked, what didn't, and why
- Prompt follow-up with struggling students

Asking for End-of-Year Value-Added Reports

As I argued earlier, the SLO process used by many schools in the Race to the Top era was corrupted by the high-stakes nature of the process (Campbell's law) and was in many cases ineffective. But the idea of a teacher team taking collective responsibility for their students' learning has potential if it's handled differently. I urge supervisors to encourage same-grade/same-subject teacher teams to consider using this process:

- Agree on a good way of measuring their students' learning—for example, a leveled reading assessment, a comprehensive math test—and get the principal's approval.
- Do a baseline assessment of all students.
- Set a SMART goal for the year—for example, a second-grade team might aim for having 85 percent of their students reading at level M on the Fountas/Pinnell scale by June.
- Keep track of progress with interim assessments during the year, learn from each other, and advocate for additional classroom resources (books, tutors, technology).
- Do an end-of-year assessment of all students.
- Meet with the principal and present the before-and-after data, including whether the team met its SMART goal.

At the end of the school year, if the value-added results from the team are positive, the principal might give an overall, medium-stakes assessment to the team (*One for all and all for one*), and add it informally to each teacher's individual performance evaluation (*You were part of a team that worked effectively together and boosted all students' reading achievement*). Here are the salient points in this process:

- Assessments are used that teachers have chosen, trust, and believe in.
- Medium stakes ensure that Campbell's law doesn't kick in.
- Teacher teamwork is encouraged.
- The focus throughout the year is on student learning, not teacher evaluation.
- This process can be used by all teachers, from kindergarten to physical education to calculus.

- There's meaningful goal setting by the team—a goal teachers care about.

- Learning is measured from the beginning to the end of that school year, so what happened in previous grades is not part of the discussion.

- Learning data can be gathered and used throughout the year.

- If one member of the teacher team is not performing well, there's a strong incentive for the team to support that person's development.

- The principal or other supervisor is involved from the beginning and can monitor and support progress in mini-observations and visits to team meetings.

- At the end of the school year, the principal has a more manageable number of goals to review—five or six teacher teams versus thirty individual teachers.

More Strategies to Keep the Focus on Learning

Here are some additional practices that I've observed in school visits that can supplement the impact of mini-observations, always looking for ways to support student learning:

Daily walkarounds. Frequent mini-observations are an excellent way to get a random sampling of each teacher's work and have substantive conversations about teaching and learning through the year. But mini-observers see less than 1 percent of a teacher's time with students. Having face-to-face conversations after every visit helps widen the observation window; so does looking at unit plans and dropping in on teacher team meetings as they discuss student work and assessments. But there's still a huge amount of unobserved time. Although we trust teachers, there's still a nagging feeling that we need to be in classrooms more.

The answer, I think, is making a daily sweep through all classrooms—micro-observations of less than a minute to say hi to teachers and students, normalize the supervisor's presence, and catch a glimpse of teacher-student interactions, curriculum, and the general vibe. Most often supervisors will see initiatives being implemented well. They might stumble on a wonderful teaching/learning moment, making their day. Very occasionally they'll see something troubling—a teacher's harsh tone, a student being disrespectful to an adult, a hazard of some kind. These walkarounds can include an immediate action (fixing a tech problem), a quick compliment to an adult or student, and maybe a note to self to follow up with a longer classroom visit, a directive, or a face-to-face meeting. A daily walkaround is an important complement to mini-observations.

Invitation to full-lesson visits. It's a sign of a healthy school culture when teachers invite an administrator to watch a lesson—perhaps when they're trying out a new idea or launching a curriculum unit, or when students are presenting their performance tasks. If a supervisor is invited to observe a particular lesson, it would be rude to treat it as a mini-observation and leave after a few minutes. Instead of a full-blown write-up, the best follow-up would be the four-part conversation recommended earlier: a specific compliment, getting the teacher talking about the lesson with a well-chosen prompt, talking about a leverage point (if appropriate), and deciding on an actionable next step.

Intensives. When he was a middle-school principal in Brooklyn, New York, Herb Daughtry Jr. got into a regular rhythm of mini-observations and appreciated spot-checking instruction. But Daughtry wanted to get a more-detailed picture of the curriculum, so each week he picked one class—for example, a seventh-grade homeroom—and did a mini-observation of that class during social studies on Monday, Tuesday, Wednesday, Thursday, and Friday. These *intensives*, as he called them, let him see (and discuss with the teacher) more than he could see in a single visit—how the curriculum was unfolding over five days and the kind of work students were producing. This is an excellent enhancement of the mini-observation process.

Shadowing a student for a day. Following a student through their schedule for a full day is a powerful experience for educators. Educators who have done this report seeing golden moments of teaching and learning, but also notice different behavioral expectations from class to class, variations in curriculum quality and rigor, passive learning, less-effective pedagogy, instances of a negative student interactions, and more. I highly recommend that supervisors clear their calendar and shadow a student at least once a year. It sharpens supervisors' observational lens by seeing instruction from the kids' point of view.

Tutoring students. Here's an idea I picked up from Holly Corsentino, a principal in Pueblo, Colorado. Every year, she picks two students and regularly has lunch with them while helping them with their work. She says this keeps her in touch with curriculum materials and the kinds of struggles some students are having. It also provides substantive support to a few students and wins points with teachers.

Student surveys. In its 2013 report, the Measures of Effective Teaching (MET) project made the case for using student surveys as one of three factors in teacher evaluation. Many educators have doubts about this idea: Are students going to be unfair to teachers who demand a lot? Will students hide behind anonymity to be mean? Will students give positive evaluations to teachers who are "nice" and don't demand much from them?

Following a student through their schedule for a full day is a powerful experience for educators.

But there's no denying that students are with their teachers way more than even the most energetic administrator. Harvard professor Ronald Ferguson and his Tripod Project colleagues report that students are quite astute at sizing up instructional competence when they are asked about observable classroom behaviors in kid-friendly language (Ferguson, 2012). Here are some sample questions, using a five-point strongly agree to strongly disagree scale:

- Our class stays busy and does not waste time.
- I understand what I am supposed to be learning in this class.
- If you don't understand something, my teacher explains it another way.
- My teacher pushes everyone to work hard.
- My teacher takes the time to summarize what we learn each day.

These are not questions about teacher popularity; they go to the heart of effective instruction and correlate strongly with student achievement. Ferguson reports that students taught by teachers with high student ratings gain four to five months more learning in a year than students whose teachers get low ratings (Ferguson, 2012).

But here are three concerns. Students sometimes don't appreciate tough, demanding teachers until years later. Could high-stakes student surveys lead teachers to reduce their work demands, dial back on behavioral standards, and shy away from unpopular classroom decisions? In addition, there's evidence that although high student ratings correlate with high achievement that year, they correlate less well with success in the next grade or course (Glenn, 2011). Finally, the real issue is not what students think of their teachers' actions; it's whether they are learning.

That's why I disagree with using student survey data as a formal part of the teacher-evaluation process. Pittsburgh's decision to count student surveys as 15 percent of teachers' evaluation turns the temperature up too much, in my view, and runs the risk of corrupting the process (Campbell's law again).

But teachers can learn a lot from their students' comments. Here's a way to use student input that avoids the problems just mentioned:

- Have all teachers survey their students anonymously twice a year, perhaps November and June, using high-quality questions (Tripod and Panorama have released banks of selected items), with the option to add some questions of their own.
- Shortly after each survey, teachers look over their data with their supervisor (or a critical friend) and consider three questions: What are you glad to see in the results? Which responses might be inaccurate (students misunderstood the question or were clearly being unfair)? And what are one or two takeaways for improving instruction? Teachers might follow up with discussions with their students, asking for more detail on areas where students had concerns.

If conversations about student survey results took place with a supervisor, they could be part of the teacher's evaluations on rubric item (Fg): "Listens thoughtfully to other viewpoints and responds constructively to suggestions and criticism." That's the Effective level; Highly Effective level reads, "Actively seeks out feedback and suggestions from students, parents, and colleagues and uses them to improve performance."

★

In the ways described in this chapter, student learning can be a central and legitimate element in supervision and coaching—and even, in a medium-stakes way, teacher evaluation. Looked at this way, accountability shifts from a threatening, mysterious, and distorting process, as it was in the Race to the Top era, to a credible, day-by-day part of a school's culture and a reflection of teachers' and administrators' deep commitment to their students.

Ian Beatty et al. (2004) coined the phrase *agile teaching* and Dylan Wiliam (personal communication) added *minute by minute, day by day*. The result: teaching and learning continuously improve—and so do test scores and students' success in school and in life.

Questions to Consider

- *Has your school moved on from VAM and SLOs?*
- *What do you think are the most effective ways to include student learning in the mini-observation process?*
- *What part do you think student surveys should play?*

9 | Coaching Results–Focused Teacher Teams

*School improvement is most surely and thoroughly achieved when teachers engage in fre-
quent, continuous, and increasingly concrete and precise talk about teaching practice.*

—Judith Warren Little

Imagine this scenario: A teacher completes a six-week unit of the US Revolutionary War
and gives an assessment to see how well students learned. Here is a tally showing the number
of students who scored at the *advanced, proficient, needs improvement,* and *failed* levels (*proficient*
is mastery, about 80 percent). The takeaway: only 52 percent of students scored *proficient*
and above—hardly a smashing success. What does the teacher do next? This is a defining moment
for teachers—the moment of truth.

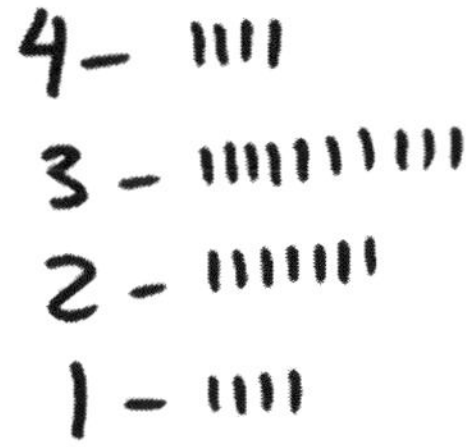

4 – IIII
3 – IIIIIIIII
2 – IIIIIII
1 – IIII

We all know what a teacher *should* do, but in the real world, most teachers record the grades
and move on to the next unit. Why? There's a lot of pressure to cover the curriculum and get
students ready for high-stakes tests. Most teachers feel they don't have the luxury to slow down

and work with the students at level 2 who haven't fully mastered the material, much less the students at level 1 who outright failed.

And there are other reasons. Some teachers believe this pattern of achievement reflects differences in intelligence that won't be changed by any amount of teaching. Some are concerned that high-achieving students will be bored if they have to go over material again and their parents will complain to the principal. Some teachers aren't confident they have the skills to help students who didn't get it the first time around. And some believe that if they have done a good job presenting the material, they've fulfilled their obligation.

These reasons are all at work in classrooms, but let's be blunt: every time a teacher moves on with half the class below mastery, the proficiency gap widens. That's because the students at levels 2 and 1 are most often the students who were already having difficulty in this and other subjects; have special needs or language barriers; are subject to stereotype threat based on class, race, and gender; and entered school with learning disadvantages stemming from home and community factors beyond their control. The teacher could probably have predicted which students were going to be below mastery before the first day of instruction.

What happens when teachers move on? This quote from Paul Black and Dylan Wiliam (1998, p. 140) paints a troubling picture: "The worst scenario is one in which some pupils who get low marks this time also got low marks last time and come to expect to get low marks next time. This cycle of repeated failure becomes part of a shared belief between such students and their teacher." The students who enter with disadvantages tend to be the ones who are confused after initial teaching, and they are the ones who are harmed the most when teachers proceed with the curriculum without checking for understanding and following up.

Few teachers have the mandate, the training, or the tools to pause when significant numbers of students are below mastery and fix what they don't understand before the gap widens even more.

In short, a powerful gap-widening dynamic is at work in most classrooms. It's not caused by evil people or incompetence. It's caused by a deeply embedded Darwinian paradigm of teaching—the one most of us experienced in school: teaching, testing, recording the bell-shaped curve of grades, and moving on. Few teachers have the mandate, the training, or the tools to *pause* when significant numbers of students are below mastery and fix what they don't understand before the gap widens even more.

I believe the principal's most important moral and professional challenge is changing the teach-test-move-on pattern. But where to begin? In an ideal world, all students would be well behaved and attentive and only need to be told once. But in the real world, a significant number of students walk into classrooms with a variety of distractions, impairments, and learning gaps, and we're lucky if initial teaching produces mastery in half of them. Jayne Boyd-Zaharias and Helen Pate-Bain said it well (2008, p. 43)—and hinted at the implications:

> No matter what the instructional format—lecture, small-group activity, or individual assignment—students make their own sense of what they're taught. Ideas don't fly directly from teachers' minds into learners' minds. Effective teaching requires teachers to assess what students are taking away from instruction to meet the differing needs of students.

Benjamin Bloom (1984) addressed this phenomenon in his research in the 1970s. If the teacher doesn't address learning problems and moves on, he said, students below mastery (defined as scoring 80 percent or above on a preliminary test) enter the next segment of the curriculum that much more confused, that much more discouraged, and that much more likely to think they're not very smart, adopt a negative attitude, and act out in class.

Bloom proposed "mastery learning" as the solution: teachers should pause instruction after a preliminary test, he said, reteach as needed, and try to bring all students up to mastery before moving on with the curriculum. Unfortunately, mastery learning didn't take off, with only a few teachers able to take the time to follow up with failing students.

Why? I believe it was because Bloom didn't link mastery learning to teacher *teamwork*, which left teachers to implement the reteaching loop on their own—a difficult challenge under the best circumstances. Richard DuFour, an Illinois principal and district leader, saw the missing piece and successfully advocated for same-grade/same-subject teacher teams—dubbed professional learning communities (PLCs)—using interim assessment data to catch up struggling students and improve the quality of teaching. DuFour's catechism is now widely known:

- What do we want each student to learn?
- How will we know when each student has learned it?
- How will we respond when a student experiences difficulty in learning?
- How will we respond if they are proficient?

Tony Flach (personal communication, 2023), a disciple of DuFour, puts it more bluntly: *Which students know what? What are we going to do about it?*

DuFour's theory of action spread like wildfire. Becky DuFour, Mike Schmoker, Robert Marzano, Douglas Reeves, Jeffrey Howard, Jay McTighe, and others have contributed to the effort, making PLCs a "hot" item in recent decades, touted as a powerful lever for equity and achievement.

Thinking back to when I was a Boston sixth-grade teacher in the 1970s, I can easily picture the transformational effect that common interim assessments and a reteaching loop would have had on our sixth-grade corridor. Instead of working in isolation, my nine colleagues and I would have had common instructional targets and could have had amazing conversations every six to seven weeks about effective and ineffective practices. Sure, we would have been concerned that the test was a good one, and yes, we would have grumbled about having to teach the curriculum in the same sequence, but as long as we were free to experiment and try new things in our classrooms, the process would have boosted our students' achievement beyond our wildest imaginings.

Unfortunately PLCs and interim assessments have often been misinterpreted and poorly implemented in many schools.

Unfortunately PLCs and interim assessments have often been misinterpreted and poorly implemented in many schools. In my work coaching principals in a number of cities and suburbs, I'm seeing a slew of implementation glitches that result in cynical and discouraged teachers—and disappointing student achievement. Some of these problems stem from misinterpretation of the basic concept. Others have to do with the quality of tests, the way they are scored, and how the data are used to follow up.

Here are poll responses from a group of educators on what they believe has gone wrong with their interim assessments:

Check any problems with your interim assessments:

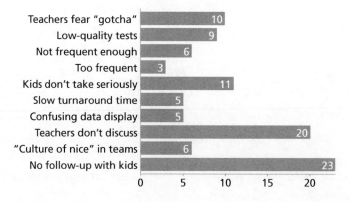

Here's an additional criticism. Assessment expert Dylan Wiliam believes the research for the impact of on-the-spot (formative) assessments is much stronger than the research on PLCs and interim assessments. Wiliam is right; on-the-spot assessments do have a better track record. But in schools that successfully address the problems listed in the poll, I've seen PLCs having a very positive effect on teaching and learning. Interim assessments, implemented well, provide an ideal *complement* for on-the-spot assessments. Here's how:

- Interim assessments are more formal and rigorous.

- They check on whether students remember and apply material several weeks after it was taught.

- They enable teachers to measure students' progress or lack thereof as the year unfolds.

- The data from interim data can be displayed in spreadsheets and wall charts, which means they can be analyzed more thoughtfully than fleeting formative data.

- Data displays make it possible for same-grade and same-subject teams of teachers to discuss collaboratively what students misunderstood, why they misunderstood it, what's confusing them, and how the material can be taught more effectively.

- Team discussions take assessment data out of the privacy of the classroom and make possible a synergistic sharing of best practices across several classrooms.

- When teachers confront specific data on their students' short-term errors and confusions, admit that certain teaching practices aren't working, and listen to colleagues who have better ideas ("Have you tried this?"), teaching can improve dramatically.

- PLC meetings enable administrators and instructional coaches to get involved in the process, contributing their wisdom and experience—and helping with scheduling, materials, and timely professional development.

- Administrators who have taken part in interim assessment discussions are much more perceptive observers in classrooms. ("It's like putting on 3-D glasses" said Paul Bambrick-Santoyo [personal communication, 2008].)

- Interim assessment data contain the names of struggling students and the specific areas in which they are having difficulty, making it easier to provide small-group tutoring and focused interventions.

- Interim assessments that simulate the content, format, and rigor of state tests can help reduce students' stress level when they take the real thing and boost their confidence when they take any kind of test.

- Because the results of interim assessments are shared within the school, they prod teachers to be on the same page in their curriculum pacing and level of rigor.

- Common assessments and open discussions of student results implicitly challenge teachers to do the very best they can in the classroom and see if their methods and materials pass the ultimate test: all students learning at high levels.

Team discussions take assessment data out of the privacy of the classroom and make possible a synergistic sharing of best practices across several classrooms.

So it's not either-or: teachers and teacher teams need to use *both* on-the-spot *and* interim assessments; each can improve teaching and learning in powerful ways. On-the-spot and interim assessments are a natural fit with mini-observations, with supervisors seeing on-the-ground action in classrooms and how teachers are processing it and following up at the team level.

Alas, as I've watched well-intentioned, hard-working educators attempting to implement interim assessments, I've realized that PLCs are a lot harder to implement than advocates naively believe. Paul Bambrick-Santoyo says the idea "hasn't traveled well" (personal communication, 2010). Working with educators in a number of schools, and reading research on effective implementation, I've summarized the most important steps to implementing interim assessments in a way that will produce the best results:

- Teacher understanding and trust
- Clear learning outcomes
- Short- and long-term goals
- High-quality assessments
- Time scheduled for assessments, data meetings, and follow-up
- Teacher involvement
- User-friendly data display
- Candid team discussions
- Involving students
- Immediate, effective follow-up with students

Here are the details, all of which need active, ongoing support from administrators and instructional coaches.

Build Understanding and Trust

The principal needs to explain interim assessments to the leadership team and staff so that everyone has a good conceptual understanding of the PLC/interim assessment process. (*What's the problem to which this is the solution?*) I've found that the "moment of truth" scenario described earlier is an effective way of making this point. In addition, teachers need *repeated* assurances that interim assessments are low stakes and will not be used as part of the performance evaluation process.

This helps create what Hector Calderon, a former New York City principal, called a "data without blame" culture in which continuous adult learning can take place (personal communication, 2004). One way of demonstrating trust in teachers is distributing copies of interim assessments well before students take them and involving teachers in refining and improving the tests; this approach is in marked contrast to the mistrustful, secret way tests are usually handled.

Clarify Learning Outcomes

As described in Chapter Eleven, all teachers need clear, manageable, standards-aligned descriptions of what their students should know and be able to do by the end of the year—not on websites or in hulking three-ring binders but in slim booklets right on their desks. Teachers need to make these standards visible to students and parents, accompanied by exemplars of proficient student work. No surprises, no excuses.

Set a Multiyear Target and Annual SMART Goals

Boosting student achievement significantly takes three or more years, so it's very helpful for the leadership team and teachers to agree on an ambitious yet attainable long-range goal—for example, 85 percent of graduating fifth graders reading at Fountas-Pinnell level W (instructional level) four years down the road. Grade-level teams can then set annual SMART goals (specific, measurable, attainable, results-oriented, and time-bound)—for example, 85 percent of first graders will be reading at Level L by the end of June. SMART goals should gradually ratchet up each year as higher-achieving students progress through the grades.

Use High-Quality Tests

Whether interim assessments are home-grown or provided by a vendor, there are important criteria to consider. Tests should be able to accomplish the following:

- Cover reading, writing, and math (and other subjects at the secondary level)
- Cover the skills and content tested in high-stakes state assessments at the appropriate level of rigor
- Have open-response as well as multiple-choice questions and writing prompts
- Incorporate user-friendly scoring rubrics
- Define on-the-way-to-college-and-career-success standards aligned with state standards
- Be aligned with the sequence of school-based curriculum materials
- Reassess previous standards, as well as new learning, to provide ongoing, cumulative review and a way of measuring progress

Finding the right length for interim assessments is a Goldilocks dilemma: they should have enough items so teachers can have substantive conversations about the results, but not so many that they're overwhelming for students to take and teachers to administer, score, and analyze. Interim assessments are low stakes and don't have to meet the same psychometric standards as state tests (for example, having seven items per standard). But interim assessments should be good enough to provide teachers with real insights for classroom follow-up.

It's also important that interim assessments not duplicate unit tests or classroom tests, resulting in overtesting and wasted classroom time. *Less is more* is a good rule of thumb. These poll results from a recent webinar show the discontent that many educators have with the quantity of tests their students take:

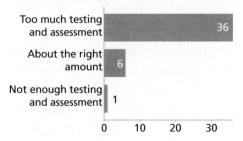

In your school, counting classroom and external assessments, is there:

The leadership team should put all the school's assessments on a master calendar—diagnostic tests, interim assessments, unit tests, teachers' classroom tests, state tests, and practice tests—and push hard to eliminate redundancy and consolidate tests to the absolute minimum needed to give teachers timely information on student proficiency as the year progresses. Using an elongated Excel spreadsheet calendar of all the weeks in the year (as recommended in Chapter Eleven) is very helpful for spreading out tests so the workload is manageable for students, teachers, and administrators.

How are commercial interim assessments working out? My sense from talking to scores of principals, teachers, district leaders, and testing experts is that K–12 assessment experts James Popham and Dylan Wiliam are right: the assessments produced by test companies are not going well in most schools because of problems with item quality and alignment, slow turnaround, and clunky data display. One exception to this gloomy picture is Formative, a small company that is doing a good job creating well-aligned interim assessments, scoring them rapidly, and training teachers and administrators to use the data effectively.

The PLC/interim assessment process is most often working well (and producing some extraordinary gains in student achievement) in small schools, often charters, that create their own tests and do the scoring in-house. This approach is labor-intensive, and many schools can't replicate it.

So where does that leave a principal whose school district mandates commercial interim assessments that have slow turnaround or low-quality items, or both? I have worked with principals in several major districts who found themselves in this position, and they've taken a variety of approaches: hand-scoring district tests to speed up turnaround, creating their own interim assessments (and deemphasizing the district's tests), getting permission from the district to use alternative assessments, and "leading up"—attempting to persuade the district to improve its assessments. Unfortunately, some principals become cynical and give up on interim assessments altogether, which means they are abandoning a powerful way to improve teaching and learning.

Let's hope that, in the years ahead, technology and enlightened district leadership will make it possible for schools to customize interim assessments from high-quality commercial or state item banks and then do all scoring and analysis locally to minimize turnaround time and maximize teacher involvement and ownership. ChatGPT and other AI tools can do a remarkably good job producing assessments, from classroom quizzes to unit and interim assessments. We need to make intelligent use of this technology.

Schedule Time for the Assessments and Immediate Follow-Up

The first scheduling priority is blocking out regular meeting times for teacher teams for ongoing discussion of student work, among other issues. As principal at the Mather, I struggled with this for years. We were able to schedule common planning time for each grade-level team K–5, but forty-five minutes was never enough time for a substantive PLC-type discussion of student work, and after-school meetings were expensive and couldn't always include teachers with family responsibilities.

> *The first scheduling priority is blocking out regular meeting times for teacher teams for ongoing discussion of student work, among other issues.*

Finally, with the help of Mary Scott, a scheduling expert, we figured out how to give an uninterrupted ninety-minute meeting for each grade-level team, and our specialist team (art, computer, music, library, and physical education), once a week. How was that possible? By putting each grade's specials next to lunch once a week, convincing our union reps to agree to one working lunch, and organizing escorts of students between specials and the cafeteria so team meetings weren't interrupted and they could do high-quality PLC work. Here's what the schedule looked like—the bold numbers are when each grade level went to specials, and the ovals show the weekly team meetings.

Mather School Master Schedule 2001–2002 - | Oct. 15, 2001   REVISED

	Pre 9:30-9:45	1 9:45 - 10:30	2 10:30 - 11:15	3 11:15 - 12:00	4 Kind lunch/recess 5th recess/lunch 12:00 - 12:45	5 4th lunch/recess 1st recess/lunch 12:50 - 1:35	6 2nd lunch/recess 3rd recess/lunch 1:40 - 2:25	7 2:25 - 3:10
Mon.		Art - 26+17 Com. - 27+17 Music- 18+17 Phys.. - 25+17	Comp. - 9 Library - 10 Music - 11 Phys. Ed. - 12	Art - 21 Comp. - 22 Library - 24 Music - 19 Phys. Ed. - 20 (Grade 5 Team Meeting)		Art - 34+14 Libr. - 13+14 Music- 15+14 Phys. - 23+14	Art - 1+36 Comp. 2+36 Libr - 6+36 Music- 16+36	Art - 3 Comp. - 4 Library - 5 Phys. Ed. - 8
Tues.		Art - 23+14 Comp. 34+14 Library - 22 Music -13+14 Phys. - 15+14	Art - 25+17 Comp. 26+17 Libr - 27+17 Music - 24 Phys. - 18+17	(Specialist Team Meeting)		Art - 12 Comp. - 21 Library - 9 Music - 10 Phys. Ed. - 11 (Grade 2 Team Meeting)	Art - 20 Comp. - 1+36 Libr. - 2+36 Music 6+36 Phys. - 16+36	Art - 8 Comp. - 3 Library - 4 Music - 5 Phys. Ed. - 19
Wed.		Art -11 Comp.- 12 Library - 21 Music - 9 Phys. Ed. -10	Comp. - 20	Art - 19 Comp. - 8 Library - 3 Music - 4 Phys. Ed. - 5 (Kindergarten Team Meeting)	Art - 16+36 Library - 1+36 Music - 2+36 Phys. - 6+36	Art - 15+14 Comp. 23+14 Libr - 34+14 Music - 22 Phys. - 13+14 (Grade 3 Team Meeting)		Art - 18+17 Comp. 25+17 Libr - 26+17 Music- 27+17 Phys. Ed. - 24
Thurs.		Art - 6+36 Comp. 16+36 Library - 20 Music - 1+36 Phys. - 2+36		Art - 13+14 Comp. 15+14 Libr - 23+14 Mus - 34+14 Phys. Ed. - 22	Comp. 18+17 Libr. - 25+17 Mus. - 26+17 Phys. - 27+17	Art - 10 Comp. - 11 Library - 12 Music - 21 Phys. Ed. - 9 (Grade 4 Team Meeting)	Art - 24	Art - 5 Comp. - 19 Library - 8 Music - 3 Phys. Ed. - 4
Fri.		Art - 4 Comp. - 5 Library - 19 Music - 8 Phys. Ed. - 3	Art - 27+17 Comp. - 24 Libr - 18+17 Mus - 25+17 Phys. - 26+17	Art - 22 Comp. 13+14 Libr - 15+14 Mus - 23+14 Phys. - 34+14		Art - 9 Comp. - 10 Library - 11 Music - 12 Phys. Ed. - 21 (Grade 1 Team Meeting)	Art - 2+36 Comp. 6+36 Libr - 16+36 Music - 20 Phys. - 1+36	ASSEMBLY 2:50 - 3:10

Principals also need to block out time in the calendar for interim tests every four to nine weeks and also schedule time for prompt scoring and teacher analysis and data meetings, ideally within twenty-four hours. It's also important to allocate several days for reteaching after each round of interim assessments. Unless these dates are on everyone's calendars, interim assessments will constantly be pushed aside by other events, and teacher teams won't look at data with any regularity.

Over several years, Greater Newark Academy, a Grades 5–8 charter school in Newark, New Jersey, scheduled its interim assessments every six weeks following this pattern:

- Wednesday and Thursday: students took interim assessments.

- Friday was an early-dismissal day (11:30 a.m.) and teachers scored, analyzed, and discussed tests and wrote their follow-up action plans, leaving at 4:00 p.m.

- The next Monday and Tuesday teachers regrouped students for reteaching and enrichment.

This school saw spectacular gains in the percent of students scoring proficient and advanced on New Jersey tests, largely attributable to its thoughtful use of interim assessments. Here are their achievement gains from 2004 to 2007 (graphic from *Driven by Data 2.0* by Bambrick-Santoyo, 2019):

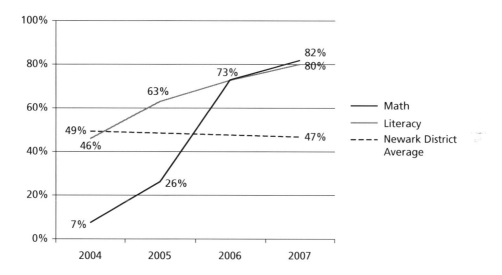

Get Teachers Involved in Making Sense of the Assessments

Teacher involvement in the interim assessment process is vital. Farming it out to a test company runs the risk of teachers not learning from their students' data. Some might complain about the work involved in scoring and analyzing interim assessments, but if professional time is blocked out that doesn't take them away from their students, teachers will end up appreciating and learning a great deal from working on their own students' tests.

Of course, schools should take advantage of scanners and other test-scoring technology to save needless paperwork—but it's essential that teachers score students' written responses and stay close to the item analysis process so they can celebrate their students' successes and form initial hypotheses about why students did poorly on some items. The heart of the interim assessment process is for teachers to be able to make better instructional decisions based on timely information.

The heart of the interim assessment process is for teachers to be able to make better instructional decisions based on timely information.

Display Data Effectively

Succinct spreadsheets and wall charts should make students' current status and progress graphically clear to teachers, administrators, students, and parents, and answer these questions: How did students do on each test item? How did students do on each standard? What's the big picture of achievement at this point? (That is, what percentage of students are *proficient* and above?) Graphic display of data, which Robert Marzano (2006) has found to be a powerful factor in boosting achievement, is especially effective when teachers and administrators see student learning data displayed by name and need.

Hold Candid Data Meetings and Plan for Follow-Up

As noted, it's vital that discussions of interim assessment data take place as soon as possible after each round of tests in same-grade and same-subject teacher teams (or, in very small schools, in one-on-one meetings between teachers and supervisors or instructional coaches). To be effective, these meetings need to be hard-hitting, honest, test-in-hand, and low stakes—celebrating successes and then looking at *what* students didn't understand and figuring out *why*. Data meetings should bring teachers out of their isolation and get them working smart to solve common learning problems. When there is only one teacher of a particular subject, Zoom is an excellent way to communicate with same-subject teachers in other schools.

Many schools have found that it's helpful to have data meetings facilitated by someone from outside the team; focused data conversations rarely happen without a guiding hand. Out of each meeting should come specific plans for next steps—an action plan for regrouping for reteaching of concepts that were widely misunderstood, small-group explanations for pockets of confusion, tutorials and after-school work for students with multiple learning problems, and distributed before-class work, mini-lesson, and homework topics in areas where most students need refreshers.

When supervisors and instructional coaches attend interim assessment data meetings, they don't have to be content experts to plunge into the conversation. Any competent educator can look at interim learning results with teacher teams and be a thought partner as teachers look for the items that caused students the most trouble, diagnose problems, brainstorm and share solutions, and decide how to follow up. This is good news for young supervisors, who are sometimes insecure about supervising teachers with many more miles on their odometers.

Instructional coaches, who are most often specialists in literacy or math, are ideal helpers in interim assessment data meetings. Their subject-area expertise is most powerful when they work with teams analyzing detailed student achievement results and planning strategies for improving student understanding.

It's crucial that PLC reports (whether they are delivered in person or in writing) be brief, low stakes, and nonbureaucratic, including, for example, the following:

- The standard taught
- How we assessed it
- Specific data on students' proficiency levels
- Students who need help and enrichment—by name and need
- What worked and what didn't work, and new ideas on teaching this unit

Teams shouldn't be bogged down in paperwork and must feel they can be creative, try new things, admit mistakes, and engage in an informal give-and-take about what's working and what needs to be improved.

Involve Students in the Process

Curriculum goals and interim assessment data have even greater impact when they are shared with students. Ideally, each child should know the following (Stiggins, 2007):

- What does proficiency look like?
- Where am I now compared to that goal?
- How am I going to close the gap?

In elementary and middle schools, it's very helpful, for example, for students to know their Fountas-Pinnell or Lexile reading levels and have a target for the end of the year. (This leads them to ask, "How do I get to be a better reader?"—a question their teachers are ready to answer.) Middle and high school students can conduct a postmortem on each interim assessment, listing which items they got wrong, whether their mistakes were careless or based on faulty understanding, and what their study strategy will be for the weeks ahead. A powerful after-test strategy for multiple-choice tests is to have students prove and disprove each answer choice, which gets them thinking through the tricks and distractors and reinforcing what makes the right answers right.

Students at all levels should have copies of the rubrics used to assess their writing and become expert at self-evaluation, tracking

A powerful after-test strategy for multiple-choice tests is to have students prove and disprove each answer choice, which gets them thinking through the tricks and distractors and reinforcing what makes the right answers right.

their progress in each of the rubric domains, and continuously improving their writing. This can prevent a frequent and depressing scenario: the teacher spends hours grading writing assignments, and students glance at the grade and throw their papers in the trash. Teachers who get their students to use rubrics to assess their own writing before handing in final work are truly working smart.

Relentlessly Follow Up

Each interim assessment provides a wealth of information that can be put to strategic use in classrooms. Assessments are a waste of time if teachers don't implement their action plans for reteaching (teaching things *differently* the second time around), follow up to see if students improve, and reflect on the data to improve their teaching. Richard DuFour and his colleagues have done some of the best work in the area of follow-up, giving detailed descriptions of schools that refuse to let students fail (DuFour et al., 2004). The strategies they describe include do-now beginning-of-class work, mini-lessons, reteaching to the whole class, tutorials, more effective use of outside tutors, peer tutoring, and parent work.

Summing Up

These ten keys to effective implementation of interim assessments are a formidable to-do list for a school. It's clear that doing this right is a complex and demanding business, and it takes focused and determined leadership to get all the moving parts functioning properly. What should supervisors look for when they visit team data meetings?

- Teachers with copies of spreadsheet reports and test items in front of them
- Drilling down on individual test items asking why students had difficulty
- Teachers admitting frankly what didn't work, and sharing methods and materials that got results (*Your kids did better than mine—what did you do? Why don't we all try that?*)
- Teachers mapping out specific action plans and pushing each other to find the best possible solutions to learning problems
- An informal, collegial atmosphere with plenty of humor

If these elements are present, supervisors can be pretty confident that things are going well and the school is on the way to dramatic gains in student achievement.

Schools that have this engine of improvement running are no longer going through the motions or implementing "one right way" to teach: they are engaged in what FDR called "bold, persistent experimentation"—trying new approaches, judging their success, discarding what didn't work, and continuously improving teaching and learning. Teacher investment is vital, because changes in classroom practices are deeper and more lasting when they come from within, as part of an ongoing, low-stakes, collegial dialogue about the best ways to get all students to high levels of achievement.

The synergistic combination of on-the-spot assessments, high-quality conversations about interim assessment data, and team accountability for SMART goals ripple out to all aspects of school improvement, helping teachers plan better, teach better, and really help struggling students. It also sharpens supervisors' vision when they visit classrooms, greatly improving the power of mini-observations.

Face-to-face teacher feedback and brief summaries are vital to the instructional impact of mini-observations. But if follow-up is limited to individual conversations and write-ups, part of the potential of these classroom visits is lost. Supervisors can get a multiplier effect by using what they learn in mini-observations and debrief conversations to broach ideas with teacher teams, forge links with team curriculum planning and results analysis (more on these in Chapters Eight and Eleven), and bolster the school's overall plan for improving student achievement.

Questions to Consider

- *Which are making the biggest difference in your school: in-the-moment or interim assessments?*
- *How well is the PLC assessment process working in your school?*
- *What are key considerations in convincing teacher teams to do this work?*

10 | Coaching Differentiation

Differentiation is classroom practice that looks eyeball to eyeball with the reality that kids differ, and the most effective teachers do whatever it takes to hook the whole range of kids on learning.

—Carol Ann Tomlinson

When supervisors walk into a classroom for a mini-observation, their five senses are flooded with information—as is a sixth sense of the hard-to-define "vibe" in the room. Liberated from the requirement to write down every detail or score the teacher on a rubric, mini-observers can take a more holistic approach, smelling the roses, watching the teacher, chatting with kids, looking at what's on the walls, and thinking about the conversation with the teacher afterward.

In Chapter Five, I suggested a very short mental checklist so mini-observers can keep their heads up and focus on what matters most:

- **Content.** Is this the right material and rigor for this grade and subject?
- **Pedagogy.** Is this the best way to teach the content?
- **Learning.** Are all students on track to mastering the content?

Supervisors are frequently reminded to look for differentiation in classrooms. It's an article of faith that teachers should differentiate their instruction—that is, teach in ways that meet their students' individual needs. Every teacher-evaluation rubric includes the idea, and administrators often look for differentiation when they visit classrooms.

But what exactly are they looking for? Do we know good differentiation when we see it? And given the challenge meeting the needs of twenty to thirty students, when have teachers differentiated enough? Researchers haven't given much guidance on these questions, and

195

there's plenty of confusion and misunderstanding in schools. Let's see if we can unpack this important issue and help mini-observers focus on what counts.

For starters, what is the problem to which differentiation is the solution? Clearly it's the fact that students walk into school with a wide range of differences in prior knowledge, vocabulary, reading proficiency, fluency in English, attitudes toward school, mindset about learning, tolerance of frustration and failure, learning-style preferences, special needs, and distracting things on their minds. And each student has a unique profile on Howard Gardner's eight intelligences: linguistic, logical-mathematical, visual-spatial, bodily-kinesthetic, musical, interpersonal, intrapersonal, and environmental awareness. The differentiation challenge is daunting!

Teachers in one-room schoolhouses on the nineteenth-century prairie had to do all that and more, catering to the needs of students from age six to sixteen.

Underwood Archives, Inc/Alamy Stock Photo

With the advent of mass education, the trend has been toward more-homogeneous classrooms, with students sorted by age, intelligence, achievement, giftedness, gender, and special needs.

Nevertheless, most teachers today still face a wide range of student differences—even in "tracked" classes. Trying to get a group of students doing the same thing—by lecturing, assigning the same twenty-five spelling words to all students, or having everyone read "Romeo and

Juliet"—can be inefficient. All too often, higher-achieving students are bored and below-level students become increasingly frustrated. A teacher aiming for the middle is lucky if half the class achieves mastery, and as students move through the grades, proficiency gaps get wider.

From this perspective, differentiating would seem to be a moral imperative. Surely all teachers should assess students' individual needs and learning styles, customize instruction to those needs, and get students working at their Vygotsky sweet spot of difficulty. University of Virginia professor Carol Ann Tomlinson, the leading expert on the issue, puts it this way:

> Differentiation is effective attention to the learning needs of each student. The purpose of developing a differentiated classroom is to make sure there's opportunity and support for each student to learn essential knowledge and skills as effectively and efficiently as possible. The key is getting to know each student and orchestrating the learning environment, curriculum, assessments, and instruction so all students learn what's being taught (personal communication, 2016).

Tomlinson and other advocates of differentiation go a step further, suggesting that teachers should differentiate by content (what's being taught), by process (how it's taught), and by product (how students are asked to demonstrate their learning).

The Critique

The goals of differentiation seem unassailable, but in recent years, serious questions have been raised about its practicality and efficacy. Among them: Can a teacher really tailor instruction for twenty to thirty different students? Does attempting to differentiate exhaust teachers, pushing them out of the profession? Is gearing the curriculum to students' current levels really tracking in sheep's clothing? Does differentiated instruction spoon-feed students, undermining their self-reliance and initiative? Does it balkanize classrooms, reducing the sense of community, collective experiences, and peer interaction? Finally, and perhaps most important, has research demonstrated that differentiation improves student learning?

Can a teacher really tailor instruction for twenty to thirty different students?

In a provocative 2010 article in *Education Week,* author/consultant Mike Schmoker asserted there was no credible research evidence that differentiation works. In his view, the case for differentiation is based "largely on enthusiasm and a certain superficial logic" (p. 22). In classrooms he'd visited around the country, Schmoker described how differentiation seemed to complicate teachers' work, requiring them to procure and assemble multiple sets of materials. I saw frustrated teachers trying to provide materials that matched each student's or group's presumed ability level, interest, preferred "modality," and learning style. The attempt often devolved into a frantically assembled collection of worksheets, coloring exercises, and specious "kinesthetic" activities . . . . With so many groups to teach, instructors found it almost impossible to provide sustained, properly executed lessons for every child or group. (p. 22)

What disturbed Schmoker most was seeing classrooms where differentiation was a way for teachers to expect less of some students. "In English," he said, "creative students made things or drew pictures. Analytic students got to read and write" (2010, p. 22).

Responding to Schmoker's article, Tomlinson and David Sousa acknowledged that some teachers have taken the idea too far. Trying to customize worksheets and coloring exercises to students' supposed learning styles, they said, is "regrettable and damaging" (Tomlinson & Sousa, 2010, p. 28). They also agreed with Schmoker on the importance of clear objectives, high standards, and frequent checks for understanding followed by appropriate instructional adaptations. But they defended differentiation's track record, citing research evidence that students learn better when the work is at the right level of difficulty, personally relevant, and appropriately engaging.

This rejoinder hardly resolved the matter. John Hattie's comprehensive meta-analysis, *Visible Learning* (2008), ranked 138 classroom instructional variables and put individualization (roughly synonymous with differentiation) 100th from the top—with an effect size of only 0.23. Cognitive psychologist Daniel Willingham debunks the idea of catering to students' individual learning styles (2005). And professional development guru Jon Saphier calls differentiation a "low-impact strategy" that's not the best target for professional development if other fundamentals aren't in place (personal communication, 2015). The debate continues, leaving many teachers and supervisors without authoritative guidance on what's best for students.

The debate continues, leaving many teachers and supervisors without authoritative guidance on what's best for students.

Reframing the Question

Let's step back and analyze the challenge of teaching heterogeneous classes from a broader perspective. Consider these twenty instructional scenarios:

- A college professor delivering a lecture to seven hundred students
- A class in a circle discussing a bullying incident
- A class standing in a circle outdoors engaging in a trust exercise

- Small groups of second graders doing an experiment with batteries and bulbs
- A teacher strategically cold-calling students
- First graders sprawling on a rug engrossed in books they chose
- Groups of fourth graders solving a math problem and reporting their strategies
- An elementary class watching a movie together
- Ninth graders reading the same article at four different reading levels using Newsela
- Students solving a math problem on 5×3 cards; the teacher going over one wrong answer
- Fifth graders using a computer program that adapts the difficulty to their responses
- A high-school physical education class doing jumping jacks in unison
- In an elementary music class, students playing guitars
- A docent at a city art museum teaching visiting tenth graders about a Renoir masterpiece
- High school biology students working individually or in groups on a "layered" unit
- A flipped classroom, students watching the teacher's lecture at home, discussing in class
- Students taking a number and coming up for individual help with the teacher
- Students having an individualized schedule for the day based on the previous day's test
- Students getting one-on-one tutoring

How much differentiation is there in each scenario? Here's how educators in a recent webinar rated these scenarios in an anonymous poll, after looking at photos of each one:

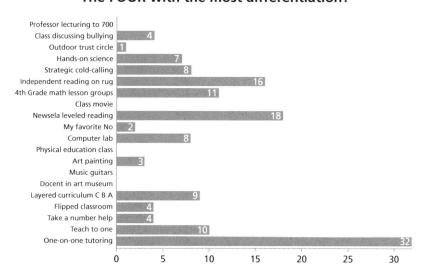

The FOUR with the most differentiation?

These responses make sense. Viewed through the lens of differentiation, individual tutoring does best, with customized Newsela reading levels and individually chosen books not far behind. On the flipside, the least differentiated would clearly be the college professor holding forth to seven hundred students, a class movie, mass exercise in a physical education class, and a group-taught music class and museum lecture.

But here's a different question: In which setting were students *learning* the most? Well, it depends. To answer that question, we'd need more information: How skillfully was each teacher handling instruction? What were the interpersonal dynamics? What were the learning objectives, and were they appropriate to that grade level? Each of the scenarios has the potential for excellent learning: a brilliant and charismatic college professor like Harvard's Michael Sandel can have every student in a large lecture hall on a steep learning curve. A one-on-one tutor can have a harsh demeanor and do all the work for the student. In the hands-on science lesson, learning would depend on whether the teacher set up just the right experiment and then moved around the class observing and prompting. With each scenario, *it depends*.

A big takeaway: differentiation is just one way of evaluating instruction—and perhaps not the most helpful. The problem with observing a class and asking how differentiated it is (or looking for any other item on a checklist of good teaching) is that it narrows our field of vision and runs the risk of missing what's really happening. Wouldn't it be better to ask three broader questions:

- What are students supposed to be learning?
- Is the teacher using the most effective way to teach it?
- Are all students learning?

Asking these questions—especially the third—focuses teachers and supervisors on these key elements of effective teaching:

- Appropriate cognitive and noncognitive unit and lesson goals
- A standard for mastery (usually 80 percent)
- Effective learning experiences
- The best mode: whole-class, small-group, individual, or digital
- Checking for understanding
- Fixing learning problems during the lesson
- Following up with students who aren't successful
- Continuously fine-tuning teaching

With this broad focus on learning intentions, pedagogy, and student learning, teachers' work—and supervisors' support and evaluation of that work—falls logically into three phases:

- Unit and lesson planning
- Delivery of instruction
- Follow-up with unsuccessful students

Let's look at each one with an eye to a manageable teacher workload, teacher teamwork, the orchestrating role of principals—and what supervisors should be looking for in classrooms.

Phase 1: Planning Units and Lessons

A good curriculum unit plan—ideally crafted by a team of same-grade/same-subject teachers—has several key elements: relevant external standards; clarity on what students should ultimately know, be able to do, and understand; a preassessment that helps anticipate misconceptions and possible learning problems; essential questions to guide students to the key understandings; a lesson-by-lesson game plan of well-chosen learning experiences; on-the-spot and summative assessments, ideally including a performance task; and a hook to grab students' interest at the outset. For unit planning, Grant Wiggins and Jay McTighe's (2005) *Understanding by Design* backward-planning protocol is widely used and admired (more on this in Chapter Eleven).

For lesson planning (ideally done the afternoon or evening before, building on the learning outcomes of the previous lesson, with the unit goals in mind), the most helpful conceptual tool is universal design for learning (UDL). The essence of UDL is crafting lessons that make the content accessible to as many students as possible.

A well-designed lesson has clear goals; thoughtful task analysis; chunked learning; modalities appropriate to the content (Demonstration? Hands-on experiment? Lecture? Textbook passage? Group work? Film? Field trip? Visiting speaker? Internet research?); links to students' interests and experiences; novel experiences to spark interest; thoughtful use of whole-class, small-group, and individual work; assessments to check for understanding; a plan B if some students don't get it; accommodations and modifications for students with special needs (including assistive technology); and perhaps texts at different levels and student choice of projects and measures of learning.

Daniel Willingham (2005) says teachers' challenge is finding the right modality for the subject matter being taught (versus differentiating for students' learning preferences). For example, lessons on atomic structure could have students using marshmallows and toothpicks to build models of atoms and molecules; students studying the Civil War could work with maps and Matthew Brady photos and watch the film *Gettysburg*; with a Langston Hughes poem, listening

"All students learn more when content drives the choice of modality."

to an audio recording might be the most powerful medium; for *Macbeth*, putting on the play. Willingham sums up this key point about planning instruction: "All students learn more when content drives the choice of modality" (2005, p. 31).

Another part of unit and lesson preparation is preparing visuals to scaffold instruction. These might include learning goals, essential questions, exemplars of student writing, worked problems, word walls, commonly misspelled words, times tables, inspirational posters, maps, and a globe.

The planning phase is where there's the greatest likelihood of falling prey to overthinking, overworking, and more overworking. Here are several ways to prevent that, which supervisors should orchestrate and support:

- Working with same-grade or same-subject colleagues (principals play a key role in scheduling common planning time for team collaboration)

- Using efficient, well-thought-out templates to streamline unit and lesson planning

- Tapping into resources that are available in print and on the internet, including Chat-GPT and other large language models, which do a remarkably good job coming up with essential questions and crafting lesson and unit plans

- Saving and sharing good unit and lesson plans for future years

- Knowing when enough is enough—not letting the perfect be the enemy of the good—and getting enough sleep

Phase 2: Delivering Instruction

Lessons are where the rubber meets the road, and a major factor in student success is a set of in-classroom moves that effective teachers have always used: effective classroom management, knowing students well, being culturally sensitive, making the subject matter exciting and relevant, being succinct and clear, taking advantage of visuals and props, involving students and getting them involved with each other, having a sense of humor, and nimbly using teachable moments (see Domain C of the teacher evaluation rubric in Chapter Eight).

But skillfully implementing these teaching skills is not enough. Teachers must check for understanding—it's always the unexpected—and work on fixing learning problems in real time. Research tells us that this is one of the most important factors in student achievement.

Fortunately, there are lots of low-tech and high-tech ways to do this, such as dry-erase boards; whole-class response systems like Kahoot and Socrative; asking probing questions (*What makes you say that?*); having students think, write, and pair-share; cruising around looking over students' shoulders and intervening (or not); getting students working on group projects that tap multiple skills; teaching students how to self-assess and improve their own work; organizing peer tutoring; and using a growing number of computer programs that personalize instruction.

These are the critical success factors in Phase 2—all of which supervisors should looking for during mini-observations:

- Energetic and sensitive lesson execution (which is why it's so important that teachers arrive at school sharp and fresh, not exhausted from overpreparing the night before)

- Building students' ability to work independently and in groups—essential for the teacher to be able to move around the classroom providing individual help

- A classroom culture in which students are comfortable making mistakes, asking for help, and helping each other

- Checking for understanding and following up

- Resisting the urge to do too much for students, gradually releasing responsibility, and pushing them to engage in productive struggle and do most of the intellectual heavy lifting

Phase 3: Following Up After Instruction

No matter how well teachers plan and teach, some students don't achieve mastery by the end of a lesson or unit. This is the moment of truth: if the class moves on, unsuccessful students will be that much more confused and discouraged and fall further and further behind, widening the gap between the haves and the have-nots. Teachers and teacher teams need the time and support to use data from exit tickets, quizzes, and unit or interim assessments to organize timely, focused interventions for those students. Examples: lunchtime help, pullout tutoring, small-group after-school help, Saturday school, and other venues to catch students up.

Teacher teams looking at assessment data is also an opportunity to reflect on methods and materials, learn from colleagues, and continuously fine-tune how they plan and teach. Team collaboration for student work (PLCs) is widely used around the country, but it's often not reaching its full potential (more on this in Chapter Twelve). The critical success factors (always on supervisors' radar) are as follows:

- Carving out time to work with same-grade/same-subject colleagues (again, the principal's key role as scheduler-in-chief)

- Having prompt access to data from well-crafted common assessments that students take seriously

- Analyzing what students had problems with and why

- Organizing effective help for struggling students

- Honestly assessing teaching techniques in light of the results

If these factors aren't in place, the PLC process can result in a cycle of repeated failure: the same students are unsuccessful each time, they sit through remediation that doesn't change results, and they become a permanent underclass of failure.

A Long-Term Goal: Student Self-Reliance and Intrinsic Motivation

> *Well-intentioned, dedicated teachers often fall into the trap of helping students too much.*

At the beginning of this chapter, I mentioned that differentiation is sometimes criticized for spoon-feeding students and undermining their ability to learn independently. Well-intentioned, dedicated teachers often fall into the trap of helping students too much. Underlying all good instruction, especially in middle and high school, should be building self-monitoring and executive functioning skills in all students. These are items for teachers to focus on in their planning, execution, and follow-up, and supervisors to look for in mini-observations and visits to team meetings—students' ability to do the following:

- Self-assess and know their strengths and weaknesses
- Understand the concept of fixed and growth mindset
- Take responsibility for managing their time
- Implement the best study skills, including the retrieval effect
- Deal with difficulty, frustration, and failure
- Have one or two passionate interests

Wrapping Up

Every day, teachers face the challenge of reaching students who have a wide range of abilities and needs. When those needs aren't met, the proficiency gaps with which students enter school get wider and wider. Tomlinson is absolutely right that we need to know students, tune in to their unique learning needs, and orchestrate the learning environment, curriculum, instruction, and assessments so all students learn essential knowledge and skills.

But as Tomlinson acknowledges, there is such a thing as too much differentiation, and as we saw in the previously described scenarios, differentiation is not the biggest driver of student success. When supervisors are too focused on differentiation, they might not see the bigger picture of what's going on in classrooms. For teachers, obsessing about differentiation can lead down an exhausting and largely unproductive rabbit hole of overthinking individualized instruction and not using a well-chosen repertoire of instructional strategies for what they are teaching.

A more effective approach is for supervisors to keep everyone focused on those three big questions: What are students supposed to be learning? Is this the best way to teach it? And are all students learning? Then supervisors, lead teachers, and other support staff members can help teachers balance their energy and creativity across the three phases: frontloading success into every unit and lesson, pulling out all the stops during instruction, and following up afterward, refusing to let students fail. All of this is hard work, but it's *effective* work that will fuel teachers' energy, sense of professional efficacy, and long-term passion for the mission of preparing all students for life success.

Questions to Consider

- *Has this chapter given you a new way of thinking about differentiation?*
- *Which of the three phases needs most work in your school—planning, execution, or follow-up?*
- *Do the three lesson observation questions make sense—content, pedagogy, learning?*

11 | Coaching Curriculum Unit Planning

Uneven, scattered curriculum isn't just boring or confusing; it can widen the gaps between students from affluent backgrounds and their peers from low-income families.

—Sonja Santelises, Baltimore City superintendent

When a supervisor walks into a classroom for a mini–observation, one of the most important questions is where the lesson fits into the curriculum unit and the larger game plan for the year. This is something children wonder about, too, as in this *New Yorker* cartoon.

"Please, Ms. Sweeney, may I ask where you're going with all this?"

Robert Weber/THE CARTOON BANK

How can supervisors know the answer to this big-picture question for every classroom they visit? How can they be sure the right curriculum content is being taught at the right level of rigor? One way is to hold a pre-observation conference in which the teacher spells out the standards covered and has a chance to talk about the broader context. This gives a sense of the lesson's purpose, but it comes with all the disadvantages of pre-announced classroom visits discussed in Chapter Three. In addition, these conferences occur only when formal observations are scheduled, which is certainly not often enough to give a sense of whether the curriculum is appropriate day by day and week by week.

Another way to know where the lesson is going is asking that lesson objectives be posted. This nudges teachers to clarify the aim of each class, helps students know what they are supposed to be learning, and enables visitors to see the purpose of the lesson at a glance. But if Ms. Sweeney had a lesson objective on the board, the inquisitive student wouldn't be satisfied. What the kid wanted to know—and what a thoughtful supervisor also wants to know—is the longer-range purpose of those addition and subtraction problems. Lesson-specific objectives (SWBAT—students will be able to . . .) are too narrow to answer that question.

Consider this actual dialogue between a science teacher and Keith, an average fifth grader, toward the end of a four-month teaching unit on the solar system:

Teacher:	Where is the sun after it sets?
Keith	*(pausing):* I don't know . . .
Teacher:	*(pointing to the student-made colorful globes with attached labels hanging from the classroom ceiling and to students' pictures and drawings on the walls):* Is there anything in our classroom exhibit that can help you think about this?
Keith	*(looking around):* No . . . but I know it doesn't go into the ocean.
Teacher:	How do you know that?
Keith:	Because it would splash the water.
Teacher:	Oh. So where does it really go?
Keith	*(pausing):* Maybe to China?
Teacher	*(relieved):* And where is it when it sets in China?
Keith	*(troubled):* I don't know . . .

—Meir Ben-Hur, *Phi Delta Kappan* (May 1998)

Not a good moment for the teacher. How could Keith have missed such an important concept after four months of instruction? How could all those hands-on experiences building model planets and moons have failed to teach this central idea? If you were a supervisor overhearing Keith and the teacher, you'd wince—and it would get you thinking about improved curriculum planning.

When you visited the fifth-grade classes during the solar system unit, things looked good. Students were engaged, artifacts were being created, and the teaching seemed creative and effective. After your mini-observations, you probably complimented the teachers. Now you find that Keith—not a student with major learning problems—is uncertain about a concept that is at the heart of the solar system unit. How could your mini-observations have missed such important information?

My hunch is that this happened because the unit plan hadn't been thought through. Lessons contained lots of engaging, hands-on activities, but teachers hadn't articulated a few "big ideas" and anticipated likely misconceptions—for example, that the sun orbits the Earth. When the learning objectives of a unit aren't clear, it's much harder to pick up on students' learning problems along the way—and assess how much they've learned at the end.

Without seeing the unit plan, it's difficult for a mini-observer to know what to look for. Even the most sharp-eyed observer will be guessing about the bigger curriculum picture. This means that comments to teachers afterward will be limited to the *process* of teaching—which is interesting and important—rather than the content, alignment, and rigor—which are key to student achievement.

Let's unpack the different levels of curriculum: macro curriculum planning, year-end expectations, unit plans, lesson plans, and the contentious issue of test prep.

Macro Curriculum Planning

In my school visits over the last two decades, I rarely see good curriculum unit planning. Why? Because although teacher preparation programs might touch on the subject, principals don't ask for unit plans (I never did) and engage in fuzzy thinking when it comes to *curriculum mapping*. When I hear that term, I never know whether people are referring to year-end expectations, the scope and sequence, unit plans, lesson plans—or some combination. Teachers rarely have structured time to work with their colleagues thinking through unit plans and assessments.

> *Teachers rarely have structured time to work with their colleagues thinking through unit plans and assessments.*

The result is that most teachers, under intense time pressure (*all that curriculum to cover, all those papers to correct!*), do their lesson planning the night before, aiming toward vaguely defined unit goals, and write unit tests shortly before students take them. Supervisors unwittingly reinforce this by inspecting lesson plans rather than unit plans, rarely looking at teacher-made tests, and supervising and evaluating teachers based on how well they perform in one or two lessons a year, not on how curriculum units and assessments are planned and executed over time.

All this can produce a worst-case scenario in classrooms: teachers, students, and principals working hard, but a big discrepancy between the *intended* curriculum, the *taught* curriculum, and the *learned* curriculum, as shown here. Many important understandings don't end up in students' long-term memory.

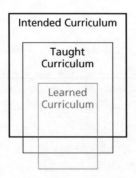

Clearly supervisors need to pay as much attention to *what* is taught as they do to *how* it's taught. In my years at the Mather, I was a slow learner in this area (despite having been Boston's citywide curriculum director for several years!) and didn't provide teachers with nearly enough guidance and support. Since leaving the principalship, I've steeped myself in the literature on curriculum and unit planning, especially the work of Grant Wiggins and Jay McTighe (authors of the seminal book *Understanding by Design*, 2005), attended numerous workshops, and begun to coach principals on ways to supervise curriculum content more thoughtfully than I did.

The next graphic shows the big picture of curriculum. At the bottom are the K–12 learning expectations, which are now quite clearly delineated in all states. I picked one grade and subject—sixth-grade math—and depicted the end-of-year learning expectations—what students need to know and be able to do by the end of the year to be successful at the next grade level.

Above that is a game plan of the math curriculum units for the year. This kind of linear display—an Excel spreadsheet with a column for every week and all the school vacations included—is very helpful in working out the length and timing of the year's curriculum units (a template for this calendar is available free at www.marshallmemo.com; click on Kim's Writing and scroll down to Classroom Materials).

Next is a unit plan for fractions, consisting of twenty lessons. And finally, there is the individual lesson—part of which the supervisor sees in a mini-observation. It should be clear (in the conversation with the teacher afterward if not during the lesson) how that lesson is part of a unit plan that is part of the year's game plan, moving students to mastery of sixth-grade math standards along a well-planned K–12 continuum of learning.

Let's look at each of these components in more detail.

Year-End Learning Expectations

The arrival of the Common Core State Standards in 2010 and the Next Generation Science Standards in 2013 ushered in a new era for US educators. Attempting a de facto national curriculum was ambitious, and after a brief honeymoon, there was pushback. Even though the standards were not a federal initiative (they were developed by the National Governors' Association, the Council of Chief State School Officers, Achieve, and both major teacher unions) and even though adopting them was voluntary, opponents branded CCSS as a top-down federal takeover. When the dust settled, all states had much more rigorous standards and assessments, heavily influenced by Common Core, but they went by different names.

Standards—and how they are assessed—are the North Star when it comes to school-level curriculum planning. They clarify *what* students should learn in K–12—the skills, knowledge, and

When the dust settled, all states had much more rigorous standards and assessments, heavily influenced by Common Core, but they went by different names.

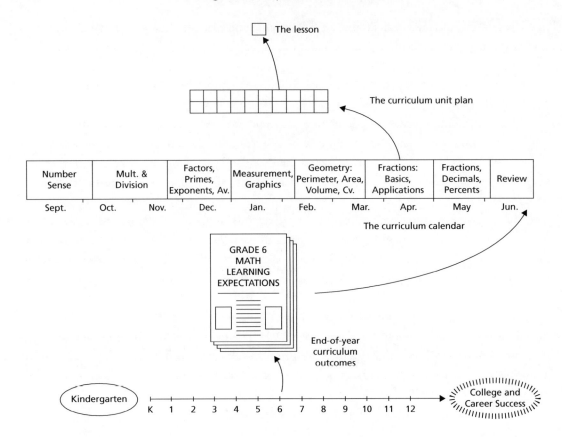

understandings—not *how* it will be taught, which is decided by districts, schools, and teachers, informed by research and best practices. The push for standards in recent years represents a major shift from the previous era, when school-based educators often lacked clear guidance on what was expected.

For independent-minded teachers like my younger self, the earlier era provided a heady degree of freedom, but it undoubtedly widened the proficiency gap by allowing expectations to be watered down for many students and leaving gaps in the curriculum as teachers pursued what interested them and entertained their students, rather than what was appropriate in a coherent, comprehensive K–12 learning sequence.

Clear statewide learning standards have the potential to put a dent in America's perennial curriculum equity problem. It's now easier for districts and schools to put in teachers' hands the kind of learning-outcomes summaries we developed at the Mather in the late 1980s. Our slim, grade-by-grade learning expectations booklets, complete with exemplars of on-grade-level reading passages and proficient student writing and problem solving, were extraordinarily helpful to teachers and parents, playing an important role in bringing about significant gains in our students' achievement. Imagine the power of documents like this aligned to state standards and assessments! They answer the teacher's most basic request of the district—*Just tell me what to teach!*—and liberate teachers to put their full energy into figuring out the most creative and effective ways to teach it.

Almost every school district has a "scope and sequence" for major subjects, but it often gathers dust. That's because it's usually written in the central office and doesn't reflect classroom realities. Pacing guides get more respect, especially if principals are the enforcers, but they're often bitterly resented by teachers, who feel pressured to march through the curriculum without discretion to take extra time to solidify learning, reteach, and help struggling students. Arguments over pacing guides sometimes involve imprecations about who has low expectations of students, who is out of touch with classroom realities, and who needs to pick up the pace by using better teaching methods.

Thinking through the curriculum calendar is an important schoolwide project, and teachers need to be involved every step of the way. Here is a step-by-step plan for how principals can make that happen:

- Provide teacher teams (grade-level and subject-area) with at least a half-day of uninterrupted time just before the school year begins and ask them to create a calendar of their curriculum units for the year.
- Start by having each team spell out their end-of-year expectations as specified by state standards and, if available, state tests.
- Each team divides their curriculum into units and estimates how many weeks each one will take.
- Use an elongated Excel grid with a column for each week of the school year, including all school vacations, marking periods, report card times, state tests, and other important events.
- Ask each team to rough out how the units will fit onto the calendar strip (being sure that tested material is covered before state tests are given). Here is an example of what this looked like in one New York City elementary school.

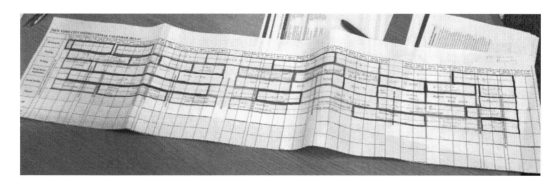

- Compare notes with other grades and teams, thinking about the coherence of a student's experience moving through the grades, and make any necessary tweaks—for example, students reading *Of Mice and Men* the same year they study the Great Depression.

- Get the information from all units entered into a composite Excel document, make copies, and distribute them to teams with instructions to figure out areas for cooperation and cross-fertilization between teams (and suggestions on curriculum units that might be shifted on the calendar to create a more-coherent experience for students).

- Discuss the composite curriculum calendar with an eye to identifying times and ways that teams might collaborate during the year.

- Finalize the whole-school composite calendar, put it on the school's website, print multiple (full-size) copies, and post them in the teachers' room, the curriculum center, and all administrators' offices for easy reference. Following is a New York City middle school's hallway display of sixth-, seventh-, and eighth-grade units.

- Revise the calendar as needed each year.

This kind of curriculum planning can be enormously helpful to teachers and administrators, leading to ongoing conversations about pacing, content, cross-fertilization, and more. But it's just the beginning.

Curriculum Unit Plans

Once the curriculum calendar is figured out, grade-level and subject-area teams can begin to plan their lead-off curriculum units, ideally using the approach developed by Grant Wiggins and Jay McTighe in *Understanding by Design* (2005). The key feature of UbD is planning each unit "backwards"—that is, starting with the final learning goals and assessments and working back through the steps necessary to get students to mastery. Here are the critical components that a team would decide on as it produces a first-rate unit plan (the sequence is up to each team):

- The name of the unit and how long it will last
- The state standards covered by the unit (written out verbatim)
- The most important factual knowledge students will acquire (preceded by *Students will know . . .*)
- A list of skills to be taught or reinforced, including habits of mind (preceded by *Students will be able to . . .*)
- Three or four big ideas or enduring understandings (each preceded by *Students will understand that . . .*) to guide teachers throughout the unit and keep the bigger picture in mind (*Ms. Sweeney, where are you going with all this?*)
- Three or four essential questions, written in provocative, student-friendly language, to be posted on the classroom wall during the unit, leading the class toward "discovery" of the big ideas
- Assessments (unit tests, a performance task) *written in advance* to assess student mastery formatively and summatively, accompanied by exemplars of proficient student work and a scoring guide
- A lesson-by-lesson game plan (not detailed lesson plans) showing when some or all of these components will be used: lectures, mini-lessons, read-alouds, independent reading, discussions, dialogues, debates, partner or small-group work, student presentations, reports, journals, reflections, films, website exploration, visiting speakers, field trips,

in-class assessments, student presentations, written reports, essays, research, journals, reflections, and homework

UbD unit planning has huge payoffs in terms of the quality of instruction and student achievement.

UbD unit planning has huge payoffs in terms of the quality of instruction and student achievement. Who among us wouldn't want our children or beloved nieces and nephews taught by teachers thinking through each curriculum unit in this fashion? But backwards design is time-consuming and intellectually challenging, and it's not something most teachers have the time or training to do on their own. The default in most schools is last-minute lesson planning. Here's a recent poll of a group of teachers' self-assessment of their proficiency with backwards curriculum design:

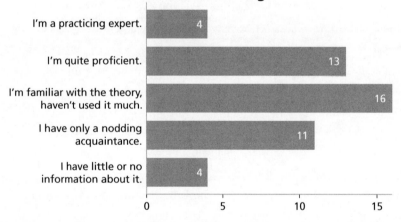

How familiar are you with backwards curriculum unit design?

I'm a practicing expert.	4
I'm quite proficient.	13
I'm familiar with the theory, haven't used it much.	16
I have only a nodding acquaintance.	11
I have little or no information about it.	4

Fortunately, there are excellent resources to support UbD, including Wiggins and McTighe's books and Jay McTighe's resource-rich website, https://jaymctighe.com, with access to hundreds of curriculum units developed by teachers around the world. Some school districts have done exemplary work with UbD, including West Windsor Township and Ramsey School District in New Jersey and Cataline Foothills in Arizona. And artificial intelligence (AI) chatbots like ChatGPT can do an amazingly good job generating essential questions and other components of UbD curriculum units—if prompts are detailed and specific.

The principal plays a critical role in good unit design. The first step is getting teachers working in same-grade and same-subject teams to plan *common* units (*no more Lone Ranger!*). UbD planning is difficult to do alone, but it becomes manageable when teachers pool their content-area expertise, share ideas and insights, and bring their collective brainpower and resources to the task—textbooks, web resources, AI, reference books, and more.

Unit-planning meetings should be part of the regular cycle of grade-level team meetings, preferably run by teachers or instructional coaches, with supervisors making regular visits, partly for quality control but also for the pleasure of watching substantive, collegial meetings. Here are other key steps for the school's leadership team:

- Giving teacher teams the mandate, perhaps in the context of a long-range goal of having all major units in the school backwards-planned within two or three years

- Providing the training and the support they need to be successful

- Giving teacher teams enough time to design units over the summer and during the school year

- Making unit design one element in the regular rotation of weekly meeting agendas (the others might be looking at interim assessment data and student work, discussing effective teaching strategies, and dealing with logistics, discipline, and student culture issues)

- Buying a school subscription to one or two good curriculum websites so teachers can download units in their area

- Arranging to have each new curriculum unit subjected to peer review (UbD materials have a helpful protocol for this)

- As part of their unit planning, having teachers develop standard ways for students to store their work (for example, a reading log, a reading response journal, a writing portfolio, or a math folder)

- Supervisors reviewing each unit before it is finalized

- Monitoring the implementation of units via mini-observations, visits to team meetings, and debriefs with team leaders, with feedback at every stage

- Collaboratively analyzing the learning outcomes of each unit: what went right and what can be improved

The most challenging part of UbD is framing the big ideas of a curriculum unit and writing matching essential questions. I once watched a group of experienced Brooklyn eighth-grade social studies teachers struggle for almost an hour to come up with the big ideas of a unit on the Civil War that they had taught for years; they had never been asked to think at that conceptual level and became better Civil War teachers for having done so. Teacher teams need time and guidance to do this work well—and should use AI tools like ChatGPT to accelerate the process.

> *The most challenging part of UbD is framing the big ideas of a curriculum unit and writing matching essential questions.*

As an example, here are the big ideas and enduring understandings for a fifth-grade unit on the solar system.

Big Ideas

Students will understand that:

- The sun's gravity has held the planets and other objects in regular orbits for billions of years, which is what makes our solar system a system.
- If the sun were the size of a large beach ball, the Earth would be the size of a pea; the great distance between them makes the sun appear much smaller.
- The Earth's distance from the sun is just right for life to develop; if we were closer, we'd burn up, and if we were farther out, we'd freeze.
- Day and night are caused by the Earth turning on its axis every twenty-four hours, not by the sun going around the Earth; it's daytime on the side facing toward the sun, night-time on the side facing away.
- A year is the amount of time it takes a planet to orbit around the sun; the length of a year is different on every planet because each planet takes a different amount of time to orbit around the sun.
- Moonlight is actually reflected sunlight, and the moon's phases (waxing from new moon to half moon to full moon and waning back again) are caused by the angle at which the sun's rays strike the moon relative to a human observer.

Essential Questions to Evoke the Big Ideas

Students will keep considering:

- Why are the sun and the planets called the solar system?
- How are most diagrams and models of our solar system inaccurate? Why?
- Why has life flourished on the planet Earth and not on other planets, moons, and asteroids in our solar system?
- What causes night and day on Earth?
- If you lived on Mars, would a year be the same length of time as on Earth? Explain.
- Why does the moon change shape over the course of each month?

The first time a team creates a UbD unit, there should be a half-day of professional time, a common unit-design template to work with, and support from consultants, instructional coaches, or administrators familiar with the process. McTighe recommends that teams start by designing one unit, teaching it, discussing learning outcomes, and making revisions. Once a good unit plan has been created, it's money in the bank; it can be used by the team that created it—and by other teams.

Then teams can focus on the next unit plan—but not every unit has to be written from scratch. Successfully creating one UbD unit makes it much easier to adopt and adapt units from colleagues, other schools, ChatGPT, or a website, saving valuable time. It's unrealistic to expect every teacher team to write a year's entire curriculum in high-quality UbD style—that would take years. But once the pump is primed, teachers can build on and adapt the work of others and spread high-quality curriculum units throughout the school in a fairly short time.

Some educators, feeling the pressure of high-stakes tests, say they can't afford the "luxury" of UbD unit planning; they say they need to focus on test preparation. But thoughtful planning and higher test scores are not an either-or choice. Good backwards curriculum planning supports better teaching, higher achievement, and a trajectory toward college and career success.

Of course, unit planning has little value if it's not aligned to standards. When teachers design impressive units and then go looking for standards that plausibly match, that's the wrong way around! Standards should come first, along with a sense of how those standards are assessed by state tests and what is aligned to a college-and-career-ready curriculum. The unit's knowledge and skill objectives and essential questions should flow directly from those high standards. Creating linear curriculum calendars, as described, is a good way to make sure standards are embedded in grade-by-grade instructional plans.

Team unit planning time is one of the best forms of professional development for teachers—and supervisors. A rigorous backwards-planning process, skillfully facilitated, gets teachers thinking about every aspect of their craft—the intended, the taught, and the learned curriculum—and how to bring them into alignment. Unit planning improves teacher collaboration, the quality of teaching, and student achievement.

Team unit planning time is one of the best forms of professional development for teachers—and supervisors.

In schools that have begun to use systematic unit design, classroom teaching is much more focused and results-oriented, and a mini-observing supervisor can concentrate on the most important thing: how well the material is being *taught* and how well students are *learning*. With three or four essential questions on the wall, frequently referred to by the teacher, any student, if asked, should be able to articulate the big picture of what the class is learning.

Lessons: Where the Rubber Meets the Road

Clearly, supervising and supporting unit planning is a high-value use of supervisors' time. Observing lessons (through frequent mini-observations) is equally important, because lessons are the vehicle that delivers all that curriculum planning, constituting 90 percent or more of instruction. But what about lesson plans? Is inspecting them a valuable exercise?

Lesson plans matter. The principal has every reason to expect that teachers plan thoughtfully for every class they teach, aligning instruction with the unit plan and end-of-year standards. But I have serious doubts about the wisdom of a principal requiring teachers to submit lesson plans in advance and spending lots of time going through them.

First of all, a lesson plan can be brilliant on paper and implemented poorly (and vice versa). Second, it's a waste of time critiquing lesson plans based on a unit plan that's poorly thought through or nonexistent—better to work with the team to improve the quality of the unit plan so that high-quality lesson plans will flow from it.

Third, in the same way that an army battle plan rarely survives contact with the enemy, a teacher's lesson plan rarely survives contact with students. What counts on the battlefield is knowing the "commander's intent"—the overall goal of the operation (Heath & Heath, 2007); what counts in the classroom is knowing the essential learning outcomes in the unit plan; having these clearly in mind leads to inventive, intelligent adaptations as conditions change on the ground—and to successful outcomes.

Then there's the sheer number of lesson plans. In a school with thirty-five teachers, about seven hundred lessons are taught each week, which means seven hundred lesson plans, which adds up to 24,500 a year. Inspecting them all would be ridiculous micromanagement, not to mention masochistic.

In a school with thirty-five teachers, about seven hundred lessons are taught each week, which means seven hundred lesson plans, which adds up to 24,500 a year.

Finally, inspecting lesson plans involves the supervisor working with one teacher at a time, while nurturing team UbD planning increases collegiality and empowers teachers to take collective responsibility for student learning.

Of course teachers should plan their lessons well, and supervisors should spot-check lesson plans during mini-observations and watch for signs that instruction isn't well planned. Some teachers need help planning good lessons, and this is a high-value activity for instructional coaches and mentor teachers. (The Achievement First lesson checklist in Chapter Five is a good starting point for teachers who don't already have a good template.)

But supervisors' time is best spent working with teacher teams on unit plans and getting into classrooms to see how units are being implemented. In the same school with 24,500 lesson plans just mentioned, grade-level teams might teach six common units per subject in the course of the year. That's a total of only about twenty-five unit plans every six weeks. If the supervisor collaborates with teacher teams on polishing each of those unit plans—and uses mini-observations to look for evidence that unit plans are being skillfully executed—there will be handsome dividends in the quality of teaching and learning.

Test Preparation: Good or Bad

In recent years, a debate has raged on the impact of high-stakes testing on the everyday life of US classrooms. Critics say that "teaching to the test" is ruining the quality of instruction and making schools into sweatshops. Supporters say the tests have raised curriculum expectations and focused much-needed attention on struggling students. Who's right?

As an educator and a parent, I'm convinced that when high-stakes tests are handled well (as I believe they have been in Massachusetts, where my own children went through public schools K–12), they are an engine of school improvement, raising standards, spotlighting inequities, and bringing order out of curriculum chaos.

What about teaching to the test? If low-quality "test-prep" materials and recycled test items are being used to drill and kill the subject matter, that's a problem. But if teachers are using first-rate classroom methods and materials to teach to worthwhile standards that are measured by the tests, that's great. If students who have fallen behind are getting skilled tutoring that boosts their confidence and performance, excellent! If nervous students are given test-taking tips and familiarized with the test format a couple of weeks before testing time, no problem.

How much teaching to the test is going on? We don't have precise data, but one thing is clear: wherever drill-and-kill is happening, it's not good for kids. Bad test prep is like junk food: it can give students a quick burst of energy (short-term test score gains), especially if kids were malnourished (deprived of good teaching and learning), but all too quickly, students get that empty feeling (their achievement sags). Test prep is like junk food if it:

- Bores students and turns them off school (tests, tests, tests all the time)
- Demoralizes teachers, making them feel like they're working in a test-prep factory
- Promotes lazy pedagogy: just assign and correct
- Uses decontextualized passages so kids don't read whole stories and books
- Overuses multiple-choice questions in daily classroom teaching
- Drills lower-level skills and skimps on writing and teaching for understanding
- Focuses on memorizing facts rather than expressing ideas in an authentic voice

Bad test prep is like junk food: it can give students a quick burst of energy (short-term test score gains), especially if kids were malnourished (deprived of good teaching and learning), but all too quickly, students get that empty feeling (their achievement sags).

Why would any self-respecting educator indulge in the junky kind of test prep? Why are some schools wasting precious time and resources that could be devoted to high-quality teaching and materials? Why is it even necessary to have a parallel test-prep curriculum to teach kids what they should cover in their regular classes?

First, most districts' learning expectations contain far more material than it's humanly possible to teach. Researcher Robert Marzano (2003) calculated that it would take roughly 15,500 hours to teach the average K–12 curriculum—and there are only about nine thousand hours of classroom learning time available from kindergarten through high school. Teachers can only cover a portion of the total curriculum—and the tests can only assess a portion. For students to do well, the portion that's taught needs to overlap with the portion that's tested. Test prep seems like the easiest way to make this happen.

Second, some school districts have not taken the obvious step of fully aligning their curriculum with test expectations. In addition, textbooks written for a national market are not perfectly aligned with the curriculum of individual states, and marching chapter by chapter through the book (which some teachers still do) can leave big gaps. Test prep thrives on this kind of misalignment. In the years ahead, clear state standards should take care of a lot of these alignment problems.

Third, even when school districts have aligned with the standards, some principals and teachers aren't confident that following the curriculum on a day-to-day basis will produce good test scores. They fall prey to the misconception that students will score high only if they are fed a steady diet of worksheets with cloned test questions.

Fourth, there's a lot of talk about how awful the tests are. In states that are using off-the-shelf tests or tests that don't include writing and higher-order thinking, this distaste is understandable. Test prep can be seen as a way to game the system and beat the test.

Finally, educators' anxiety about high-stakes tests can create a kind of group panic attack: *if we don't take desperate measures, our kids will fail! Gotta have some test prep—even if it displaces good teaching.* Superintendents, principals, and teachers have been known to succumb to this kind of thinking and make unwise curriculum choices.

These are the reasons why junky test prep has found its way into all too many classrooms and after-school programs. Opponents of high-stakes testing pounce on this. They argue that low-level "drill-and-kill" teaching is an inevitable by-product of such tests. They say that when a state spells out what should be taught and holds everyone accountable with tests, it basically dictates how it should be taught—poorly. Their solution? Get rid of the tests!

But dumping high-stakes tests would slow the positive momentum of education reform. Scary testing might seem like a strange way to help children, but state-level assessments with some consequences attached to them are the only way that has yet been discovered to get schools to focus their curriculum and take responsibility for teaching all students to high standards.

True, teachers have less freedom in what they teach, and some have had to give up beloved (sometimes excellent) curriculum units that didn't fit the standards. But something had to be done to forge a more-coherent K–12 curriculum sequence, eliminate overlap and fill some gaps, and make the high school diploma a more meaningful document. There is a strong equity dimension to this: the students who suffer most from an individualistic, chaotic curriculum and a lack of clear standards are the least advantaged. If standards are handled well, they can be a powerful lever for closing the proficiency gap.

A caution: interim assessments don't need to be clones of external tests. To be sure, students should be familiar and comfortable with the look and feel of high-stakes tests. When the big day arrives and they open up their test, their reaction should be, *This is challenging stuff, but it's what we've been learning, I'm used to answering questions like these, and I can handle it.*

But interim assessments can also take the form of performance tasks, essays, and presentations. Members of a track team who specialize in sprints don't prepare for the hundred-meter dash by doing nothing but hundred-meter dashes. They run a variety of distances, do weight training, and eat a balanced diet. In the same way, students should be getting a variety of instructional and assessment approaches. This will produce the best possible performance on the narrower bandwidth of actual tests—and prepare them for success in high school, college, and beyond.

Critics of high-stakes state testing complain that it narrows the curriculum. But as noted previously, US K–12 curriculum expectations are so extensive that it would take twenty-two years of schooling to cover them. An intelligent paring down of standards is a good thing—unless it means the elimination of art, music, physical education, and high-quality field trips. Students need a balanced curriculum to succeed in the twenty-first century; this is especially important for students who enter school with disadvantages.

Is it right for schools to "teach to the test"? If that means "test prep"—forcing students to do pages and pages of sample test items week after week—the answer is no; that's educational malpractice. If "teach to the test" means aligning the curriculum to standards and paying particular attention to the standards that are tested, I see no problem—provided the standards are robust, the tests are high quality, and teachers use good pedagogy to prepare their students.

Teachers *don't have to teach badly* to raise test scores. Tests dictate the *what*, not the *how-to*, of teaching. The research is clear that what produces well-educated graduates and high test scores is good teaching. Junky test prep is a shortcut that doesn't work. Students need the real thing—challenging subject matter; engaging, hands-on classroom activities; and energized teachers who know their subject and make it exciting and relevant.

Teachers don't have to teach badly to raise test scores.

Having students do a lot of writing is especially important. Doug Reeves, a national expert on standards, has found that writing develops the kind of higher-order thinking and understanding that translates directly into better performance on all kinds of tests—including those with multiple-choice questions (2000).

Anti-testers do have a point: the pressure of high-stakes testing can lead some educators to make unwise curriculum choices. But with a little prodding, these educators will come to their senses and do the right thing. If you are a school administrator with your pen poised to sign a requisition for test-prep materials, use the checklist in this section to determine the level of junkiness. If it's high, just say no!

If you are a teacher, student, parent, or community leader and you see junky test prep in your school, speak up! It's not good for your school—and it's not going to produce high test scores in the long run.

The path to good teaching and really solid achievement is clear. Schools need to accept the reality of high-stakes tests—and work to improve the quality of those tests where they fall short. They need to align their grade-by-grade curriculum with test expectations, reducing what's required of teachers to a manageable amount. They need to ensure that 99 percent of classroom time is devoted to high-quality, aligned instruction with no cheesy test prep. They need to put a premium on creative, involving, relevant pedagogy and teacher teamwork, trusting that excellent teaching is the best way to get and sustain high scores—even on tests that are not perfect. And they need to provide teachers with the support, training, and materials to do the job.

Let's swear off the junk food of test prep. Let's give our children the kind of education that

Let's swear off the junk food of test prep.

will prepare them for any kind of test—including the real world. Let's ensure that high test scores mean that students are truly proficient, not just good test-takers. And let's give them a classroom curriculum that will nourish them for years to come. They deserve no less.

Taking Stock

In schools that have clear end-of-year outcomes, curriculum calendars, a growing number of backwards-designed units, and a sharp focus on how all this comes together in each individual lesson, teachers are focused on the most important issues: high expectations; the knowledge, skills, and understandings students must acquire; predictable misunderstandings; and how learning will be assessed.

When supervisors do mini-observations with this broader perspective in mind, they have far greater insight and significantly enhance their supervisory power. Their follow-up conversations (and year-end evaluations) are more efficient and helpful, and they are more effective cross-pollinators as they move from class to class and grade to grade.

Questions to Consider

- *In your school, how often are teachers' lesson plans reviewed? Unit plans?*
- *Are essential questions for units displayed in classrooms?*
- *How much pressure do teachers feel to use test prep materials?*

12

Should Supervisors Get Involved During Mini-Observations?

Withholding feedback is choosing comfort over growth.
—Adam Grant

As more schools shift from traditional, full-lesson teacher evaluations to short, frequent, unannounced classroom visits, an interesting question comes up: Should supervisors get involved during a lesson if they see an opportunity to improve or affirm teaching? On-the-spot interventions rarely happen during formal evaluations because of the need to take detailed notes. But during a mini-observation, supervisors might be inclined to speak up if:

- They want to draw attention to something particularly praiseworthy.
- They have an interesting idea or anecdote that will enrich the lesson.
- The teacher is missing an opportunity to make an important point.
- Some students seem confused and the teacher isn't noticing.
- The teacher makes a consequential error.
- A student's behavior is seriously disrupting the lesson.

This chapter has been adapted from Marshall, K. (2015). Should supervisors intervene during classroom visits? *Kappan* (October), 8–13.

Here are some examples of supervisors getting involved during a lesson, and one who's trying to decide whether to do so:

- A middle-school US history teacher finishes explaining a Civil War event and asks, "Is everyone with me?" One student says, "Yes," and the teacher takes this as representative of the whole class and starts to move on. But the principal at the back of the room senses that many students lack some essential prior knowledge. He asks the teacher, "Do you mind if I ask your students a couple of questions?" The teacher nods (she has no choice), and in a few minutes, the principal is able to fill in the gaps so students will understand the rest of the lesson. The teacher sees her mistake and is able to improve the remaining classes she teaches that morning.

- A Massachusetts principal is unable to contain herself as she watches a math teacher mixing up perimeter and area and corrects it on the spot. The principal believes her intervention didn't embarrass the teacher.

- A New York City principal blurts out during a class, "There's a spelling mistake on the board." The principal is able to frame it as a challenge to students, who may have thought the teacher misspelled the word intentionally to see if they were paying attention.

- In a New York City high school history class, the teacher is explaining latitude and longitude with a flat map and an observer exclaims, "Get the globe!" Startled and clearly annoyed, the teacher complies.

- An eighth-grade history class is discussing Martin Luther King Jr.'s "I Have a Dream" speech, and an observer realizes that the teacher isn't mentioning one of the most important things about the speech: that King, encouraged by Mahalia Jackson to his left *("Tell them about the dream, Martin, tell them about the dream!")*, put aside his prepared text and ad-libbed the last and most acclaimed part of the speech. The observer really wants to jump in and describe this intriguing fact. Should he?

Advocates of "real-time coaching" believe there are lots of teachable moments like these and that praising or redirecting a teacher on the spot is a powerful way to bring about short- and long-term improvements. A leadership coach I know likens it to coaching in professional baseball, football, and basketball games. During-class coaching has become the go-to supervisory model in some schools, especially charters, with supervisors routinely jumping in during classroom visits and sometimes taking over the class to model a more-effective approach.

A few years ago, a district in Arizona took the idea a bit further. Three supervisors—the principal, assistant principal, and an instructional coach—visited classrooms together, observed for five to seven minutes, and then asked the teacher to pause the lesson. The coach kept an eye on the class while the administrators took the teacher out into the corridor for immediate feedback. When they returned, the coach demonstrated with students how that lesson segment should have been taught.

Whenever I describe this practice to groups of educators, I hear gasps and lots of disapproval. Won't correcting teachers during a lesson undermine their authority and embarrass them in front of students? Won't interruptions throw teachers off stride and compromise the lessons they've planned? Won't students be distracted from curriculum content as they tune in on interesting adult dynamics?

In addition, when visitors get involved, doesn't that change what they're observing, producing less-accurate snapshots of everyday instruction? (In physics, this is called the Hawthorne effect—the instrument of measurement changes what's being measured.) Finally, isn't it possible for teachers to game the process, nimbly showcasing what they know the supervisor is looking for—turn and talk, check for understanding, asking higher-order questions—but not changing the way they teach day to day?

The strong consensus among educators I work with, as shown by this recent poll, is that unless safety is an issue, supervisors should zip their lips and give feedback afterward. In fact, this is the way most athletic coaches work with their players, talking privately to the pitcher on the mound or quarterback on the sidelines (quarterbacks' radio link to the coach is turned off during play action).

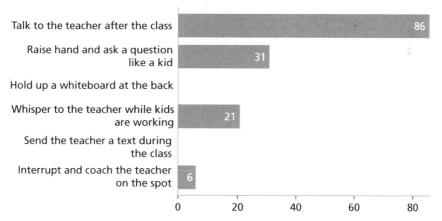

If students seem confused during a lesson, should the supervisor ...

Talk to the teacher after the class	86
Raise hand and ask a question like a kid	31
Hold up a whiteboard at the back	
Whisper to the teacher while kids are working	21
Send the teacher a text during the class	
Interrupt and coach the teacher on the spot	6

A former Alaska principal and superintendent summed up his concerns: "Improving adult practice is complex and requires lots of trust, time, and care. I fear advocates of real-time coaching are looking for a silver bullet, an easy way." A veteran Ohio teacher was more passionate: "To praise or correct a teacher in front of students drives a stake into whatever relationship the teacher and the students have. Even if it's praise, it's demeaning."

*"Improving adult prac-
tice is complex and
requires lots of trust, time,
and care."*

Advocates of real-time coaching disagree. *Seize the moment*, they say. When supervisors wait until the post-observation conference, feedback loses its immediacy and won't have nearly as much effect. Besides, post-observation conferences are cumbersome and bedeviled by checklists and rubrics, and people are so busy that several days might pass before they meet, if they meet at all. Supervisors need to help teachers improve their practice *now*, when the situation is fresh in their minds.

This is especially important, they say, with novice teachers whose undeveloped skills in classroom management and content mastery urgently need to get better. One observer in New York City said that critics of classroom interventions are too concerned with teachers' feelings and should be focusing on the students whose education is being compromised by ineffective teaching.

Of course, real-time coaching can be done in less-intrusive ways. A supervisor can whisper in the teacher's ear while students are doing group work (*This would be a great time to mention that essential question on the wall*), slip the teacher a note (*The kids over by the window are not engaged*), gesture unobtrusively at a student who is having difficulty (*You might want to come over and help her*), or quietly intervene with a noncompliant student. (A Massachusetts principal described how she beckoned a surly adolescent to step out, learned he'd been up late the night before at a family wedding, and told him to pull up his pants, fix his face, and do his best back in the classroom.)

Another approach (this was an option in the poll) is for the supervisor to raise a hand like a student, get called on, and ask a question that subtly redirects the teacher (*Maybe it's just me, but I didn't get that; can you please go over it again?*). A supervisor can also text the teacher from the back of the room (*Time to check for understanding*) or even talk quietly into a cellphone, coaching the teacher via a Bluetooth earpiece. This is akin to an on-air newscaster getting direction from a producer that the TV audience can't hear.

But, even using these kinder and gentler approaches, is real-time coaching a good idea? In the absence of good research, school leaders need to think this one through. Let's start at the thirty-thousand-foot level: What is the ultimate goal of supervision and evaluation? More good teaching in more classrooms more of the time. How can we best accomplish this? Because even the most energetic supervisors observe teachers less than 1 percent of teaching time, we need to create intrinsic motivation in teachers to use effective practices the rest of the time. How can school leaders optimize day-to-day instruction and instill a continuous-improvement mindset for those who don't already have it? Here are some possibilities, in roughly descending order of effect:

- Hiring and retaining teachers with an inner drive to get good results, a willingness to constantly reflect, and a growth mindset about improving practice

- Orchestrating teacher teamwork that produces high-quality unit and lesson plans and fosters ongoing reflection about content and process

- Ensuring that teacher teams and instructional coaches regularly look at assessments and student work, identify best practices, and constantly improve instruction

- Creating a professional culture in which teachers visit each other's classes and engage in nondefensive discussions about what's working and what isn't

- Providing helpful professional development

- Conducting official evaluations

Why is teacher evaluation ranked last? Because research tells us that, with a few exceptions, traditional evaluations have not played an important role in improving teaching and learning. Alas, administrators' time is often consumed by documentation, evaluation, and compliance—and the myriad other things they need to do to keep their schools running smoothly.

Because even the most energetic supervisors observe teachers less than 1 percent of teaching time, we need to create intrinsic motivation in teachers to use effective practices the rest of the time.

Real-time teacher coaching is a well-intentioned attempt to improve this dismal record. The idea is that when supervisors correct less-than-effective practices on the spot (and praise what's working well), the feedback is much more likely to stick in teachers' minds. On-the-spot interventions are also very appealing to busy administrators because they take less time. Teachers and administrators are busy and anything that gets feedback to teachers more quickly is a boon.

But might real-time coaching be a false efficiency? There are several reasons to doubt its effectiveness as a supervisory tool.

First, scoping out what's going on in a classroom during a visit is complex and demanding work, and coming up with wise and helpful feedback on the spot is a high bar. Supervisors enter with some knowledge of the teacher, the students, and the curriculum, but there's a lot they don't know about a particular lesson. They need to watch and listen carefully, examine what's on the board or screen, look over students' shoulders to understand the instructional task, check in with one or two students (*What are you learning today?*) when the teacher is not interacting with the whole class, and jot some notes to remember key points and quotes. To decide on the best coaching points usually takes a few minutes of reflection, preferably in a quiet place outside the classroom. Shooting from the hip during the class seriously risks getting it wrong and undermining the kind of trust that's essential for teachers to be receptive to the input.

Second, supervisors who speak up during classes tend to focus on classroom management problems and teachers' tactical moves and not deeper curriculum and pedagogical issues. During short classroom observations, visitors can only guess at what occurred before and after the visit and might not understand the broader curriculum goals or a teacher's on-the-fly adaptations. Having access to unit and lesson plans is helpful, but the best way to get missing information is to have a private chat with the teacher, who can fill in important contextual information (why that girl was upset; why it seemed wise to depart from the lesson plan; how the discussion changed after you left; why I'm having a bad day). Hearing from the teacher greatly improves the quality and credibility of the supervisor's feedback, but it's simply impossible to delve into classroom dynamics, student work, and effective practices during an actual lesson.

Third, real-time coaching can come across as a power trip by administrators: *Not only can I walk into your classroom any time, but I will interrupt your teaching whenever I feel like it.* From the teacher's point of view, especially for those who are used to being left alone, supervisors' interjections might seem annoying, disrespectful, and 99 percent about administrative convenience. A former principal and superintendent told me that if a supervisor had acted this way early in his teaching career, it would have driven him out of the profession.

Fourth, teachers will find observations more stressful if there's always the possibility of being interrupted. Administrators are never going to be invisible during classroom visits—students and teachers are well aware of their presence—but the dynamic is heightened if supervisors frequently jump in.

Finally, let's be frank, some principals, assistant principals, and department heads don't have a good eye for instruction, lack an understanding of the essentials of good pedagogy, are opinionated about one best way to teach, and lack the skill set needed to have helpful feedback conversations with teachers. In the hands of supervisors like these, real-time coaching can do serious damage to teaching and learning, not to mention faculty morale. Superintendents, heads of school, and their designees need to be aware of problem supervisors and immediately address their shortcomings. How? By regularly (at least once a month) making brief classroom visits with school-based administrators, debriefing, observing or role-playing feedback conversations with teachers, and replacing administrators who are persistently ineffective in this vital part of their jobs.

Superintendents, heads of school, and their designees need to be aware of problem supervisors and immediately address their shortcomings.

The Importance of Timing

But what about the time lag and the bureaucratic nature of post-observation conferences? Doesn't that provide a compelling rationale for real-time coaching? Not if supervisors shift to mini-observations and much shorter debrief conversations and strive to do them within twenty-four hours of each classroom visit. Ten minutes is usually plenty of time for a high-quality feedback chat, provided the supervisor has thought through a few key points, planned how to launch the conversation (see the four quadrants approach described in Chapter Six), and uses language that makes it a genuine conversation about teaching and learning: *Tell me a little about your thinking at that moment. How did the lesson turn out? What did you hope I would notice? Let's look at some of the kids' work.*

Coaching suggestions are much more likely to be heard and acted on if the teacher has a chance to explain the context and the bigger picture in a face-to- face conversation. These conversations might include strong redirection (*I didn't hear a single higher-order thinking question while I was there*), and supervisors can learn a great deal from how teachers react to criticisms and reflect on their work. In short, high-quality debriefs are golden opportunities to get inside teachers' heads and strengthen instruction.

Of course, having this kind of conversation will be difficult if supervisors have too many teachers to evaluate and are required to use a time-consuming evaluation process, which can take four hours or more for one teacher. Superintendents and heads of school need to take steps so that each supervisor has a manageable caseload and is liberated from the notoriously ineffective traditional evaluation process. Then school administrators can give their full attention to a couple of short, frequent, unannounced visits a day, followed by high-quality, follow-up conversations and brief narrative documentation.

Proponents of real-time coaching tend to agree on a manageable span of control and dumping the traditional evaluation process, but they continue to press their point about getting involved during lessons. Some successful charter leaders say real-time coaching is a key factor in high student achievement. It works, they contend, because teachers know what the deal is up front (*this is the way we do things in our school*), students see it as a model of adults learning together (*my principal is a teacher, and my teacher is a learner*), and trusting professional relationships have been established.

I'm skeptical. Isn't it possible that successful schools using real-time coaching are getting high test scores *in spite of* this practice, not because of it? That in their impatience to fix problems in the moment, practitioners of real-time coaching are turning teachers off, undermining trust, and missing out on post-lesson coaching conversations that can have much greater impact? That real-time coaching is contributing to teacher attrition, one of the biggest problems in struggling high-poverty schools—and in many other schools in the wake of the pandemic?

Another Way

The bottom line: supervisors need to exercise great restraint during classroom visits. If I were still a principal, here's what I would explain to teachers and work hard to implement:

- I'll visit each classroom at least once a month so that all teachers receive a timely, coherent stream of support, affirmation, and helpful feedback throughout the year.

- During classroom visits, I'll be as unobtrusive as possible, observe carefully, check in with students, jot a few handwritten notes, and zero in on the most important affirmations and one possible suggestion.

- I'll interrupt instruction only in emergencies and, even then, avoid undermining you with your students.

- Very occasionally, I might communicate with a you via a note or whispered suggestion.

- I'll strive to have a brief face-to-face conversation after a visit—ideally in your classroom when students aren't there and within 24 hours—listen carefully to your point of view, make a coaching point if appropriate, and follow up promptly with a brief narrative summary.

- I'll sometimes take videos of classroom interactions (with your prior agreement) so we can dissect classroom dynamics afterward.

- My feedback will not involve a checklist or rubric scoring, which I've found undermines a good coaching dynamic.

- I'll encourage you to invite me in to take part in discussions, read to students, or share my own experiences and insights on the curriculum, but such visits will be separate from my short observations.

- I'll mesh the classroom observation process with teams' curriculum unit planning, analysis of assessments and student work, and what students have to say about their teachers in twice-a-year surveys.

When it comes to affirming and improving teaching, there are no shortcuts. With real-time coaching, the skill threshold is too demanding, the risks of being superficial or getting it wrong too high, the probability of upsetting and alienating teachers too great, and the chances of not having deeper conversations about teaching and learning too real.

When it comes to affirming and improving teaching, there are no shortcuts.

The good news is that supervisors can avoid these pitfalls by taking a little more time, reflecting a little more carefully, and engaging teachers in face-to-face coaching after each observation. Fitting in these conversations is challenging, and they are sometimes stressful on both sides, but this is the core work of supervisors. Doing it well will result in—let's hear that again—more good teaching in more classrooms more of the time.

Questions to Consider

- *When, if ever, do you think it's appropriate for supervisors to get involved during visits?*
- *What has been your experience with this as a teacher?*
- *What policy would you implement as a principal?*

13 | Time Management

Fitting It All In

You'll never get into classrooms if you wait until there's nothing else to do; you'll always have unfinished tasks that compete with the work of visiting classrooms and talking with teachers. If you don't plan ahead, and instead decide moment by moment what most deserves your time and attention, you'll naturally gravitate to low-priority, high-urgency tasks.

—Justin Baeder

How can a dedicated school leader work really hard and fail to get significant gains in student achievement? The answer is obvious: by spending too much time doing the wrong things and not enough time doing the right things. That sounds pretty straightforward—but in my fifteen years as a principal, I wasn't clear enough about the "right things" and often fell victim to HSPS—hyperactive superficial principal syndrome. As a result, I didn't give enough of the right kind of support to teachers, and our students didn't do nearly as well as they could have.

Over the years, I've come at the time management challenge in three ways. The first was working *longer and harder*—finding ways to fit more into each day and increasing stamina and endurance. The second was working *smarter*—learning time-management tricks and becoming more efficient. The third was working *deeper*—trying to figure out the practices that were most likely to get results.

By the end of my principalship, I was a lot more efficient in how I managed my time, was zeroing in on the practices that would move student achievement. And I was exhausted. There was clearly a need for a better balance among these three ways of working! A frazzled, swamped

237

A frazzled, swamped principal won't lead effectively, get into classrooms, and provide the right kind of support to teachers.

principal won't lead effectively, get into classrooms, and provide the right kind of support to teachers.

Don't get me wrong—our school made solid progress. But it was only after I left the Mather, immersed myself in the research, and watched a variety of school leaders in action that I developed a more balanced understanding of instructional time management. This chapter presents detailed suggestions in three broad areas for working *deep* and *smart*—without burning out:

Set big-picture goals and stay focused:

- Decide on the "big rocks" for each year.
- Plan for the year, month, week, and day.
- Monitor progress.

Continuously improve teaching and learning:

- Clarify curriculum and discipline expectations.
- Orchestrate and support teams meetings and professional development.
- Frequently visit classrooms and give feedback.

Hone priority management skills:

- Write it down, prioritize, and follow up.
- Delegate to competent people.
- Minimize time-wasting crises and activities.
- Take care of yourself.

These align with an instructional time management rubric I've developed. At the end of each section, I've inserted the matching rubric line and invite you to self-assess and think about areas of strength and goals for improvement.

Set Big-Picture Goals and Stay Focused

Decide on the "Big Rocks" for Each Year

You're probably familiar with the big rocks story, a classic in time management workshops. A speaker puts three big rocks into a mason jar and asks if it's full.

Yes, say some in the audience, but she pours gravel between the big rocks. Is it full now? The audience is catching on and is not surprised that quite a bit of sand fits between the cracks of the big rocks and gravel. Full now? There's room for a gallon of water.

What's the moral of the story? "You can always fit more in!" is the gullible response. No! The moral (especially for beleaguered K–12 school administrators) is to put the big rocks in first. Otherwise your day will be filled with the gravel, sand, and water of a busy school—things that are not the key priorities.

How to decide on the big rocks? At its simplest, strategic planning consists of putting the brutal facts on the table, choosing no more than three major priorities for the year, setting measurable goals, and deciding who's responsible for each and a timeline for action.

In terms of teacher supervision, coaching, and evaluation, a supervisor's personal big rocks might include a numerical goal for mini-observations per day or week, planned visits to teacher teams, and certain areas of the curriculum that need particular attention. Here's the rubric line for focus:

Focus	I have a laser-like focus on student achievement and my strategic plan for the year.	I keep student achievement and my strategic plan in mind every day.	I periodically remind myself of my strategic plan and the goal of student achievement.	Each day is driven by events, not by my long-term goals.

Plan for the Year, Month, Week, and Day

David Allen's book *Getting Things Done* is a classic for leaders in all arenas. Allen advocates writing down a master to-do list for both professional and personal domains (a "total life reminder system" reduces stress, he says), sorting and prioritizing the list, and weekly review of progress (a "critical success factor"). This is how the year's goals (the Big Rocks) cascade to the week's goals and day-by-day execution.

> *"The key is not to prioritize what's on your schedule but to schedule your priorities."*

Inherent in the work of K–12 supervisors is a constant juggling of the "gravel, sand, and water" of the school day, always fighting to make room for the Big Rocks. Stephen Covey (2004, p. 161) said it well: "The key is not to prioritize what's on your schedule but to schedule your priorities." Covey popularized President Dwight Eisenhower's 1954 observation (that urgent problems are often not important and important problems are rarely urgent). The key to being effective is doing the stuff in quadrant 2—what's important but not urgent—for school leaders, which includes relationship building, data tracking, and professional reading.

	Must do right now	Don't have to do right now
Important to student achievement	I	II
Not important to student achievement	III	IV

David Allen acknowledges that there are things we don't like to do and put off (the 1950s cartoon character Pogo Possum coined the phrase, "We have met the enemy and he is us."). Allen's suggestions: analyze why we are avoiding something (perhaps the discomfort of confronting a teacher on a mediocre classroom practice), ask ourselves how we would feel about not doing it (the kids!), deciding on the *next action* (planning the mini-observation and follow-up chat), and pushing ourselves to do it.

Here's the rubric line for planning:

Planning	I have an effective personal planning system for the year, month, week, and day.	I write down a list of what I want to accomplish each week and day.	I come to work with a list of what I want to accomplish that day.	I have a list in my head of what I want to accomplish each day but sometimes lose track.

Monitor Progress

Allocating time for reflection and self-assessment is difficult (another time-management challenge!), but it's essential to getting better. There are a number of ways of tracking progress and thinking about what's working and not working. As a principal, I jotted notes in a personal diary every weekend, kept track of the number of classroom visits I was making, and regularly revisited my goals for the year, asking myself if I was putting my time and energy into the right activities. At the end of each year, I went through my diary and extracted twenty key words that described the most important events of the year. Over my years as principal, it was fascinating to look back and remember the contours of each year.

I also suggest using the principal evaluation rubric in Chapter Fourteen, which parallels the rubric lines included in each section of the current chapter. You might highlight the three strongest areas and the three that most need improvement, develop a strategy for improving in your areas of need, and then (perhaps every three months) score yourself on the rubric again to see if you've made progress. The goal is to have all your ratings at the Effective and Highly Effective levels. If you do, it means you're working smart and working deep, which are the key to getting results.

For supervisors, among the many other demands on their time are: a system for keeping track of mini-observations and follow-up; monitoring the work of teacher teams; and taking note of grade/team trends and progress on student achievement. Perhaps there's a data wall with students' reading levels and math achievement broken down by name and need.

One of the most helpful initiatives for K–12 instruction management is the National SAM Innovation Project (NSIP). Each participating school has a SAM—the school administrative manager—who meets briefly with the principal every day and goes over how they are spending time in three areas: instruction, management, and taking care of themselves. The SAM's job is to nudge the principal to devote more time to instruction—classroom visits, follow-up with teachers, visiting team meetings—less on management, and to take care of themselves. Wow, do I wish I'd had a SAM at the Mather!

Here's the rubric line for monitoring:

Monitoring	I regularly evaluate progress toward my goals and work on continuous improvement.	I periodically review how I am doing on my weekly goals and try to do better.	I try to keep track of how I am doing on my goals.	I occasionally berate myself for not accomplishing my long-range goals.

Continuously Improve Teaching and Learning

Clarify Curriculum and Discipline Expectations

When teachers freelance on curriculum and need to be reminded to teach what their grade level and course is responsible for, that's not a good use of administrators' time. A key supervisory role is making sure every teacher knows what they need to teach—not *how* to teach it, but *what* their role is in the K–12 curriculum sequence—so that students move from grade to grade and course to course with fundamental skills, knowledge, and understandings. Mini-observations are an ideal way to frequently monitor curriculum content and focus on the quality of instruction.

When teachers freelance on curriculum and need to be reminded to teach what their grade level and course is responsible for, that's not a good use of administrators' time.

Discipline expectations are also vital—otherwise administrators' time will be spent dealing with students who should not have been sent to the office. Educators at Centennial High School in Oregon came up with a one-pager clarifying what teachers must deal with in their classrooms and what issues require the involvement of administrators.

Teacher managed

- Excessive talking
- Being off task
- Chewing gum/eating
- Drinking non-alcoholic
- Missing homework
- Unprepared for class
- Name-calling
- PDA
- Passing notes
- Backtalk to adults
- Cheating, plagiarism
- Sleeping
- Shutting down
- Noncompliance
- Minor disobedience, disruptive behavior
- Minor vandalism
- Electronic device

Office managed

- Insubordination
- Fighting
- Vandalism
- Verbal or physical intimidation
- Carrying a weapon
- Making threats
- Gang representation
- Cutting class, repeated tardies
- Theft
- Drug/alcohol violation
- Directed profanity
- Harassment, including sexual
- Security threat/breach
- Passing lewd notes
- Repeated backtalk
- Repeated PDA
- Dress code violation
- Creating a fake pass

Every school should have something like this to maximize the number of discipline issues that are dealt with in classrooms, freeing administrators up to do the big rocks work of visiting classrooms and teacher teams and talking with frontline educators about the heart of the matter—teaching and learning.

Here's the rubric line for expectations:

Expectations	Staff know exactly what is expected of them in terms of class-room instruction and discipline.	Most staff know what is expected in terms of class-room instruction and discipline.	I often have to remind teachers of policies on instruction and discipline.	I am constantly reminding staff to use better procedures for instruction and discipline.

Orchestrate and Support Teams and Professional Development

Meetings are not the most popular part of the work day, but if they are well run and center on teaching and learning, they are a vital part of the enterprise. A key administrator role is setting the right frequency, length, and participant list for these meetings:

- Grade-level and course teams for personal learning community (PLC) work
- Department and subject-area teams for vertical curriculum work
- Leadership team
- Individual check-ins
- All-faculty
- Off-site retreats

"Teaching is a collective effort, and the most powerful predictor of a student's performance in a subject in any given year is what they learned in the previous grade."

The meetings with the most potential to improve teaching and learning are PLCs by grade level and course, analyzing student work and planning follow-up as described in Chapter Eleven. This is where supervisors doing mini-observations have the most important role, bridging the work of teams with the daily work in classrooms. This quote highlights the crucial role of administrators who work across teacher teams:

Teaching is a collective effort, and the most powerful predictor of a student's performance in a subject in any given year is what they learned in the previous grade. What any one teacher or school can achieve with students is critically dependent on the teaching quality of their colleagues. (Pettersson & Briggs, 2019)

For "lonely singleton" teachers—a small high school has only one physics teacher—supervisors should encourage and facilitate getting on regular Zoom calls with other same-subject teachers around the region so PLC work happens even for these potentially isolated teachers.

Here's the rubric line for collaboration:

Collaboration	All key team meetings are scheduled and regularly do high-quality work together.	Key team meetings are scheduled and take place regularly.	Each month I have to schedule key meetings because they are not in people's calendars.	I call grade-level, curriculum, and other meetings when there is a crisis or an immediate need.

Frequently Visit Classrooms and Give Feedback

This whole book is devoted to effective classroom visits, so I won't go into detail here. Suffice it to say that allowing mediocre and ineffective teaching to continue drags down the learning of all students, especially those who enter school with disadvantages. Getting into classrooms and following up is a moral imperative.

Mini-observations take time, but as I've argued, the time is spent much more effectively, with teacher evaluation distributed differently through the school year. Here is a schematic comparison, showing how the traditional system usually involves a large amount of work in the weeks just before the evaluation deadline—last-minute teacher observations and write-ups—whereas with a mini-observation regimen, about the same amount of time is spread through the entire year, with more time allotted for mid-year check-in conferences and end-of-the-year summatives.

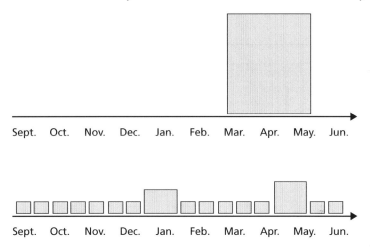

Of course supervisors using the traditional model are walking around their schools from September to June, but those informal glimpses of teaching don't "count," and there are vastly fewer opportunities for coaching and one-on-one PD. With mini-observations, that's going on every week of the year.

Here's the rubric line for observations:

Observations	I visit several classrooms a day and give prompt face-to-face feedback to each teacher.	I get into a few classrooms almost every day and give helpful feedback to teachers.	I try to get into classrooms but am often distracted and rarely give feedback.	I only observe teachers in formal evaluations.

Hone Priority Management Skills

Write It Down, Prioritize, and Follow Up

The four-fold time management challenge for supervisors is (1) remembering and following up on the most important stuff, (2) dealing with email, (3) having the right information at their fingertips, and (d) confronting the tendency to POUT (put off unpleasant tasks). Mastering the flow of information and being organized makes a leader credible and effective.

But even supervisors with brilliant memories can't retain all the information that floods their brains every day. As principal, I quickly learned that when I lost track of things and failed to follow up, my credibility with teachers, students, and parents went out the window—and my blood pressure spiked.

> *As principal, I quickly learned that when I lost track of things and failed to follow up, my credibility with teachers, students, and parents went out the window—and my blood pressure spiked.*

Most rookie supervisors learn an ironclad rule: *you have to write things down.* But fashion can conspire to prevent principals from carrying around the right equipment. Women's pants, shirts, and jackets rarely have pockets designed to hold pens, notepads, cellphones, and smartphones—and a surprising number of men refuse to put a pen and piece of paper in their shirt pockets (when they were teenagers, kids who did this were mercilessly teased).

So what's a supervisor to do? *Get over it!* Buy practical clothes, use your shirt pocket, carry around a clipboard, or use an electronic device clipped to your belt. Without ready access to a pen and paper (or a device with a stylus or a thumb-pad), you'll forget important things and get a reputation as an unreliable flake.

When I first started as principal, I wrote down everything on various pieces of paper and then at the end of the day spent more than an hour unpacking my lists (it was sometimes difficult to read my own handwriting in notes I'd jotted on the fly). I finally developed a system of keeping several 5×3 note cards in my shirt pocket and writing incoming information on one of several designated cards—one for immediate action items, one for email I needed to send that afternoon, one for staff memo ideas, one for parent letter ideas. At the back of my slim stack I kept a few blank cards for random ideas.

This system saved an hour a day because everything was already sorted: when I sat down to do email, all the reminders were on one card; when I wrote the staff memo, all the ideas I needed to remember were right there on one card. Same with the parent letter. Miscellaneous ideas jotted on the blank cards (for example, a quote that I could use at the next year's opening staff meeting or an idea for a different bell schedule) could be popped straight into files in my office and when I needed information on that area, everything would be in one place. Now I might use a digital product like Evernote for this presorting process, although I do like 5×3 cards.

One of the shibboleths of time management is that you should handle every piece of paper only once. This might work for people in high-level government and business positions with adequate support staff, but it absolutely won't work for school leaders. Supervisors who follow this rule will never leave their desks!

So what happens to all those notes and pink phone messages and US mail and bits of *stuff* that come in during the day, not to mention the email and social media? How can a supervisor be a *people person*, not a paper-pusher, in the heart of the school day? My approach was to quickly scan the contents of my in-basket several times a day and use a fifteen-second rule: if an item couldn't be signed, delegated, or thrown away within fifteen seconds, it went onto my after-hours pile.

How can a supervisor be a people person, not a paper-pusher, in the heart of the school day?

In the late afternoon, when things quieted down, I began to make my way through this material, and what didn't get finished, I took home—and what couldn't be finished in the evening went to the weekend pile (along the way, I ditched the less important stuff).

Another useful time-management tool is sorting incoming items into "bins"—conceptual categories—and getting them off the mental desk and onto an organized list or into someone else's hands as quickly as possible. Like my presorted 5×3 pocket cards, bins help make sense of information and keep me sane. Here are some bins for sorting incoming stuff:

- An individual email
- A group email
- A text, tweet, or Facebook post
- A paper note in a mailbox
- A PA announcement in the morning
- A mini-lecture at a student assembly
- For the staff bulletin
- For the weekly parent newsletter
- For a face-to-face conversation
- For a visit to a particular classroom
- For a faculty meeting
- For a grade-level team meeting
- For a planned staff retreat
- For a team meeting

- For the leadership team
- For the assistant principal
- For the secretary
- For the counselor
- For the late-afternoon paperwork pile
- For next year's beginning-of-the-year staff meeting
- For the next Survey Monkey staff questionnaire

There are two other categories: politely say no and drop everything and do now.

Mentally (and physically) sorting hundreds of incoming bits of information into these bins is helpful to clearing your desk, getting other people helping you out, and being able to get your hands on the right information at the right time.

A regular staff memo—weekly seems to be most schools' rhythm—is an exceptionally valuable tool. It's a convenient bin for all sorts of information that the leadership team wants to pass along to colleagues, from the mundane to the inspirational: reminders of paperwork deadlines, upcoming fire drills, welcoming new staff members and bidding farewell to those who depart, recognizing colleagues for above-and-beyond contributions, staff and student birthdays (this was one of my trademarks as principal), lost items, professional development (PD) opportunities, positive stories about teachers and students, asking for reactions to ideas, best practices and interesting research findings, good quotes, and reinforcement of the school's vision and mission.

> *A regular staff memo— weekly seems to be most schools' rhythm—is an exceptionally valuable tool.*

A brief, well-written memo gives everyone the same information at the same time, squashes rumors, deals with a lot of routine matters without taking up precious time in face-to-face meetings, and is an opportunity to bind the community together. In the *Mather Memo* that I published throughout my principalship, I regularly shared cartoons with an educational theme, bringing a smile to many of my colleagues' faces. Even serious leaders need to lighten up occasionally!

Email is the next challenge. Most administrators are flooded with it 24/7—more than a hundred a day. Here's a recent poll on time management, with email the most commonly cited challenge:

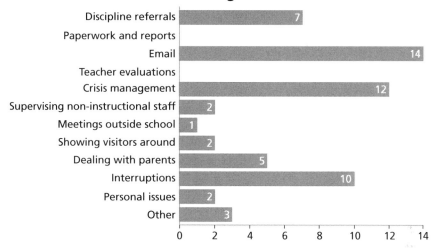

Your top THREE time management challenges?

There's a strong tendency to work on email during the day to keep it from building up, but time management gurus are unanimous in saying that this is a mistake. Why?

- Dealing with email in dribs and drabs is inefficient because we put aside messages that require time and thought and end up reading and thinking about them twice. Email should be tackled when there's time to concentrate and deal decisively and thoroughly with all of it—that is, late afternoon, evening, or early morning.

- Constant interruptions keep leaders from focusing on the people, issues, and projects that matter. Psychologists have found that electronic distractions undermine concentration, high-level thinking, and retention (Begley, 2009).

- Checking email (especially checking a hand-held device) is annoying—even rude—to the people you're talking with; it makes them feel they are less important than this anonymous person who has commandeered your attention.

- It's much more satisfying and affirming to read and respond to a tranche of email in the late afternoon than to read messages one or two at a time.

So here's how I suggest dealing with email:

- Turn off the chime or beep or vibration that announces the arrival of new email. An email message is not like an incoming phone call; the beauty of email is that it's *asynchronous*; twenty-four hours is a widely accepted response time.

- Schedule a couple of thirty-minute blocks (perhaps early morning and late afternoon) to do email in concentrated, efficient bursts. It's amazing how quickly we can make our way through fifty or more emails when we have the time to really focus.

- Superiors and colleagues should not expect an immediate response to an email during the school day. An automatic reply message can say something like this: "I check email each weekday afternoon after 3:00 p.m. If your message is urgent, please call me on my cell phone at XXX-XXX-XXXX." If I were a superintendent and one of my principals responded to my email in the middle of the school day, I would be concerned. *Why are you on your computer? You should be in classrooms and team meetings!*

> *Superiors and colleagues should not expect an immediate response to an email during the school day.*

All right, so you've established an efficient system for writing things down and relegating paperwork and email to blocks of times outside the heart of the school day. It's still possible to drop the ball on important matters. Why? POUT.

We all have things we hate to do—and are quite creative at putting them off. Mine were financial planning and notes from upset people; I dreaded dealing with them and would handle any number of easier, lower-priority tasks before finally addressing them, sometimes days later. Principals I know confess to putting off teacher evaluations, the school improvement plan, scheduling, parent communication, or filing.

How to deal with POUT? Identify your demons and develop a strategy to deal with them in a timely manner. Eric Dawson, the head of Peace Games, hated working on the budget, so when it was time to finally do the dirty deed, he put on a special hat so everyone in the office knew to leave him alone. Another approach: "Do the worst first."

Filing away paperwork is a chore many people avoid as long as possible. When paper and emails build up—on our desks or computers—we can't find important information when we need it, sometimes with dire consequences. In my time as a principal, my pile built up inexorably, and every month or so, I would come in on a Saturday morning, put on some music, and get it done. It was actually very satisfying, and I reaped the reward every time I was able to quickly put my hands on the items I really needed.

On the question of whether to take work home, there are two distinct styles among supervisors I know. Some like to stay late at school, finish off as much as possible, go home in the early evening, and relax. Others prefer to go home in the late afternoon, take a break (exercise, watch some TV or other entertainment, spend time with family), and then do another two or three hours of late-evening work at home. It's six of one, half a dozen of the other. The bottom line is getting the really important stuff done every day—and having a life.

Here's the rubric line for follow-up:

Follow-Up	I have a fool-proof system for writing things down, prioritizing, and following up.	I almost always write important things down and follow up on the most critical ones.	I try to write things down but am swamped by events and sometimes don't follow up.	I trust my memory to retain important tasks, but I sometimes forget and drop the ball.

Delegate to Competent People

Some supervisors have a strong urge to do everything themselves and are impatient when others don't do things just right. This tendency needs to be curbed! The reality is that school leaders can't inspire every child, observe every classroom, scrutinize every lesson plan, plan every unit, look through every student's portfolio, take out every splinter, analyze the results of every test, lead every training workshop, and facilitate every team meeting.

Far from it! Given the impossible number of academic challenges and the even more overwhelming number of operational demands, they must empower colleagues to do the bulk of this work—otherwise, they will fall victim to HSPS and preside over a fragmented staff, low morale, and disappointing student achievement.

The key to long-range sanity and effectiveness is hiring good people, nurturing their talents, staying involved with their work—and refraining from micromanagement. Colleagues' competence is always an issue; my favorite cartoon on time management shows a boss saying to a subordinate: "Tell you what—I won't micromanage if you don't macro-mess up." For principals who have taken over schools with less-than-stellar staff members or have made hiring mistakes, it might be several years before optimal delegation is possible, but the goals are clear:

- Teachers handling instruction and all but the most serious discipline problems
- Teacher teams planning high-quality curriculum units and using interim assessment data to continuously improve teaching and learning
- Counselors preventing or dealing with students' socio-emotional problems
- Custodians keeping the school clean and safe
- Students taking increasing responsibility for their own behavior and learning
- The principal freed up to orchestrate the whole process and focus relentlessly on the big rocks (while occasionally picking up a piece of paper)

The key to long-range sanity and effectiveness is hiring good people, nurturing their talents, staying involved with their work—and refraining from micromanagement.

Of course, teachers and other staff members can't do their jobs when they are constantly pulled out for PD and other meetings. I'm a big advocate of *time on task* for school staff—on the job with children 95 percent or more of the time. Educators' PD and administrative meetings should not encroach on contact time with students.

The same goes for principals, who need to be in their buildings almost all the time. I believe the only reason for a superintendent to hold an administrative meeting during the school day is to allow principals to observe another school in action and discuss what they've seen. Otherwise, meetings should be after hours.

Delegation is essential to good time management, but there are certain things that principals should do themselves. Among those are being out front to greet students as they enter school in the morning, personally wishing them well as they go home, being in the cafeteria during a portion of lunchtime, and attending key student and community events. In each of these situations, the principal's presence has great symbolic value, and they can also use these occasions to take the pulse of the school and be available for informal chats with students and staff members. Visibility and accessibility really matter.

Delegation is essential to good time management, but there are certain things that principals should do themselves.

It's also important that staff members know they have permission to tell the principal things that won't necessarily be pleasant to hear. Some of the worst management failures (the Space Shuttle *Challenger* disaster, for example) occur when leaders wall themselves off from honest feedback.

Here's the rubric line for delegation:

Delegation	I have highly competent people in key roles and delegate maximum responsibility to them.	I give key staff people plenty of responsibility for major items.	I have trouble letting go and delegating a number of key tasks.	I end up doing almost everything myself.

Minimize Time-Wasting Crises and Activities

Kenneth Freeston and Jonathan Costa (1998) believe that school leaders' work falls into three buckets:

- **Value-added work.** These tasks improve teaching and boost achievement for all students (supervising and coaching teachers, discussing curriculum and assessment results, focusing on big rocks).

- **Necessary work.** These tasks aren't sexy but keep the school running (supervising the cafeteria, ordering supplies, doing the budget, school safety).
- **Waste work.** These tasks include redoing things that weren't done right the first time.

The principalship is a constant struggle to maximize value-added work, minimize waste work, and get the necessary work done as efficiently as possible.

It's astonishing how much time a screw-up can consume. One morning in my principalship, I was walking briskly down a corridor to see a teacher, and as I passed a classroom, I thought I heard the teacher say the word *jackass* in front of a roomful of students. I was distracted by my immediate task and didn't focus on what I had just heard, but the next day, there was a huge ruckus on this corridor: a parent had stormed into the school (no locked door and security camera in those days, and no social media to immediately broadcast the incident to the world), bypassed the office, and confronted the teacher outside his classroom for calling her daughter (you guessed it) a jackass.

There ensued a chain of events, starting with my physically separating the teacher and parent and coaxing her down to my office, that consumed about twenty hours of my time. Had I been more attentive and promptly asked the teacher about his comment (his defense was that he told the girl that she was acting *like* a jackass) and phoned the mother immediately, the next few days would have been far more productive. Some crises can't be avoided, but anything we can do to prevent or deflect time-wasting activities saves precious energy that can be devoted to the real work.

There are lots of other ways to cut down on wasted time: meeting agendas and crisp closure with teacher teams and the faculty, multitasking (within reason), and spending very little time in the office—thus avoiding those frequent drop-ins that invariably start with the words, "Got a minute?" A sitting principal is a sitting duck.

> *A sitting principal is a sitting duck.*

It is possible for principals to get so focused on being efficient that they lose sight of how their colleagues see them. In a charming *Phi Delta Kappan* article, principal Autumn Tooms (2003) described how a consultant gently told her that she was charging around the halls of her school in a way that made her staff think she was angry. "Had I told anyone I was angry?" asked Tooms. "No. Had anyone ever asked if I was angry? No. Did it matter that my assistant principal walked the same way when she was on a mission? Again, no." Tooms realized that she needed to modulate her intensity, and she wrote *Stroll* on the back of her office door and on her walkie-talkie. She still got a lot done every day, but her staff no longer thought she was angry at them.

There are also times when immediate action is not the best time-management strategy. This is analogous to the choices the person who washes the dishes in a household has when confronted with a deeply encrusted pan after dinner: scrubbing it for ten minutes, or filling it with water, letting it soak overnight, and then spending thirty seconds finishing the job in the morning. Certain school crises benefit from strategic procrastination; others need to be dealt with immediately. Knowing which is which is always a judgment call.

Certain school crises benefit from strategic procrastination; others need to be dealt with immediately.

And, of course, there are times when an event trumps everything else—a child is seriously injured, a suspicious-looking person enters the school, a staff member's parent dies—and the most important thing is to drop everything and be there. This is perhaps the highest time-management skill: knowing when to shift gears.

Here's the rubric line for prevention:

Prevention	I have effective strategies for preventing or deflecting time-wasting crises and activities.	I am quite good at preventing or deflecting most time-wasting crises and activities.	I try to prevent them, but crises and time-wasters sometimes eat up large chunks of time.	Much of each day is consumed by crises and time-wasting activities.

Take Care of Yourself

School leadership is an intensely demanding job, and there are no shortcuts; even skillful and strategic time managers are exhausted at the end of most weeks. But burned-out supervisors don't serve students and staff members well. Good time management includes knowing one's limits, planning for the long haul, and finding ways to maintain a good personal energy level. Here are a few suggestions:

- Exercise regularly (twenty minutes of aerobic time three times a week or thirty minutes of moderate exercise five times a week is plenty, say most doctors).
- Eat healthy most of the time (breakfast is the most important meal).
- Get enough sleep.
- Carve out regular time for relaxation and fun (one of my nonnegotiables was watching a good movie every Friday evening).

- Build a support system—friends who give you candid feedback, a mentor, and a sensitive and devoted significant other.
- Orchestrate small and large wins; there's nothing like success to produce an extra shot of optimism and energy.

Here's the rubric line for balance:

Balance	I am sharp and fresh because I attend to family, friends, fun, exercise, nutrition, sleep, and vacations.	I am mostly successful in balancing work demands with healthy habits and a life outside school.	I'm not always attending to family, health, exercise, sleep, and vacations.	Work and/or personal life are suffering because I rarely exercise, don't sleep enough, and am in poor health.

Questions to Consider

- *In which three of the rubric areas are you strongest?*
- *In which two do you most need to improve?*
- *What are the most helpful time management insights you've picked up from this chapter?*

14 | The Role of the Superintendent

We're from the central office and we're here to help you.
—Robert Spillane, former Boston and
Fairfax County superintendent

This ironic quip by my late boss (which always got a big laugh) captures the ambivalence of many school-based public-school educators about the district office. When I was Spillane's curriculum director in Boston, my colleagues and I were acutely aware of the resistance that met some of our initiatives in the schools. No wonder! This graphic shows how many different constituencies—state officials, district officials, professional development providers, families, teachers, and others—bring their bright ideas, mandates, agendas, and concerns to school leaders.

This chapter is geared to leaders of public school districts, but many of the points apply to heads of school.

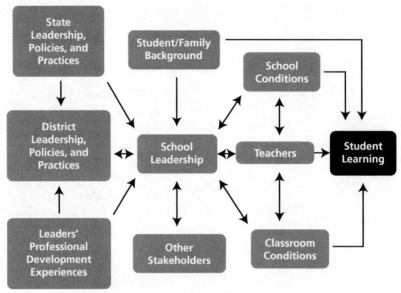

Source: *University of Minnesota. (2010).* Learning from leadership: Investigating the links to improved student learning. *Retrieved from www.cehd.edu/CARE/Leadership/Learning-from -Leadership_Final-Research-Report_July-2010.pdf*

The figure also shows how many layers there are between district leaders and the ultimate goal—student learning. Superintendents have to work *with* school leaders and teachers to get results in classrooms. Trying to bring about change from the central office, I learned, can feel like pushing a string. When school-based administrators and teachers have the same set of beliefs and strategies as the superintendent, it's much more likely that change will happen.

So one of the superintendent's most important jobs is providing clarity, coherence, and direction. That's a big job, and books have been written about it. This chapter will focus on improvement in one key area: teacher evaluation. If a district is to shift from the traditional model to mini-observations, the superintendent plays a key role. Here are the main challenges:

Leader buy-in. Building support among school-based administrators and teacher union leaders, perhaps by doing a book study, bringing in a persuasive advocate, sending people to visit other districts implementing mini-observations, or tapping maverick administrators within the district who are already pioneering the idea.

The contract. Working with the teachers' union to negotiate language that will support mini-observations. This might start with a pilot program in one school with teachers willing to volunteer, and then spread to the whole district.

Teacher support. In the FAQ section of Chapter Fifteen, I recommend a step-by-step meeting in which the principal or an outside consultant works on persuading teachers, many of whom will initially be skeptical of mini-observations.

Staffing. An essential task is getting the supervisor/teacher ratio to no more than one to twenty-five, preferably lower. This might involve adding assistant principals and other staff, but more often it's a question of delegating teacher supervision to all administrators, school- and central-office-based, spreading out responsibility, and eliminating overlaps. There's great variation in this ratio from school to school, as shown by this poll from one of my webinars with school administrators:

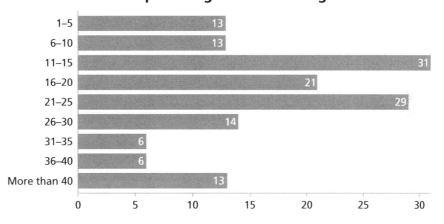

How many teachers are you personally responsible for supervising and evaluating?

Evaluation software. It's very helpful to have an electronic platform like T-EVAL that will simplify the mini-observation process and minimize paperwork. An important feature pioneered by T-EVAL limits the supervisor's summary of debriefs with teachers to no more than one thousand characters (about 160 words)—which can be written in ten to fifteen minutes. Once mini-observations begin, monitoring supervisors' write-ups is important to staying in touch with instructional issues and quality-controlling the process.

Training. Watching, analyzing, and role-playing with short classroom videos is the best way to bring people up to speed on mini-observations. I've had success with the double role-play: supervisors watch a video, brainstorm effective teacher actions and possible coaching points, pair up and do a five-minute role-play, debrief with partners (body language, getting to the point, choice of leverage point, etc.), switch partners and switch roles and role-play with a different person in a different role, debrief again, and discuss key takeaways with the full group.

School visits. The superintendent's boots-on-the-ground participation in mini-observations is a key success factor—making sure, in frequent school visits, that school-based supervisors are getting into classrooms, observing perceptively, and debriefing skillfully. Questions to ask the principal:

- How are your mini-observation visits going? Let's take a look at your log.
- What's your daily target? Are you able to hit that most days?
- When you don't, what's getting in the way? How can I help?
- How are the feedback talks going? How are teachers reacting? Give me a couple of examples from the last week or two.
- How are your follow-up summaries going? Let's take a look at one or two.
- What are you noticing in classrooms? Any building-wide trends?
- Are there classrooms where your impressions from mini-observations don't match student-achievement results—for example, a teacher who looks good but whose students aren't doing as well as expected?
- Are there any teachers you're especially impressed with?
- Any teachers having difficulty?
- Let's go visit one of each of those right now and afterwards talk about what's going on.

> *An essential task is getting the supervisor/teacher ratio to no more than one to twenty-five, preferably lower.*

If possible, it's helpful to occasionally sit in on a feedback conversation (with the teacher's permission) to get a sense of whether supervisors are providing effective feedback.

Four other look-fors in school visits: (1) Curriculum unit planning: Is there evidence that teacher teams are thinking through their units at a high level? (2) Teacher teamwork on assessment analysis: Are PLCs giving good assessments and following up with analysis and action? (3) End-of-year rubric evaluation of teachers: Are principals accurately and fairly assessing their teachers and using the data to improve performance and make wise personnel decisions? And (4) time management: Are supervisors putting first things first, while keeping some balance in their lives?

Principal meetings. Once launched, an essential way to monitor and support the mini-observation process is making it a regular agenda item for district leadership meetings. Having one or two supervisors read their debrief summaries and get feedback from the group is a helpful exercise to fine-tune the skills of making these write-ups succinct, to the point, and effective in communicating appreciation and one leverage point to each teacher.

Feedback and fine-tuning. Polling all teachers at least once a year will provide helpful information on how the program is going and what needs to be tweaked.

For mini-observations to have an impact on teaching and learning, each component has to be short—class visits, debriefs, and write-ups—and supervisors need continual monitoring and feedback.

Principal Evaluation Rubric

Are principals accurately and fairly assessing their teachers and using the data to improve performance and make wise personnel decisions?

For end-of-year evaluation of principals, I recommend that superintendents use a rubric that I've developed specifically for this purpose. This principal rubric parallels the teacher rubric introduced in Chapter Seven—six domains, nine criteria in each, and a four-level rating scale (without numbers at the top). The rubric is designed to give principals and other school-based administrators an annual assessment of where they stand in all performance areas—and detailed guidance for improvement. I suggest that its use parallel the teacher evaluation process:

- Introducing the rubric at the beginning of the year and having each principal self-assess and agree with the superintendent on three professional goals for the year.
- Conducting regular school visits and following up with a brief narrative summary sent electronically. I recommend the one-thousand-character (160-word) ceiling on the length of these summaries.
- Having a midyear check-in meeting and comparing the principal's self-assessment on the rubric with the superintendent's tentative ratings and discussing any lines on which they disagree.
- Continuing a regular rhythm of school visits and then at summative evaluation time, again comparing the principal's self-assessment with the superintendent's ratings, discussing disagreements and evidence, and finalizing the evaluation.

Here's a sample summary sent after a superintendent's visit with a principal:

Good visiting Tony Hardel's sixth-grade classroom with you today. As you pointed out, Tony is struggling. I know you have made an effort to visit her classroom frequently, and you were insightful in identifying her strengths and weaknesses—good work! We also discussed that you were frustrated with Tony for not showing improvement despite your repeated feedback. Having reviewed your written feedback to her, I think you need to provide more specific action steps, for example, ask her to cold-call students who haven't yet raised their hands and ask eager students to write answers in their notebooks. Asking her to observe one of your high-performing teachers might also work, and I would suggest providing her with specific things to look for. Finally, I've also found that vide-otaping struggling teachers and asking them to review their own performance is a great way to get them to see where they can do better. I look forward to hearing how things unfold when we meet next month.

The rubric is not a checklist for school visits. To knowledgeably evaluate a principal at the end of a school year, a superintendent (or designee) needs to be in the school frequently (at least once a month), have lots of formative feedback conversations, and look at other information, including staff surveys. It is impossible (and irresponsible) to fill out the rubric based on one or two visits.

The rubric is not a check-list for school visits.

The rubric covers principals' actions, not their personal qualities. Underlying these fifty-four manifestations of leadership are the principal's vision, firm beliefs, access to research, a network of support, interpersonal and communication skills, cultural competence, courage, decisiveness, resilience, and wisdom.

Here is the rubric, which is available as a PDF at www.marshallmemo.com: click Kim's Writing and scroll down to the rubrics section. If you want to tweak the rubric, e-mail Kim at kim.marshall48@gmail.com for an Excel version.

As with the teacher rubric, the Effective level is expected, solid performance. When review-ing each row, that is the first cell that should be read. If it's not an accurate description of per-formance, read to the left or right to find the closest match.

A. Strategy

The principal	Highly Effective	Effective	Improvement Necessary	Does Not Meet Standards
a. **Team**	Recruits a strong and diverse leadership team and develops its skills and commitment to a high level.	Recruits and develops a diverse leadership team with a balance of skills.	Enlists one or two like-minded colleagues to provide advice and support.	Works solo with little or no support from colleagues.
b. **Diagnosis**	Involves stakeholders in a comprehensive diagnosis of the school's strengths and areas for growth.	Thoroughly assesses the school's strengths and areas for development.	Makes a quick assessment of the school's strengths and weaknesses.	Is unable to gather much information on the school's strong and weak points.
c. **Gap**	Challenges colleagues by presenting the gap between current student data and a vision for college/career success.	Motivates colleagues by comparing students' current achievement with external standards.	Presents data without a vision or a vision without data.	Bemoans students' low achievement and shows fatalism about bringing about significant change.
d. **Mission**	Wins staff and student buy-in for a succinct, inspiring, results-oriented mission statement.	Produces a memorable, succinct, results-oriented mission statement that's known by all staff.	Distributes a boiler-plate mission statement that few colleagues remember.	Does not share a mission statement.
e. **Theory**	Wins staff ownership for a robust, research-based theory of action for improving student achievement.	Researches and writes a convincing theory of action for improving achievement.	Accepts colleagues' current notions of how student achievement can be improved.	Says that hard work improves achievement, but shows doubts that progress can be made.
f. **Plan**	Collaboratively crafts and wins support for a bold multi-year strategic plan with annual goals.	Gets input and writes a comprehensive, measurable strategic plan for the current year.	Produces a bureauceatic, non-accountable strategic plan.	Recyles the previous year's bureaucratic, non-accountable strategic plan.
g. **Support**	Fosters urgency and responsibility among all stakeholders for achieving annual and long-range goals.	Builds ownership and support among stakeholders for achieving annual goals.	Presents the annual plan to stakeholders and asks them to support it.	Gets the necessary signatures for the annual plan, but there is little ownership and support.
h. **Enlisting**	Masterfully wins over resistant staff members who feared change and/or harbored low expectations.	Effectively manages resistance, low expectations, and fear of change.	Works on persuading resistant staff members to get on board with the plan.	Is discouraged and immobilized by staff resistance, fear of change, and low expectations.
i. **Revision**	Regularly tracks progress, gives and takes feedback, and continuously improves performance.	Periodically measures progress, listens to feedback, and revises the strategic plan.	Occasionally focuses on key data points and prods colleagues to improve.	Is too caught up in daily crises to focus on emerging data.

Overall rating:_____ Comments:

B. First Things First

The principal	Highly Effective	Effective	Improvement Necessary	Does Not Meet Standards
a. Planning	Plans for the year, month, week, and day, relentlessly getting the highest-leverage activities done.	Plans for the year, month, week, and day, keeping the highest-leverage activities front and center.	Comes to work with a list of tasks that need to be accomplished that day but is often distracted from them.	Has a mental list of tasks to be accomplished each day, but often loses track.
b. Communication	Successfully communicates goals to all stakeholders by skillful use of a variety of channels.	Uses a variety of means (e.g., face-to-face, newsletter, digital) to communicate goals to others.	Has a limited communication repertoire and some key stakeholders are not aware of school goals.	Is not an effective communicator and others are often left guessing about policies and direction.
c. Outreach	Frequently solicits and uses feedback and help from staff, students, parents, and external partners.	Regularly reaches out to staff, students, parents, and external partners for feedback and help.	Occasionally asks staff, students, parents, or external partners for feedback.	Rarely or never reaches out to others for feedback or help.
d. Follow-up	Has a foolproof system for capturing key data, remembering, prioritizing, and following up.	Writes down important information, remembers, prioritizes, and almost always follows up.	Captures key information but is swamped by events and sometimes doesn't follow up.	Trusts his or her memory to retain important information, but often forgets and fails to follow up.
e. Expectations	Has staff buy-in for high expectations for management, discipline, and cultural competence.	Makes sure staff know what is expected for management procedures, student discipline, and cultural competence.	Periodically reminds teachers of policies on management procedures, student discipline, and cultural competence.	Is constantly reminding and correcting staff about management, student discipline, and cultural competence.
f. Delegation	Has highly competent people in key roles, trusts them, and publicly appreciates their work.	Delegates appropriate tasks to competent staff members, monitors progress, and praises good work.	Doesn't delegate some tasks that should be done by others.	Tries to do almost everything him- or herself.
g. Meetings	Successfully gets all key teams meeting regularly and taking responsibility for productive agendas.	Ensures that key teams (e.g., leadership, grade-level, student support) meet regularly.	Needs to call key team meetings because they are not in people's calendars.	Convenes grade-level, leadership, and other teams only when there is a crisis or an immediate need.
h. Prevention	Takes the initiative so that time-wasting activities and crises are almost always prevented or deflected.	Is effective at preventing and/or deflecting many time-wasting crises and activities.	Tries to prevent them, but crises and time-wasters sometimes eat up lots of time.	Finds that large portions of each day are consumed by crises and time-wasting activities.
i. Efficiency	Deals quickly and decisively with the highest-priority e-mail and paperwork, delegating the rest.	Has a system for dealing with e-mail, paperwork, and administrative chores.	Tries to stay on top of e-mail, paperwork, and administrative chores but is often behind.	Is way behind on e-mail, paperwork, and administrative chores, to the detriment of the school's mission.

Overall rating:_____ Comments:

C. Curriculum and Data

The principal	Highly Effective	Effective	Improvement Necessary	Does Not Meet Standards
a. **Expectations**	Gets teacher buy-in on clear, standards-aligned grade and course goals with exemplars of proficient work.	Ensures that teachers know the knowledge and skills students should master by the end of each year.	Refers teachers to district or national scope-and-sequence documents for curriculum direction.	Leaves teachers without clear direction on student learning outcomes for their grades and courses.
b. **Baselines**	Ensures that all teams use assessment data from the previous year and/or fresh diagnostic data to plan instruction.	Provides teacher teams with previous-year test data and/or asks them to assess students' current levels.	Refers teachers to previous-year test data as a baseline for current-year instruction.	Does not provide baseline test data to teachers.
c. **Targets**	Gets each grade-level/ subject team invested in reaching SMART year-end goals.	Works with grade-level and subject-area teams to set measurable student goals for the current year.	Urges grade-level/ subject teams to set measurable student learning goals for the current year.	Urges teachers to improve student achievement, but without measurable outcome goals.
d. **Materials**	Ensures that all teachers have high-quality, culturally responsive curriculum materials and technology.	Procures effective and culturally responsive curriculum materials and technology for key subject areas.	Works to procure good curriculum materials but quality control is lacking.	Leaves teachers to fend for themselves with curriculum materials.
e. **Interims**	Ensures that high-quality, aligned, common assessments are regularly given by all teacher teams.	Orchestrates common assessments to monitor student learning several times a year.	Suggests that teacher teams give common assessments to check on student learning.	Doesn't insist on common assessments, allowing teachers to use their own classroom tests.
f. **Analysis**	Orchestrates high-quality data/action team meetings and thoughtful reflection after each assessment.	Monitors teams as they analyze assessment data, asking *what* students got wrong and *why*.	Suggests that teacher teams work together to draw lessons from the tests they give.	Does not ensure that teacher teams analyze test results during the year.
g. **Follow-Up**	Gets teams following up assessments with effective reteaching, tutoring, and enrichment.	Has teams follow up each interim assessment with reteaching and enrichment.	Suggests that teachers use interim assessment data to help struggling students.	Does not provide time or leadership for follow-up after tests.
h. **Monitoring**	Uses grades, attendance, and behavior data to drive continuous improvement toward goals.	Monitors data in several key areas and uses them to inform improvement efforts.	Monitors attendance and discipline data to inform decisions.	Is inattentive to important school data.
i. **Celebration**	Boosts morale and a sense of efficacy by getting colleagues to celebrate and own student gains.	Draws attention to student, classroom, and schoolwide successes, giving credit where credit is due.	Congratulates individuals on successes.	Takes credit for improvements in school performance or misses opportunities to celebrate success.

Overall rating:_____ **Comments:**

D. Talent Development

The principal	Highly Effective	Effective	Improvement Necessary	Does Not Meet Standards
a. **Meetings**	In meetings, gets teachers invested in discussing results, sharing effective strategies, and building trust and collegiality.	Uses staff meetings to get teachers sharing strategies and becoming more cohesive.	Uses staff meetings primarily to announce decisions, clarify policies, and address staff concerns.	Rarely convenes staff members and/or uses meetings for one-way lectures on policies.
b. **Ideas**	Ensures that colleagues are current on the professional literature and continuously explore effective practices.	Reads widely, shares ideas, and fosters an ongoing, schoolwide discussion of effective practices.	Occasionally passes along interesting articles and ideas to colleagues.	Rarely reads profes-sional literature or discusses best practices.
c. **Growth**	Orchestrates high-quality PD, coaching, mentoring, school visits, and other professional learning tuned to staff needs.	Organizes aligned, ongoing coaching and training that builds classroom proficiency.	Orchestrates staff development workshops that often do not engage staff or improve instruction.	Provides occasional PD, leaving teachers mostly on their own with professional growth.
d. **Teams**	Gets teams to take ownership for using data and student work to drive continuous refinement of teaching.	Orchestrates regular teacher team meetings as a key forum for professional learning.	Suggests that teacher teams work together to address students' learning problems.	Does not emphasize teamwork and teachers work mostly in isolation.
e. **Units**	Ensures that teachers backwards-design high-quality, standards-aligned units and provides feedback on drafts.	Asks teacher teams to cooperatively plan curriculum units following a common format.	Occasionally reviews teachers' lesson plans but not unit plans.	Does not review lesson or unit plans.
f. **Coaching**	Visits several classrooms a day and gives prompt, helpful, face-to-face feedback to each teacher.	Visits a few classrooms almost every day and gives helpful feedback to teachers.	Tries to get into classrooms but is often distracted by other events and rarely provides feedback.	Observes teachers only in annual or bi-annual formal evaluation visits.
g. **Courage**	Skillfully and courageously engages in difficult conversations with less-than-effective teachers, helping them improve.	Provides redirection and support to teachers who are less than effective.	Criticizes struggling teachers but does not give them much help improving their performance.	Shies away from giving honest feedback and redirection to teachers who are not perform-ing well.
h. **Accountability**	Counsels out or dismisses ineffective teachers, scrupulously following contractual requirements.	Counsels out or dismisses most ineffective teachers, following contractual requirements.	Tries to dismiss one or two ineffective teachers, but is stymied by procedural errors.	Does not initiate dismissal procedures, despite evidence that some teachers are ineffective.
i. **Staffing**	Recruits, hires, onboards, supports, and retains highly effective, diverse teachers who share the school's vision.	Recruits, hires, onboards, and retains effective, diverse teachers.	Recruits and hires teachers who seem to fit his or her philosophy of teaching.	Makes last-minute appointments to teaching vacancies based on candidates who are available.

Overall rating:_____   Comments:

E. Culture

The principal	Highly Effective	Effective	Improvement Necessary	Does Not Meet Standards
a. Expectations	Gets staff buy-in for clear, schoolwide student-behavior standards, routines, and consequences.	Sets expectations for student behavior and establishes schoolwide routines and consequences.	Urges staff to demand good student behavior, but allows different standards in different classrooms.	Often tolerates discipline violations and enforces the rules inconsistently.
b. Discipline	Deals effectively with any disruptions to teaching and learning, analyzes patterns, and works on prevention.	Deals quickly with disruptions to learning and looks for underlying causes.	Deals firmly with students who are disruptive in classrooms, but doesn't get to the root causes.	Tries to deal with disruptive students but is swamped by the number of problems.
c. Celebration	Publicly celebrates kindness, effort, and improvement, building students' pride in their school.	Praises student achievement and works to build school spirit.	Praises well-behaved students and good grades.	Rarely praises students and fails to build school pride.
d. Training	Ensures that staff are skilled in positive discipline, cultural competence, and sensitive handling of student issues.	Organizes PD and suggests articles and books on classroom management and cultural competence.	Exhorts teachers to get better at classroom management and be culturally competent.	Does little to build teachers' skills in classroom management and cultural competence.
e. Support	Is highly effective getting counseling, mentoring, and other supports for high-need students.	Identifies struggling students and gets effective support services to meet their needs.	Tries to get crisis counseling for highly disruptive and troubled students.	Focuses mainly on discipline and punishment with highly disruptive and troubled students.
f. Families	Makes families feel welcome and respected, responds to concerns, and gets some actively involved in the school.	Makes parents feel welcome, listens to their input, and works to get them involved.	Reaches out to parents and tries to understand when they have concerns.	Makes little effort to reach out to families and is defensive when parents express concerns.
g. Curriculum	Informs parents of grade and course learning expectations and specific ways they can support their children's learning.	Makes sure teachers tell parents what their children are learning and ways to support the curriculum at home.	Informs parents of grade-level learning expectations.	Does not inform parents of the school's learning expectations.
h. Conferences	Orchestrates student-led conferences in which parents and students see specific next steps for improvement.	Maximizes the number of helpful parent/teacher conferences.	Makes sure that report cards are filled out correctly and provided to all parents.	Provides little or no monitoring of the report card process.
i. Outreach	Runs an effective school website and uses digital media to showcase the school and communicate with families.	Sends a periodic school newsletter and asks teachers to have regular communication of their own.	Urges teachers to communicate regularly with parents.	Leaves parent contact and communication up to individual teachers.

Overall rating:_____ **Comments:**

F. Management

The principal	Highly Effective	Effective	Improvement Necessary	Does Not Meet Standards
a. Ethics	Sets a stellar example through impeccably ethical, professional, and culturally sensitive behavior.	Acts in an ethical and culturally competent manner and expects colleagues to do the same.	Is not sufficiently attentive to ethical standards and cultural competency, giving mixed messages to staff.	Sometimes acts unethically and/or in a culturally insensitive manner, setting a poor example for colleagues.
b. Scheduling	Creates an equitable schedule that maximizes learning time, teacher collaboration, and smooth transitions.	Creates an equitable schedule that provides meeting times for all key teams.	Creates a schedule with some flaws and few opportunities for team meetings.	Creates a schedule with inequities, technical flaws, and little time for teacher teams to meet.
c. Movement	Ensures efficient, orderly, and friendly student entry, dismissal, meal times, transitions, and recesses.	Supervises orderly student entry, dismissal, meals, class transitions, and recesses.	Intermittently monitors student entry, dismissal, transitions, and meal times, resulting in some problems.	Rarely supervises student entry, dismissal, and common spaces and there are frequent problems.
d. Maintenance	Leads staff to ensure effective, creative use of space and a clean, safe, and inviting campus.	Supervises staff to keep the campus clean, attractive, and safe.	Works with custodial staff to keep the campus clean and safe, but there are occasional lapses.	Leaves campus cleanliness and safety to custodial staff and there are frequent lapses.
e. Transparency	Is transparent about how and why decisions are made, involving stakeholders whenever possible.	Ensures that staff members know how and why key decisions are made.	Tries to be transparent about decision-making, but stakeholders sometimes feel shut out.	Makes decisions with little or no consultation, causing resentment and morale problems.
f. Bureaucracy	Deftly handles bureaucratic, contractual, compliance, and legal issues and leverages them to support teaching.	Efficiently manages bureaucratic, contractual, compliance, and legal issues.	Sometimes allows bureaucratic, contractual, compliance, and legal issues to distract teachers.	Frequently mishandles bureaucratic, contractual, compliance, and legal issues in ways that disrupt learning.
g. Budget	Skillfully manages the budget and finances to maximize student achievement and staff growth.	Manages the school's budget and finances to support the strategic plan.	Manages budget and finances with few errors, but misses chances to support the strategic plan.	Makes errors in managing the budget and finances to the detriment of teaching and learning.
h. Relationships	Builds strong bonds with key district and external personnel and gets them excited about the school's mission.	Builds relationships with district and external staffers so they will be helpful with paperwork and process.	Is correct and professional with district and external staff but does not enlist their active support.	Neglects relationship-building with district and external staff and doesn't have their support.
i. Resources	Taps all possible human and financial resources to support the school's mission and strategic plan.	Is effective in bringing additional human and financial resources into the school.	Occasionally raises additional funds or finds volunteers to help out.	Is resigned to working with the standard school budget, which doesn't seem adequate.

Overall rating:_____   Comments:

Evaluation Summary Page

Principal's name:_____ School year:_____

School:_____

Evaluator:_____ Position:_____

RATINGS ON INDIVIDUAL DOMAINS:

A. Strategy:

    Highly Effective   Effective   Improvement Necessary   Does Not Meet Standards

B. First Things First:

    Highly Effective   Effective   Improvement Necessary   Does Not Meet Standards

C. Curriculum and Data:

    Highly Effective   Effective   Improvement Necessary   Does Not Meet Standards

D. Talent Development:

    Highly Effective   Effective   Improvement Necessary   Does Not Meet Standards

E. Culture:

    Highly Effective   Effective   Improvement Necessary   Does Not Meet Standards

F. Management:

    Highly Effective   Effective   Improvement Necessary   Does Not Meet Standards

OVERALL RATING:

Highly Effective   Effective   Improvement Necessary Does Not Meet Standards

OVERALL COMMENTS BY SUPERVISOR:

OVERALL COMMENTS BY ADMINISTRATOR:

Supervisor's signature: _____ Date:_____

Administrator's signature: _____ Date:_____

(The administrator's signature indicates that he or she has seen and discussed the evaluation; it does not necessarily denote agreement with the report.)

As stated above, the Effective level describes solid, expected professional performance; any administrator should be pleased with ratings at this level. The Highly Effective level is reserved for truly outstanding leadership as described by very demanding criteria. Improvement Necessary indicates that performance has real deficiencies and must improve (some novice administrators might start here). And performance at the Does Not Meet Standards level is clearly unacceptable and will lead to dismissal if it is not improved promptly.

When assessing each criterion, it's best to start with the Effective level, and if that doesn't describe the principal, look to the left or right and circle or highlight the cell that's the best match. On each page, this will create a clear graphic display of overall performance, areas for commendation, and areas that need work. The superintendent should then write the overall rating at the bottom of each page with brief comments, and then record all the ratings and overall comments on the summary page.

Clearly, some of the criteria are more important than others—in an absolute sense and also within the context of each school and each principal's top priorities for the year. That is why it's unwise to come up with a numerical score for each page and the overall rubric. The principal and superintendent should have a clear understanding going into each school year about which areas are going to get the greatest emphasis. It's not that the others are unimportant—the principal should be rated on all fifty-four—but some are more important than others, and that should be reflected in the comments the superintendent writes at the bottom of each page and the overall comments on the summary page at the end.

End-of-year evaluation conferences are most effective when the superintendent and administrator fill out the rubric in advance and then meet and compare one page at a time. Of course, the superintendent has the final say, but the discussion should aim for consensus based on actual evidence of the most accurate score for each criterion. Superintendents should go into the evaluation process with some humility, because they can't possibly know everything about a principal's multifaceted work.

Superintendents should go into the evaluation process with some humility, because they can't possibly know everything about a principal's multifaceted work.

Similarly, principals should be open to feedback from someone with an outside perspective—all focused on whether the school is producing learning gains for all students. Note that student achievement is not explicitly included in this rubric. The fifty-four criteria are the research-based *drivers* of student achievement—the leadership inputs that, if done at the Effective or Highly Effective level, should lead directly to impressive outcomes. The rubric measures inputs; student-achievement data measure the outcomes and should be a separate component of a district's evaluation of principals.

Some superintendents sugarcoat criticism and give inflated scores to keep the peace and avoid hurting feelings. This does not help an administrator improve. The kindest thing the boss can do for an underperforming administrator is give candid, evidence-based feedback and robust follow-up support. The rubric is helpful for framing areas for improvement—as well as appreciating areas of strength.

Ratings for all the administrators in a district can be aggregated into a spreadsheet that can give an overview of leadership development needs (similar to the teacher evaluation spreadsheet shown in Chapter Seven).

When a superintendent introduces this rubric to principals for the first time, I recommend the particular-general-particular strategy described in Chapter Seven:

- Give an overview of the rubric, looking at the domains and scoring levels.
- Pick a page (perhaps *D. Talent Development*) and have principals read just the *Effective* column of that page from top to bottom.
- Pick one row on that page and read the cells horizontally from right to left to give a flavor of how the four levels of performance step up from unsatisfactory to mediocre to solid to outstanding.
- Have principals self-assess on that page.
- In small groups and then the larger group, have principals discuss the rubric's advantages (first) and any concerns they have.
- Break principals into groups and assign one page of the rubric to each group. The task (with each group reporting out at the end) is to brainstorm and write onto chart paper the evidence the superintendent would need to rate them on that page—and how that evidence might be gathered in school visits; surveys of staff, students, and parents; and a few key artifacts. Each group should also articulate the big idea of their page—the most important "bumper sticker" take-away for the domain.

Many principals find this rubric challenging when they first flip through it, and there's often some pushback on how demanding the Highly Effective level is. But there are principals who attain the highest rating on each of the criteria. When introducing the rubric (as with the teacher rubric), it's important to make clear that the Effective level is Expected performance—where every principal should be—and the Highly Effective level is above-and-beyond, superb performance.

The primary way to assess principals should be regular school visits by the superintendent or designee. Frequency is crucial—at least ten visits during each school year—to get past the dog-and-pony dynamic that occurs when visits are few and far between and everything rides on how the school looks to the boss. Many schools have a special signal to alert staff members when the superintendent is in the building—in one school, a student is sent from classroom to classroom carrying a red blackboard eraser. It's a healthy sign when superintendents' visits are so frequent that the school goes about its business and doesn't try to present anything special.

Many schools have a special signal to alert staff members when the superintendent is in the building.

Should superintendents' visits be unannounced? This is a matter for debate within each district; I can see advantages and disadvantages. The goal is for the superintendent to see daily reality and be able to spend an hour or two with the principal talking and visiting classrooms.

Gathering artifacts is also helpful—especially the school's schedule—but superintendents should be careful not to overemphasize paper and electronic documents. The main source of information and point of intervention should be face-to-face conversations in the principal's office and walking around the school.

Once or twice a year, the superintendent might also conduct an anonymous survey of teachers, parents, and students. New York City does this every year, and it's one of the most impressive legacies of the Joel Klein era (see http://schools.nyc.gov/accountability/tools/survey/default.htm).

Superintendents might also want to consider bringing in the Peer Assistance and Review (PAR) program described in Chapter Seven. This is a way of enlisting outstanding teachers in the supervision and evaluation process and lightening principals' load.

In some districts and states, there's been resistance to fully adopting the mini-observation model. Unable or unwilling to deal with pushback from unions, they are implementing a hybrid model: administrators do announced *and* unannounced observations.

This sounds like a sensible, middle-of-the-road compromise, but it has a fatal flaw: if principals continue to spend four hours or more on each traditional observation and don't get relief from their other responsibilities, they simply won't have time for more than one or two short observations—not nearly enough for teachers to trust the process and for administrators to get a true sense of what's going on in classrooms. The result: exhausted and cynical school leaders and no improvements in teaching and learning.

Let's face it: the traditional model of announced, infrequent, full-lesson classroom visits is ineffective and a poor use of administrators' time. Half-measures won't work. Districts need to make a clean break with the past and use an approach that will win teachers' trust, give them continuous feedback on their work, provide fuel for teacher teamwork for curriculum and data follow-up, and culminate in accurate end-of-year evaluations.

Some path-breaking principals have already made the shift. I salute their courage, but this needs to happen at scale—and this is where superintendents can make the difference. Only policymakers and union leaders have the power to rewrite contracts, bring teacher evaluation out of the dark ages, and turn it into a powerful tool for improving teaching and learning. Let's see some honesty and courage at the top. Our students deserve no less.

End-of-Year Rubric Evaluation of Teachers

An important step for the superintendent is getting a high-quality teacher evaluation rubric approved by key stakeholders and ensuring that principals have a good eye for assessing teaching and use the rubric well. Once a rubric is in place, these steps are essential:

- Explaining the philosophy and details of the teacher evaluation rubrics to principals.
- Walking principals through the meeting format suggested in Chapter Seven for introducing the rubrics to their teachers at the beginning of the school year.
- As suggested, using principal meetings to practice teacher feedback conversations with teachers.
- Making sure principals don't fall into the trap of gathering voluminous "evidence" on each teacher, but rather observe them perceptively and constantly *improve* their performance through face-to-face coaching conversations throughout the year.
- Holding principals accountable for having difficult conversations with teachers who are not performing well, and supporting them if personnel action is required.

End-of-year rubric evaluations of a teacher's overall performance is difficult to simulate in principals' meetings—and that's where inter-rater reliability is going to matter the most. The ratings teachers receive in one school should be close to those they would receive in another. A district-wide rubric's descriptive language will reduce the variations that probably existed in the past, using narrative or checklist evaluations, but not every principal is going to interpret the rubric the same way.

The ratings teachers receive in one school should be close to those they would receive in another.

How can a district's cadre of principals simulate watching the same teacher through an entire year of instruction and discussing appropriate rubric scores? I have a suggestion: *The Class* is an award-winning, true-to-life film about a Paris teacher's year with one group of eighth graders (the DVD can be purchased on Amazon). The movie is in French (with subtitles), and the cultural context is different, but it rings true in the US context and is the closest thing we have to seeing an entire year of instruction in a realistic setting (the teacher in *The Class* wrote the book on which the screenplay is based and plays himself in the film).

Working with groups of principals and superintendents, I've had success playing ten short clips interspersed through the film and then having everyone evaluate the teacher on two or three of the domains in the teacher evaluation rubric and comparing scores. This is an effective way to get principals discussing and justifying their ratings in light of actual classroom scenes they've watched together. Here are the ten scenes I recommend using (they can be accessed by using the scene selection menu at the beginning of the film):

- **Scene 2.** The opening minutes of the year; Mr. Marin greets students and conducts an opening activity.
- **Scene 3.** Mr. Marin is going over vocabulary that students don't know; there's a culturally fraught discussion about cheeseburgers.
- **Scene 5.** A lesson on the subjunctive tense, and a student asks Mr. Marin if he is gay.
- **Scene 8.** Students push back on the autobiography assignment that Mr. Marin is asking them to complete.
- **Scene 9.** Mr. Marin meets with a disrespectful student after class and forces her to apologize.
- **Scene 12.** Students read their autobiographies and exchange insults.
- **Scene 14.** Interactions with parents—this doesn't count as a mini-observation.
- **Scene 15.** Students are in the computer lab typing up autobiographies, and Mr. Marin has a positive interaction with Soulleman, a challenging student.
- **Scene 18.** A brief glimpse of students interacting on the playground, then soccer presentations in class.

  (Between these scenes, two girls in the class who acted as observers in a faculty disciplinary committee disclosed to their classmates that teachers had discussed Soulleman and other students' performance.)

- **Scene 21.** Mr. Marin loses his cool, insults the two girls, and a student is injured.

  (Between these two scenes, Soulleman is expelled from the school, and Mr. Marin is not disciplined.)
- **Scene 27.** In the last class before summer vacation, students say what they learned that year. One student approaches the teacher after dismissal and says she hadn't learned anything.

Time Management

Many principals struggle with making time for instructional leadership, and superintendents can provide valuable assistance. Having principals self-assess on the second page of the principal rubric ("First Things First") at the beginning of the year and zeroing in on specific areas for improvement can be a very healthy process. Checking in on the areas for improvement can be a regular part of the superintendent's visits to each school.

Many principals struggle with making time for instructional leadership, and superintendents can provide valuable assistance.

Some superintendents I've worked with praise Malachi Pancoast's two-day Breakthrough Coach time-management workshop for principals. There's a lot to be said for Pancoast's approach, especially the idea of delegating more to the school secretary, getting more organized with paperwork and meetings, and trying to get everything done during the school day.

But there's one area where Pancoast and I disagree. He says that principals should spend three full days in their offices taking care of paperwork and meetings and two full days in classrooms. I believe a more effective approach is doing about two mini-observations each day of the week and carving out a compressed, efficient chunk of time, usually after school, for paperwork.

The advantages of this approach are (1) principals have better situational awareness if they're walking around their schools every day; (2) mini-observations are spread through the week, giving a more representative sampling of each teacher's performance; (3) teachers know that the principal might walk in at any point in the week; and (4) principals are more likely to have prompt follow-up conversations with teachers because there are only about two classroom visits a day, versus five to seven a day if observations are squeezed into two days.

The school administrative manager (SAM) model described in Chapter Thirteen is another way of attacking the perennial time management challenge. This program assigns a middle-level staffer to schools (usually one per building) to take noninstructional tasks off the principal's desk and nudge them to be organized about visiting classrooms and dealing with curriculum and assessment. For information on the National SAM Innovation Project, see www.SamsConnect.com.

One of the macro tasks on each principal's priority/time management plate is creating the professional conditions that enable teachers to do their best work. Harvard Graduate School of Education professor Susan Moore Johnson (2012) argues that the professional environment is as important as teachers' credentials and previous experience in determining their success with students—perhaps more so. Superintendents need to check frequently on how well principals are dealing with the key areas that Johnson has studied (and advocating for them and allocating funding):

- **Summer planning time.** Professional time before the school year begins and after it ends is essential, and occasional full-day professional days during the year are highly desirable, preferably timed to fall immediately after interim assessments.
- **Planning time for teacher teams** (particularly important for curriculum unit development and effective analysis of interim assessment results). Provide time for teacher teams to collaborate during the school day without pulling them away from students; uninterrupted double-period meeting times are ideal.

- **Materials.** Put in teachers' hands the books and technology they need to teach standards effectively, and orchestrate professional development on the actual materials being used in classrooms.

- **Classroom interruptions.** Reduce these to near zero, and be especially tough on all-school PA announcements.

- **Reform clutter.** Home in on a small number of big rocks initiatives and help everyone focus on them. Narrowing down from the nine core leadership tasks to two or three is one that many principals find challenging. Being a thought partner in this process—looking over the needs assessment and exploring different possibilities—is where the superintendent can be very helpful.

- **Professional support.** Teachers and other staff members get updates on interesting research and best practices from the outside world.

In sum, the superintendent is essential to the success of the mini-observation model in schools. Through frequent school visits, ongoing feedback, and substantive principals' meetings, the superintendent can be a key player on the team that gets more good teaching in more classrooms more of the time.

Questions to Consider

- *Is there a secret signal in your school for when the superintendent arrives?*
- *How can the superintendent in your district be most helpful with teacher evaluation?*
- *What strikes you looking through the principal evaluation rubric?*

15

A Short Summary, Frequently Asked Questions, and a Wrap-Up

The key to improved student learning is to ensure more good teaching in more classrooms more of the time.

—Jon Saphier

A Short Summary of This Book

A key part of every supervisor's job is affirming good teaching, coaching for improvement, and evaluating overall performance. The traditional model of infrequent full-lesson observations is ineffective because of baked-in design flaws. Alternatives suggested in recent years have failed to solve the challenge of fairly and accurately evaluating a school's teachers, each of whom teaches about nine hundred lessons a year.

Mini-observations use a different design: frequent, short, systematic, unannounced classroom visits (ten to fifteen minutes in each class about once a month), each followed by a face-to-face conversation and brief narrative summary. Mini-observations and debriefs give supervisors a much more accurate sampling of day-to-day instruction and multiple opportunities to appreciate and coach teachers' work. These interactions, along with other points of contact and each teacher's self-assessment, culminate in a detailed rubric evaluation at the end of the school year.

Mini-observers also support teacher teams as they design curriculum units and lessons, analyze students' work, and learn from each other about the most effective ways to build student mastery day by day. The supervisor's job is keeping the focus on all students learning at high levels. The design of mini-observations brings out the best in school administrators and is eminently coachable by superintendents and heads of school, who also play a key role providing the staffing, training, and support to make the model work.

Mini-observations have been called a *keystone habit*—a relatively simple and low-cost change (for example, families eating dinner together) that brings about major improvement. Here's a graphic, followed by a description of the twelve ways mini-observations strengthen teaching, relationships, teamwork, and leadership:

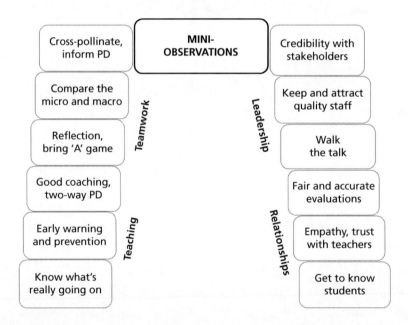

Teaching becomes more and more effective because supervisors are aware of daily classroom realities, can intervene early when they see problems, and have plenty of opportunities to coach teachers—and to be coached by them.

Relationships are nurtured with teachers because frequent visits give a clear picture of the challenges some are facing with students because supervisors frequently see them learning, and when it's time for end-of-year evaluations, teachers are likely to see them as fair and accurate.

Teamwork and reflection are constantly growing because frequent conversations about lessons get teachers thinking about their work, motivate them to bring their A game every day, and supervisors see the intersection of short classroom visits with unit plans, teacher teamwork, and schoolwide curriculum and professional development, and can spread good ideas from class to class and to the whole faculty.

Leadership continuously improves as supervisors show their support of teachers as professionals and people; the professional working conditions supported by the mini-observation process make teachers want to stay in the school, and the word gets out that this is a good school to be in; and supervisors have credibility with stakeholders because they are so familiar with what's going on in classrooms and the school as a whole.

Frequently Asked Questions

The idea of mini-observations is unconventional and raises a number of questions. Here are those I hear most often, each followed by my response:

Isn't ten minutes insufficient to see what's going on during a lesson? Watching a video of a lesson segment quickly convinces people that a *lot* happens in ten to fifteen minutes. But to get an accurate picture of a teacher's overall work, short visits need to be frequent, randomly spread through the year, and always followed by a face-to-face conversation in which the teacher can put the snapshot in context and fill in important background information.

Unannounced visits feel like a "gotcha" aimed at catching the teacher doing something wrong, showing a lack of trust. Mini-observations take some getting used to, but they allow the teacher's day-to-day work to shine through without the nervous-making once-a-year "dog-and-pony show." Supervisors build trust in the face-to-face conversations, showing that mini-observations aren't about finding fault but rather about appreciating good practices and working together to fine-tune teaching and learning.

Observers will miss the best parts of the lesson, which seem to occur just before or after a mini-observation. That can happen, but face-to-face debrief conversations give the teacher a chance to describe what the supervisor missed, filling in gaps and showing the work students produced.

The observer might see a bad moment and take that out of context. Every teacher has those moments, but if there are enough visits (once a month is a good frequency), not-so-good moments are seen in the overall context of effective teaching and learning.

Unannounced visits will distract students and throw the teacher off stride. If short visits are frequent, they become routine and students and teachers get used to them and barely notice the administrator's presence.

If short visits are frequent, they become routine and students and teachers get used to them and barely notice the administrator's presence.

Not having a pre-observation conference means the supervisor won't know the whole lesson plan. Again, the face-to-face conversation gives the teacher an opportunity to explain the context, show the lesson and unit plan, and talk about students' long-term learning. Supervisors might also be able to look over the lesson plan during the mini-observation.

What is the observer looking for in a short visit? Do they bring in a checklist or rubric? Checklists and rubrics are not appropriate for a mini-observation. The supervisor should be looking for the big picture: How is this lesson going in terms of learning objectives, pedagogy, and student learning?

What if the supervisor isn't experienced in my subject area? Nobody can be an expert in every grade and subject, and humility is important. Face-to-face conversations are an opportunity for the teacher to bring observers up to speed on content and pedagogy with which they're not familiar. With help from the teacher on grade- and subject-specific details, a perceptive administrator can make appreciative and helpful observations on pedagogy, classroom climate, student engagement, and evidence of learning.

Will busy supervisors be able to get into classrooms frequently enough? There's no question that mini-observations are a time management challenge. But with the average caseload of twenty to twenty-five teachers per supervisor, making a monthly visit to each classroom involves an average of only two mini-observations a day. If the visits are short, the debrief conversations are short, and the write-up is limited to 1,000 characters (about 160 words), it's possible to do an average of two a day, which adds up to ten per teacher each year.

Some teachers will get fewer mini-observations than others and that isn't fair. Equity—everyone getting the same number of visits per year—is an important principle to which supervisors should publicly commit. Even the best teachers appreciate feedback and can be encouraged to share their ideas with colleagues.

Shouldn't supervisors see a full lesson at some point?
Brand-new teachers benefit from a full-lesson observation, but ideally this should be low-stakes and conducted by an instructional coach or another teacher who is very familiar with their grade or subject area—and promptly followed up with a face-to-face debrief. Teachers on an improvement plan should also have full-lesson observations, perhaps by a third party to get another opinion. And if a teacher invites a supervisor to observe a lesson, they should stay the full time. But except for these three situations, mini-observations provide much more information and authenticity to the process of supervision, coaching, and evaluation.

Even the best teachers appreciate feedback and can be encouraged to share their ideas with colleagues.

It's unfair to base an end-of-year summative evaluation on mini-observations. Actually, frequent mini-observations give a much more accurate picture of a year's instruction than one or two formal, full-lesson visits—provided that the short visits are frequent, randomly spaced through the day and year, and are always followed up by a face-to-face debrief. Using a detailed evaluation rubric at the end of the school year, with teacher input and discussion, supervisors can put together a remarkably detailed and accurate picture of overall performance.

What does the research say about mini-observations? There have been very few studies of this model because researchers tend to accept the traditional model as unchangeable. However, there are strands of research on K–12 schools that support the mini-observation model, including the importance of building relational trust, positive professional working conditions, principals acting as instructional leaders, frequent and specific feedback, early intervention with classroom problems, and face-to-face coaching.

New Leaders, a US principal training and professional development program, identified fifteen research-based skills for school leaders; the mini-observation process addresses nine of them: (1) being highly visible around the school, (2) building trusting relationships with teachers and students, (3) identifying and celebrating effective practices, (4) initiating difficult conversations, (5) leading outcome-based meetings with clear protocols, (6) using time strategically, (7) setting clear expectations, (8) monitoring adult practices, and (9) delivering high-quality professional development.

Does the average supervisor have the chops to implement mini-observations? The basic design of mini-observations actually makes it more do-able than the traditional evaluation model because (1) supervisors have multiple at bats to hone their observation and feedback skills; (2) the frequency and informality of the post–mini conversations means supervisors don't have to be perfect every time; (3) in the face-to-face debriefs, teachers can "school" their supervisors about the finer points of their subject and pedagogy and also correct anything the visitor might have misunderstood; (4) feedback after each classroom visit focuses on one "leverage point" at a time so the evaluative task is more limited and manageable; and (5) when feedback conversations take place in the teacher's classroom when students aren't there, they're on their home turf and the power dynamic is more conducive to helpful give-and-take.

Okay, but who is going to supervise my supervisor and ensure quality? That's the job of the superintendent or head of school, and they need to be in your school frequently to monitor the mini-observation process. One of the best ways to check on and build supervisors' skills is conducting co-observations of several classes and then going back to the office to debrief, discuss, and role-play. Superintendents and heads of school should also conduct anonymous surveys of teachers to see how mini-observations are going.

> *Supervisors can't (and shouldn't) be robots, expected to come up with exactly the same rating for each teacher.*

What about inter-rater reliability? Isn't there too much room for subjectivity in this way of working with teachers? Supervisors can't (and shouldn't) be robots, expected to come up with exactly the same rating for each teacher. Superintendents and heads of school should select, train, and support their supervisors to have good observation and human interaction skills and use sound judgment as they give feedback to teachers.

I don't like the idea of being "graded" and put in little boxes on the rubric. Why not write a narrative evaluation at the end of the year? Traditional narrative evaluations are time-consuming and can never include the myriad aspects of a teacher's work through the year. There's also a very high skill threshold in writing good narratives, and many supervisors don't have the training and writing skills to do them well. In addition, teachers don't have input as the supervisor writes narrative evaluations (although of course they can protest afterward). The rubric is a comprehensive, research-based deconstruction of teaching (with some notable gaps on items that are too subjective to evaluate, such as sense of humor). The rubric makes it possible to give more-detailed evaluative feedback on key descriptors of teaching, with the teacher's input to fill in gaps in the supervisor's knowledge, in much less time.

Could mini-observations replace traditional teacher evaluations? Absolutely, if the key elements are in place: (1) frequent, short, systematic, and unannounced; (2) face-to-face conversations after each, with short narrative summaries sent to the teacher; (3) a midyear rubric check-in meeting to identify and address possible issues; (4) teacher input and a full discussion of rubric ratings at the end of the school year; (5) supervision of supervisors to ensure skill and fairness. There's a strong argument that this system is more accurate, fair, and supportive of teachers than traditional evaluations, and will result in high-quality, more-equitable instruction for all students.

I'm a union representative and like the idea of mini-observations, but some of my colleagues are skeptical. What are the key questions I should get answers to? I (Kim Marshall) was a union rep when I taught at the King School in the 1970s. Here are the key questions I would want good answers to in order to feel comfortable recommending mini-observations to my fellow teachers: Why are we doing this? What's the problem to which mini-observations are the solution? Will there be enough classroom visits to adequately sample the nine hundred lessons each of us teaches? Will supervisors stay long enough? Will visits be systematically spread out? How can we prevent mini-observations from being intrusive and disruptive? What are supervisors looking for during short visits? Do the supervisors in our school have a good instructional eye and are they being supervised and held accountable by their boss? Will there always be a face-to-face conversation after visits so I can put the short visit in context? Will supervisors take into account the bigger picture outside the very short visits to our classrooms? Will we have an opportunity to submit anonymous feedback on the process as least once a year? And will we have meaningful input on our final evaluations?

I'm a principal and really like the idea of mini-observations. How can I convince my teachers and superintendent? Here's one strategy: convene faculty members for a one-hour meeting, with the superintendent sitting in, and take these steps:

- Explain the basic idea of mini-observations: short, frequent, systematic, unannounced visits with face-to-face conversations and a brief narrative summary every time.
- Acknowledge that it's very different from the traditional model. Some schools are implementing it successfully, but for us it's a bit of a leap of faith.
- Have teachers get in groups and brainstorm worries about mini-observations, rational and irrational.
- Pull the group back together and elicit all the worries, with one person writing them on an easel sheet (there are usually about eleven worries). Don't argue with them; just get them out there to show candor and openness and prepare the group for the next steps of persuasion.
- Show a ten-minute video of a teacher in action, using one that has some solid teaching and areas for improvement.
- Have the whole group brainstorm first the teacher's effective actions, then possible areas for improvement.
- Ask people to discuss with one elbow partner which coaching point they believe is the most important.

- Then have everyone get up, choose a partner they don't usually work with, and do a five-minute role-play of a conversation with the teacher in the video, with one person acting the teacher, the other the supervisor. Even people who hate role-playing usually enjoy this exercise.

- After five minutes, call time, thank colleagues for engaging, have everyone sit down, and elicit comments on how the conversations felt, what were the most common coaching points, and any particularly good opening lines or funny moments.

- Explain further details of how mini-observations might work, including a brief written summary sent electronically to the teacher after the conversation, the number of visits per year, a midyear check-in with the rubric, rubric ratings at the end of the school year, with teacher input, and what might be involved contractually in implementing the plan in your school.

- Have an open discussion about next steps: perhaps a study group to read articles and think it through, a field trip to a school implementing mini-observations, a discussion of the rubric (see Chapter Seven for details), pilot with a few volunteers.

These steps usually produce a willingness to engage in further discussion and perhaps a pilot or full implementation. The *Best of Marshall Memo* website's section on performance evaluation has fourteen article summaries (available as a PDF or podcast) that can be a good starting point for a study group on the subject: www.bestofmarshallmemo.org.

I'm at teacher leader and want to gather support for mini-observations. Who do I need to convince to make this happen? Here's a word splash showing teachers' and administrators' responses to this question in a recent webinar:

Comparing Six Theories for Improving Teacher Evaluation

In the Introduction of this book, I suggested that a good teacher evaluation process should have four components: quality assurance, feedback, motivation, and good personnel decisions. In the following figure, those are on the vertical axis, and six suggested strategies for improving teaching and learning are on the horizontal axis. The size of the star (or lack of a star or a question mark) in each intersecting cell represents my estimate of the impact of each theory of action on student learning.

SUPERVISION AND EVALUATION: WHY? HOW?	Announced full-lesson classroom visits and write-ups	State test-score data to evaluate individual teachers	10 short classroom visits, talks, and brief write-ups	Student surveys, teachers learning from data	Monitoring teacher teams' curriculum unit plans	Monitoring teams' interim assessment follow-up
Quality assurance			★ (large)	☆ (small)	☆ (small)	☆ (small)
Feedback to affirm and improve	?		★ (large)	★ (large)	★ (large)	★ (large)
Teacher motivation		?	★ (large)	★ (large)	★ (large)	★ (large)
Good personnel decisions			★ (large)	?	☆ (small)	☆ (small)

My takeaway (and I hope yours after reading this book) is that traditional evaluations and using test scores (value-added and student learning objectives) contribute very little, if anything toward our goal. The biggest impact comes from frequent mini-observations followed by debriefs and short write-ups—a big star on all four. Teachers learning from data and student surveys is strongest on feedback and motivation, uncertain on quality assurance and personnel decisions. Monitoring and supporting unit planning and the PLC process are very strong on feedback and motivation, moderately strong on quality assurance and personnel decisions. It's clear where we should be investing our time and passion if we want to get results!

Wrapping Up

Do you recall the vignette in Chapter Two about the teacher who wept in a post-observation conference when told she had mixed up *mean, median,* and *mode* in a math lesson? It's a true story, and I was her principal. This took place shortly after I arrived at the Mather, long before mini-observations. With the benefit of hindsight, I can see exactly what went wrong.

The teacher was clearly putting on a special lesson for my formal observation, and although she had done a lot of preparation, an important mathematical error had crept into the lesson plan. She might have been more focused on impressing me with a razzle-dazzle hands-on activity than on the quality of her students' learning.

In fairness to her, she'd been working in isolation from other teachers at her grade level and had not been exposed to high-quality professional development. Her nervousness about the high-stakes meeting in my office undoubtedly contributed to her being devastated when (in her view) I played gotcha. Her takeaway from my criticism—"Never to take a risk"—seems defensive and wrong, but given the supervision and evaluation process we were using, it was understandable.

If we could time-shift this teacher to a contemporary US school implementing the key components advocated in this book, how might things turn out differently? For starters, she and her teammates would be operating in a standards-based environment and know that their students were going to take rigorous state math tests based on those standards. They would collaboratively backwards-design the math unit on mean, median, and mode, clarifying their big ideas and essential questions, the important facts and concepts to be learned, and the way student learning would be assessed at the end of the unit. In this process, the team would probably catch this teacher's misconception and figure out a collective classroom strategy to teach these tricky concepts, anticipating students' likely mistakes.

As she began to teach the unit in her classroom, the teacher would probably be less concerned about what I would think if I happened to drop in (mini-observations had replaced formals) and more focused on whether her students were *getting* it and how they would do on their unit assessment and on the external test at the end of the year. If I did notice a teaching error during a mini-observation, I would bring it up in the informal follow-up chat - no tears, just a helpful conversation to fine-tune the lesson. And if students did well on the end-of-unit or interim assessment, the team would report the results to me and their colleagues with real pride in a job well done. The teacher's year-end rubric evaluation would probably end up being mostly Effective and Highly Effective, and our meeting would be a candid and businesslike sharing of commendations and suggestions.

This is a far better scenario than the kind of tense confrontation I described—better for teachers, better for students, and better for the whole school community. But for it to become a reality, we have to rethink conventional teacher supervision and evaluation. Supervisors need to go beyond classroom inspection and actively supervise curriculum planning, interim assessment analysis, and follow-up, with *student learning* at the center of every conversation.

With this expanded portfolio, supervisors can spot-check classrooms with mini-observations while orchestrating a creative, low-stakes, collegial process that gets teacher teams deeply invested in continuously improving their teaching and their students' success. What fuels this engine of improvement is constantly experimenting, analyzing what's working and what isn't, refusing to let students fail. Teams must work with the realization that there isn't one right way to teach, and effective teaching must be tuned to the unique circumstances of every classroom: the teacher, the students, the subject matter, and the moment.

What would we look for in a school that has this engine running? First, that there is effective teaching in all classrooms with a constant, steady focus on results. Dylan Wiliam and Ian Beatty put it best, in an email they wrote me early in 2009:

Agile teaching,
responsive to student learning
minute by minute,
day by day,
month by month.

Second, that teacher teams are designing curriculum units and assessments with the student learning goal in sight and continuously improving instruction down to the individual lesson. Third, that teacher teams meet periodically to analyze interim assessment results, candidly discussing what's working and what isn't, pushing each other to develop the best possible practices, and making plans to follow up and get all students on track.

And at the center we would see a principal with a firm grasp on all these elements, very well informed about what is happening in classrooms, skillfully juggling myriad events and interruptions inherent in the job, and keeping the focus on the ultimate goal—all students graduating with the skills and knowledge they need to take the next step toward college and career success.

Implementing the recommendations of this book would ensure that each of these components works well. For starters, principals would have a far more accurate appraisal of the quality of instruction in each classroom, based on the rubrics' detailed definition of teaching and frequent mini-observations. Effective and Highly Effective teachers would receive frequent, authentic praise for their work, and would see the evidence in their work in students' achievement on interim assessments. Less-than-effective teachers would get early support from the principal and other supervisors, many would improve, and for those who do not, necessary steps would be taken. Finally, principals would be able to look parents and other key stakeholders in the eye and assure them that there is good or excellent teaching in every classroom.

This is teacher supervision, coaching, and evaluation at its best, showing teachers that we care about them as professionals and people, providing the conditions for continuous improvement in student achievement and happy, productive teachers. This is how supervisors can work smart, build collaboration, and close the achievement gap.

Bibliography

Allen, D. (2001). *Getting things done*. Penguin.

Ambady, N., & Rosenthal, R. (1993). Half a minute: Predicting teacher evaluations from thin slices of nonverbal behavior and physical attractiveness. *Journal of Personality and Social Psychology, 64*(3), 431–441.

Baeder, J. (2018). *Now we're talking*. Solution Tree.

Bambrick-Santoyo, P. (2016). *Get better faster*. Jossey-Bass.

Bambrick-Santoyo, P. (2018). *Leverage leadership 2.0*. Jossey-Bass.

Bambrick-Santoyo, P. (2019). *Driven by data 2.0*. Jossey-Bass.

Bambrick-Santoyo, P. (2023). *Make history*. Jossey-Bass.

Bambrick-Santoyo, P., & Chiger, S. (2013). *Love and literacy*. Jossey-Bass.

Bambrick-Santoyo, P., Settles, A., & Worrell, J. (2013). *Great habits, great readers*. Jossey-Bass.

Beatty, I., et al. (2004). *Agile teaching: A dynamic approach to classroom instruction*. Scientific Reasoning Research Institute & Department of Physics, University of Massachusetts Amherst.

Begley, S. (2009). Will the BlackBerry sink the presidency? *Newsweek* (February 16), 37.

Ben-Hur, M. (1998). Mediation of cognitive competencies for students in need. *Phi Delta Kappan, 79*(9), 661–666.

Benson, T., & Fiarman, S. (2019). *Unconscious bias in schools*. Harvard Education Press.

Black, P., & Wiliam, D. (1998). Inside the black box. *Phi Delta Kappan, 80*(2), 139–148.

Blanchard, K. (1982). *The one-minute manager*. William Morrow.

Blankenship, S. (2014). If you thought I was perfect, you weren't paying attention. *Connected Principals* (July 25).

Bloom, B. (1984). The search for methods of group instruction as effective as one-to-one tutoring. *Educational Leadership, 41*(8), 4–17.

Boudett, K. P., Murnane, R. J., & City, E. A. (2005). *Data wise: A step-by-step guide to using assessment results to improve teaching and learning*. Harvard Education Press.

Boudett, K. P., & Steele, J. L. (2007). *Data wise in action: Stories of schools using data to improve teaching and learning.* Harvard Education Press.

Boyd-Zaharias, J., & Pate-Bain, H. (2008). Class matters: In and out of school. *Phi Delta Kappan, 90*(1), 41–44.

Bracey, G. (2004). Value-added assessment findings: Poor kids get poor teachers. *Phi Delta Kappan, 86*(4), 331–333.

Brown-Chidsey, R. (2007). No more waiting to fail. *Educational Leadership, 65*(2), 40–46.

Buck, F. (2008). *Get organized! Time management for school leaders.* Eye on Education.

Burkins, J., & Yates, K. (2021). *Shifting the balance.* Stenhouse.

Campbell, D. T. (1976). *Assessing the impact of planned social change.* The Public Affairs Center, Dartmouth College, Hanover, New Hampshire.

Chenoweth, K. (2007). *It's being done.* Harvard Education Press.

Chenoweth, K. (2021). *Districts that succeed: Breaking the correlation between race, poverty, and achievement.* Harvard Education Press.

Chenoweth, K., & Theokas, C. (2011). *Getting it done: Leading academic success in unexpected schools.* Harvard Education Press.

City, E., Elmore, R., Fiarman, S., & Teitel, L. (2009). *Instructional rounds in education: A network approach to improving teaching and learning.* Harvard Education Press.

Clotfelter, C., Ladd, H., & Vigdor, J. (2007). Teacher credentials and student achievement: Longitudinal analysis with student fixed effects. *Economics of Education Review* (December), 673–682.

Coggshall, J., Rasmussen, C., Colton, A., Milton, J., & Jacques, C. (2012, May). *Generating teaching effectiveness: The role of job-embedded professional learning in teacher evaluation.* Comprehensive Center for Teacher Quality Research.

Covey, S. (1994). *First things first: To live, to love, to learn, to leave a legacy.* Simon & Schuster.

Covey, S. (2004). *The seven habits of highly effective people.* Simon & Schuster.

Coyle, D. (2009). *The culture code.* Dell.

Coyle, D. (2018). *The talent code.* Random House.

Danielson, C. (1996). *Enhancing professional practice: A framework for teaching.* ASCD.

Danielson, C. (2001). New trends in teacher evaluation. *Educational Leadership, 58*(5), 12–15.

Danielson, C. (2007). *Enhancing professional practice: A framework for teaching* (2nd ed). ASCD.

Danielson, C. (2008). *The handbook for enhancing professional practice.* ASCD.

Danielson, C. (2009). *Talk about teaching.* Corwin Press.

Danielson, C., & McGreal, T. (2000). *Teacher evaluation to enhance professional practice.* ASCD.

Daresh, J. (2006). *Leading and supervising instruction.* Corwin Press.

Darling-Hammond, L. (2000). How teacher education matters. *Journal of Teacher Education, 51*(3), 166–173.

Darling-Hammond, L., Cook, C., Jaquith, A., & Hamilton, M. (2012). *Creating a comprehensive system for evaluating and supporting effective teaching*. Stanford Center for Opportunity Policy in Education.

Downey, C., Steffy, B., English, F., Frase, L., & Poston, W. (2004). *The three-minute classroom walk-through*. Corwin Press.

Doyle, D., & Han, J. G. (2012). Measuring teacher effectiveness: A look "under the hood" of teacher evaluation in 10 sites. Conncan, 50Can, and Public Impact.

DuFour, R. (2004). What is a "professional learning community"? *Educational Leadership*, *61*(8), 6–11.

DuFour, R., DuFour, R., & Eaker, R. (2008). *Revisiting professional learning communities at work*. Solution Tree.

DuFour, R., DuFour, R., Eaker, R., & Karhanek, G. (2004). *Whatever it takes: How professional learning communities respond when kids don't learn*. Solution Tree.

DuFour, R., & Marzano, R. (2009). High-leverage strategies for principal development. *Educational Leadership*, *66*(5), 62–68.

Duhigg, C. (2012). *The power of habit*. Random House.

Dweck, C. (2006). *Mindset*. Random House.

Edmonds, R. (1979). Effective schools for the urban poor. *Educational Leadership* (October), 15–24.

Ericsson, A., & Pool, R. (2016). *Peak*. Houghton Mifflin Harcourt/Mariner.

Ferguson, R. (2012). Can student surveys measure teaching quality? *Phi Delta Kappan*, *94*(3), 24–28.

Ferguson, R., & Ladd, F. (1996). Additional evidence on how and why money matters: A production function analysis of Alabama schools. In H. F. Ladd (Ed.), *Holding schools accountable: Performance-based reform in education*. Brookings Institution Press.

Fisher, D., & Frey, N. (2007). *Checking for understanding*. ASCD.

Freeston, K., & Costa, J. (1998). Making time for valuable work. *Educational Leadership*, *55*(7), 50–52.

Fullan, M. (2003). *The moral imperative of school leadership*. Corwin Press.

Galley, L. (2011). The research vs. the rhetoric: Reasons why experts urge caution when using student test scores to evaluate teachers. *NJEA Review, 84*, 10–13.

Gladwell, M. (2005). *Blink*. Little, Brown.

Glenn, D. (2007). You will be tested on this. *Chronicle of Higher Education, 53*(40), A14.

Glenn, D. (2011). One measure of a professor: Students' grades in later courses. *Chronicle of Higher Education, LVII*(19), A8–A9.

Goe, L., Biggers, K., & Croft, A. (2012, May). *Linking teacher evaluation to professional learning: Focusing on improving teaching and learning*. National Comprehensive Center for Teacher Quality.

Goldberg, M., & Harvey, J. (1983). A nation at risk: The report of the National Commission on Excellence in Education. *Phi Delta Kappan, 65*(1), 14–18.

Goldstein, J. (2008). Taking the lead. *American Educator, 32*(3), 4–11, 36–37.

Goodwin, B., & Kristin, R. (2023). *The new classroom instruction that works.* ASCD.

Grant, A. (2016). Stop serving the feedback sandwich (May 4).

Grubb, N. (2007). Dynamic inequality and intervention: Lessons from a small country. *Phi Delta Kappan, 89*(2), 105–114.

Guskey, T. (2005). A historical perspective on closing achievement gaps. *NAASP Bulletin, 89*(644), 76–89.

Guskey, T. (2022). *Implementing mastery learning* (3rd. ed.). Corwin.

Hall, P., & Simeral, A. (2008). *Building teachers' capacity for success: A collaborative approach for coaches and school leaders.* ASCD.

Hattie, J. (2002). The relation between research productivity and teaching effectiveness: Complementary, antagonistic, or independent constructs? *Journal of Higher Education* (September/October), 603–641.

Hattie, J. (2008). *Visible learning.* Routledge.

Haycock, K. (1998). Good teaching matters . . . a lot. *Thinking K–16, 3,* 3–14.

Heath, C., & Heath, D. (2007). *Made to stick: Why some ideas survive and others die.* Random House.

Howard, J. (2004). Proficiency now! A rallying cry for all black folks in the 21st century. In J. Kamara & T. M. Van Der Meer (Eds.), *State of the race: Creating our 21st century; Where do we go from here?* (pp. 253–265). Diaspora Press.

Huberman, M. (1993). The model of the independent artisan in teachers' professional relations. In J. W. Little & M. W. McLaughlin (Eds.), *Teachers' work: Individuals, colleagues, and context* (pp. 11–50). Teachers College Press.

Hunter, M. (1986). Let's eliminate the pre-observation conference. *Educational Leadership, 43,* 69–70.

Jenkins, R. (2016). What makes a good teacher? *The Chronicle of Higher Education, LXII*(39), A26.

Jerald, C. (2012, March). *Ensuring accurate feedback from observations: Perspectives on practice.* Bill and Melinda Gates Foundation.

Johnson, J., Leibowitz, S., & Perrett, K. (2018). *The coach approach to school leadership.* ASCD.

Johnson, J., Uline, C., & Perez, L. (2011). Expert noticing and principals in high-performing urban schools. *Journal of Education for Students Placed at Risk, 16*(2), 122–136.

Johnson, S. (2012). Having it both ways: Building the capacity of individual teachers and their schools. *Harvard Educational Review, 82*(1), 107–122.

Joint Committee on Standards for Educational Evaluation, Arlen Gullickson, Chair. (2009). *The personnel evaluation standards* (2nd ed). Corwin Press.

Klein, K. (2011, September/October). Pull, don't push: Designing effective feedback systems. *Wharton Leadership Digest: Nano Tools for Leaders.*

Kotter, J., & Cohen, D. (2002). *The heart of change: Real-life stories of how people changed their organizations.* Harvard Business Press.

Lemov, D. (2021). *Teach like a champion 3.0.* Josscy-Bass.

Levy, S. (2007, June 11). When bloggers say no to a simple chat. *Newsweek.*

Liljedahl, P. (2021). *Building thinking classrooms in mathematics.* Corwin.

Maple, J. (2000). *The crime fighter.* Broadway Books.

Marshall, K. (1970). Law and order in grade 6E. *Harvard Bulletin, 73*(1), 32–41.

Marshall, K. (1996). How I confronted HSPS (hyperactive superficial principal syndrome) and began to deal with the heart of the matter. *Phi Delta Kappan, 77*(5), 336–345.

Marshall, K. (2003a). A principal looks back: Standards matter. In D. T. Gordon (Ed.), *A nation reformed?* (pp. 53–68). Harvard Education Press.

Marshall, K. (2003b). Recovering from HSPS (hyperactive superficial principal syndrome): A progress report. *Phi Delta Kappan, 84*(9), 701–709.

Marshall, K. (2008a). Interim assessments: A user's guide. *Phi Delta Kappan, 90*(1), 64–68.

Marshall, K. (2008b). Is supervising the heck out of teachers the answer? *Education Week, 27*(36), 23, 25.

Marzano, R. J. (2003). *What works in schools.* ASCD.

Marzano, R. J. (2006). *Classroom assessment and grading that work.* ASCD.

Marzano, R. J. (2007). *The art and science of teaching.* ASCD.

Marzano, R. J., Waters, T., & McNulty, B. A. (2005). *School leadership that works.* ASCD & McREL.

Mazur, E. (1997). *Peer instruction: A user's manual.* Pearson Prentice Hall.

McTighe, J., Seif, E., & Wiggins, G. (2004). You can teach for meaning. *Educational Leadership, 62*(1), 26–30.

MET Project. (2012). *Learning about teaching: Initial findings from the Measures of Effective Teaching Project.* Bill and Melinda Gates Foundation.

Mishra, A. K. (1996). Organizational responses to crisis: The centrality of trust. In R. Kramer & T. Tyler (Eds.), *Trust in organizations* (pp. 261–287). Sage.

Mooney, N., & Mausbach, A. (2008). *Align the design.* ASCD.

NPR. (2012). Lax coal mine regulation to blame for black lung: Study (July 10).

Nuthall, G. (2004). Relating classroom teaching to student learning: A critical analysis of why research has failed to bridge the theory-practice gap. *Harvard Educational Review, 74*(3), 273–306.

Nye, B., Hedges, L., & Konstantopoulos, S. (2004). How large are teacher effects? *Educational Evaluation and Policy Analysis* (November), 94.

O'Neill, J., & Conzemius, A. (2005). *The power of SMART goals*. Solution Tree.

Parker, N. (1984). *The work of public and private elementary school principals (Unpublished doctoral dissertation)*. Teachers College, Columbia University, New York.

Payne, C. (2022). *So much reform, so little change*. Harvard Education Press.

Petrilli, M. (2011, January 13). Opinion: Lights, camera, action! *Education Gadfly*.

Pettersson, H., & Briggs, K. (2019). Combating teaching attrition rates: Start locally. *The Education Gadfly, 19*(25)

Pickering, D. J., & Pollock, J. E. (2001). *Classroom instruction that works*. ASCD.

Platt, A. D., Tripp, C. E., Fraser, R., Warnock, J., & Curtis, R. (2008). *The skillful leader II: Confronting conditions that undermine learning*. Ready About Press.

Platt, A. D., Tripp, C. E., Ogden, W. R., & Fraser, R. G. (2000). *The skillful leader: Confronting mediocre teaching*. Ready About Press.

Pollock, J. (2007). *Improving student learning one teacher at a time*. ASCD.

Popham, J. (2004a). A game without winners. *Educational Leadership, 62*(3), 46–50.

Popham, J. (2004b). "Teaching to the test": An expression to eliminate. *Educational Leadership, 62*(3), 82–83.

Popham, J. (2006, October). *Defining and enhancing formative assessment*. Paper presented at the meeting of the Council of Chief State School Officers' State Collaborative on Assessment and Student Standards, Austin, TX.

Randall, C. (2020). *Trust-based observations*. Rowman & Littlefield.

Reeves, D. (1998, October). Holding principals accountable. *The School Administrator*.

Reeves, D. (2000). *Accountability in action*. Advanced Learning Press.

Reeves, D. (2004). *Making standards work* (2nd ed). Advanced Learning Press.

Ribas, W. (2005). *Teacher evaluation that works!!* Ribas Publications and Rowman & Littlefield Education.

Rice, J. (2003). *Teacher quality: Understanding the effectiveness of teacher attributes*. Economic Policy Institute.

Rivkin, S., Hanuschek, E., & Kain, J. (2005). Teachers, schools, and academic achievement. *Econometrica* (March), 471–458.

Roberts, G. (2012). Queens parents demand answers following teacher's low grades, *New York Post* (February 26).

Rubin, C. (2011, September 20). The global search for education: What did you learn today?

Rutter, M., Maughan, B., Mortimore, P., Ouston, J., with Smith, A. (1979). *Fifteen thousand hours: Secondary schools and their effects on children*. Harvard University Press.

Saginor, N. (2008). *Diagnostic classroom observation: Moving beyond best practice*. Corwin Press.

Sanders, W. L., & Rivers, J. C. (1996). *Cumulative and residual effects of teachers on future student academic achievement*. University of Tennessee Value-Added Research and Assessment Center.

Sanders, W. L., Saxton, A. M., & Horn, S. P. (1997). The Tennessee value-added assessment system: A quantitative, outcomes-based approach to educational measurement. In J. Millman (Ed.), *Grading teachers, grading schools: Is student achievement a valid evaluation measure?* (pp. 137–162). Corwin Press.

Saphier, J. (1993). *How to make supervision and evaluation really work.* Research for Better Teaching.

Saphier, J. (2005). *John Adams' promise: How to have good schools for all our children, not just for some.* Research for Better Teaching.

Saphier, J. (2017). *High expectations teaching.* Corwin.

Saphier, J., Haley-Speca, M. A., & Gower, R. (2008). *The skillful teacher.* Research for Better Teaching.

Saphier, J., & Marshall, K. (2008). Jon Saphier and Kim Marshall on supervision and evaluation: Many areas of agreement, a few areas of disagreement. *Marshall Memo.*

Sato, M., & Lensmire, T. (2009). Poverty and Payne: Supporting teachers to work with children of poverty. *Phi Delta Kappan, 90*(5), 365–370.

Schmoker, M. (1992). What schools can learn from Toyota of America. *Education Week* (May 13), 23–25.

Schmoker, M. (1999). *Results: The key to continuous school improvement* (2nd ed). ASCD.

Schmoker, M. (2001). *The results fieldbook: Practical strategies from dramatically improved schools.* ASCD.

Schmoker, M. (2004). Tipping point: From feckless reform to substantive instructional improvement. *Phi Delta Kappan, 85*(6), 424–432.

Schmoker, M. (2006). *Results now: How we can achieve unprecedented improvements in teaching and learning.* ASCD.

Schmoker, M. (2010). When pedagogic fads trump priorities. *Education Week, 30*(5), 22–23.

Schmoker, M., & Marzano, R. (1999). Realizing the promise of standards-based education. *Educational Leadership, 56*(6), 17–21.

Seider, S. (2012). *Character compass.* Harvard Education Press

Smith, V. (2012). Mining company gets 253 citations, *Boston Globe* (February 24).

Steele, C. (2010). *Whistling Vivaldi.* Norton.

Stiggins, R. (2007). Assessments through the student's eyes. *Educational Leadership, 64*(8), 22–26.

Stiggins, R., Arter, J., Chappuis, J., & Chappuis, S. (2006). *Classroom assessment for student learning.* Educational Testing Service.

Stigler, J., & Hiebert, J. (1999). *The teaching gap.* Free Press.

Stobbe, C., & St. John, L. (2004). *Professional teaching standards: California standards for the teaching profession* (rev. ed.). New Teacher Center. (Originally written by Moir, E., Freeman, S., Petrock, L., & Baron, W. [1997]).

Stone, D., & Heen, S. (2014). *Thanks for the feedback.* Penguin Books.

Stone, D., Patton, B., & Heen, S. (1999). *Difficult conversations.* Penguin Books.

Stronge, J. H. (2002). *Qualities of effective teachers*. ASCD.

Sullivan, S., & Glanz, J. (2005). *Supervision that improves teaching*. Corwin Press.

Toch, T., & Rothman, R. (2008). *Rush to judgment*. Education Sector.

Tomlinson, C., & Sousa, D. (2010). When pedagogical information trumps reason, a letter from Carol Tomlinson and David Sousa. *Education Week, 30*(12), 28.

Tooms, A. (2003). The rookie's playbook: Insights and dirt for new principals. *Phi Delta Kappan, 84*(7), 530–533.

Tough, P. (2006). What it takes to make a student. *New York Times Magazine* (November 26), 44–51, 69–72, 77.

Trimble, S., Gay, A., & Matthews, J. (2005). Using test score data to focus instruction. *Middle School Journal, 36*(4), 26–32.

Wallace Foundation. (2011, January). *The school principal as leader: Guiding schools to better teaching and learning*. Wallace Foundation.

Weisberg, D., Sexton, S., Mulhern, J., & Keeling, D. (2009). *The widget effect: Our national failure to acknowledge and act on differences in teacher effectiveness*. New Teacher Project.

Whitehurst, G. (2002, March 5). *Scientifically based research on teacher quality: Research on teacher preparation and professional development*. White House Conference on Preparing Tomorrow's Teachers.

Wiggins, G. (1998). *Educative assessment*. Jossey-Bass.

Wiggins, G. (2006). Healthier testing made easy. *Edutopia, 2*(3), 48–51.

Wiggins, G. (2012). Seven keys to effective feedback. *Educational Leadership, 70*(1).

Wiggins, G., & McTighe, J. (2005). *Understanding by design* (2nd ed). ASCD.

Wiggins, G., & McTighe, J. (2007). *Schooling by design*. ASCD.

Wiliam, D. (2007). Content then process: Teacher learning communities in the service of formative assessment. In D. B. Reeves (Ed.), *Ahead of the curve: The power of assessment to transform teaching and learning* (pp. 183–204). Solution Tree.

Wiliam, D. (2007/2008). Changing classroom practice. *Educational Leadership, 65*(4), 36–41.

Wiliam, D. (2018). *Creating the schools our children need*. Learning Science International.

Wiliam, D. (2021, April 19). Why there is no such thing as a formative assessment. *Assess for Learning EU*.

Wilkerson, J., & Lang, W. S. (2007). *Assessing teacher dispositions*. Corwin Press.

Williams, J. (2005). On the positive side: Bloomberg and Klein seek to repair a failure factory. *Education Next, 5*(4), 17–21.

Willingham, D. (2005). Do visual, auditory, and kinesthetic learners need visual, auditory, and kinesthetic instruction? *American Educator, 29*(2), 31–35, 44.

Winerip, M. (2012). On education: A way to rate teachers, with flaws. *New York Times* (February 29).

Rubric Sources

The rubric presented in Chapter Seven was developed after referring to the following similar efforts in schools and districts, and revised with input from numerous school-based educators:

Alexandria Public Schools (Virginia) performance evaluation rubrics (2003)

Aspire Charter Schools, California teacher evaluation rubrics (2003)

Australian Government Department of Education and Training, Teaching Practice Evaluation Framework (2019)

Boston Public Schools Performance Evaluation Instrument (1997)

City on a Hill Charter School (Boston) performance evaluation rubrics (2004)

Conservatory Lab Charter School (Boston) performance evaluation rubrics (2004)

Enhancing Professional Practice: A Framework for Teaching by Charlotte Danielson (ASCD, 1996)

"Indicators of Teaching for Understanding" by Jay McTighe and Eliot Seif (unpublished paper, 2005)

Linking Teacher Evaluation and Student Learning by Pamela Tucker and James Stronge (ASCD, 2005)

North Star Academy Charter School of Newark (New Jersey): Teaching Standards (2004–05)

Roxbury Preparatory Charter School, Boston: Criteria for Outstanding Teaching (2004–05)

The Skillful Teacher by Jon Saphier, Mary Ann Haley-Speca, and Robert Gower (Research for Better Teaching, 2008)

The Three Big Rocks of Educational Reform by Jon Saphier (Research for Better Teaching, 2005)

Vaughn Next Century Learning Center, Chicago performance evaluation rubric (2004)

What Works in Schools: Translating Research into Action by Robert Marzano (ASCD, 2003)

Index

Printed and bound by CPI Group (UK) Ltd, Croydon, CR0 4YY

10/06/2025

14686752-0001